PRINCIPLES OF MACROECONOMICS

Dedicated to
Mihir Rakshit and Arup Mallik

PRINCIPLES OF MACROECONOMICS

Soumyen Sikdar

OXFORD

UNIVERSITY PRESS

OXFORD

UNIVERSITY PRESS

YMCA Library Building, Jai Singh Road, New Delhi 110 001

Oxford University Press is a department of the University of Oxford. It furthers the
University's objective of excellence in research, scholarship, and education
by publishing worldwide in

Oxford   New York

Auckland Cape Town Dar es Salaam Hong Kong Karachi Kuala Lumpur
Madrid Melbourne Mexico City Nairobi New Delhi Shanghai Taipei Toronto

With offices in

Argentina Austria Brazil Chile Czech Republic France Greece Guatemala
Hungary Italy Japan Poland Portugal Singapore South Korea Switzerland
Thailand Turkey Ukraine Vietnam

Oxford is a registered trademark of Oxford University Press
in the UK and in certain other countries

Published in India
by Oxford University Press, New Delhi

ISBN-13: 978-0-19-568025-6
ISBN-10: 019-568025-1

Typeset by Archetype
Printed in India at Ram Printograph, Delhi 110 051
Published by Oxford University Press
YMCA Library Building, Jai Singh Road, New Delhi 110 001

Contents

1. Introduction

THE NATURE OF MACROECONOMICS

The study of economics is traditionally divided into a micro field and a macro field. Microeconomics deals with the behaviour of disaggregated individual decision-makers such as a single consumer or a saver or a worker or a single production unit (firm) or an industry (collection of firms producing similar or closely related products). Macroeconomics, on the other hand, takes as its subject the economic activity of the entire nation as an indivisible unit. The analysis, in contrast with microeconomics, is very aggregative in nature. Some of the most important macroeconomic variables are: national income (its size, distribution, and growth), national investment (change in the nation's stock of productive capital), changes in the purchasing power of money (general inflation or deflation), the overall state of employment in the economy (not employment in a particular business enterprise or industry), budgetary policy of the government, the condition of the nation's balance of international payments.

Macroeconomists try to understand how an actual economy operates and, on the basis of that understanding, suggest policies that may be adopted to improve the performance of the economy. Thus, understanding and policy prescription are two critically interlinked aspects of the economist's role in society. Given the complexity of a modern industrial economy, it would be too much to expect that the policy analysis would be accurate and infallible all the time. But the policies recommended on the basis of good economic reasoning are of invaluable help to policymakers most of the time. Although the actual implementation of policies belongs to the domain of the politician, the advice offered by economists supply crucial ingredients to the decision making process. In India, after independence, Prime Minister Nehru enlisted the help of economists and other social scientists in giving shape and direction to the Five-Year Plans. And after nearly 50 years of planned development, when reforms were initiated in the early 1990s, macroeconomists once again played a very important role as advisors in the complex process of restructuring the old economy and launching it on a new path of growth in a globalized world.

For the purpose of analysis, macroeconomic theory combines all the economic units engaged in myriad activities into a small number of large groups. The simplest framework or model uses only two groups—households and firms where production is organized. Subsequently, the government is introduced as a third entity and, finally, the rest of the world enters as the destination of the nation's exports and the source of its imports. In some contexts a useful division is between the private sector (households and privately-owned firms) and the public sector (government sector). Introduction of foreign trade turns the economy from a closed system into an open one.

THE MAJOR MACROECONOMIC ISSUES

The major problems engaging the economist studying the national economy are as follows.

What Determines the Overall Level of Output and Employment?

A nation's well-being depends first and foremost on the total quantity of goods and services available to its citizens for consumption. Thus, on average, Americans are able to enjoy a better standard of living than Indians because America produces more goods and services than India. More production usually goes hand in hand with more employment of factors of production, of which labour is the most important one. Therefore, it is of great importance to identify the factors that determine the level of production in an economy. Only then effective measures for raising that level can be undertaken.

How can Business Cycles be Controlled?

Actual economies all over the world have shown fluctuations in aggregative economic activity—periods of rising output (and falling unemployment) alternating with recessions in which production plummets and unemployment soars. In the post-reform era in India, the economy was clearly on an upswing during 1991–6, but a prolonged decline set in after that. Recent years have shown some signs of recovery. A major task of economists is to try to eliminate or minimize such fluctuations in economic activity (known as business cycles). This is the task of *stabilization policy*. Fluctuations are harmful because they upset the plans of economic agents by introducing strong elements of uncertainty and lead to loss of livelihood (and potential output) through unemployment. The cost falls disproportionately on the poorer sections because, in a recession, the unskilled or semi-skilled workers are the first to be thrown out of work and their unemployment tends to persist for extended periods.

There is disagreement among economists about the desirability of active stabilization policy. One group (generally known as the classicals or new classicals) have strong beliefs in the self-correcting mechanisms of a capitalist economy. The system, according to their view, can take care of business cycles on its own. Government policy, however well-intentioned it may be, only makes matters worse by crudely meddling with the inherently stabilizing forces of private enterprise. The Keynesian economists strongly disagree and deny the ability of capitalist economies to eliminate business cycles unaided by the government.

How can Inflation be Controlled?

Inflation corrodes the standard of living of the citizens of a community by reducing the purchasing power of money. While episodes of hyperinflation, like Germany immediately after the First World War or Bolivia during the early 1980s when prices rose to astronomical levels within very short periods, are relatively rare, creeping inflation at slower rates are common enough. While inflation is harmful for the general standard of living, costs of price-rise, like those of unemployment, are not evenly distributed across the different social groups. The poorer sections, without stable employment or adequate social security provisions to fall back on, are much more vulnerable in a regime of rising prices. Therefore, keeping the general price level under control is one of the most important economic responsibilities of national governments. Understanding inflation, accordingly, features as a major goal of macrotheory.

The Government of India (GOI) is fully aware of the adverse social implications of inflation and has always assigned top priority to its control through appropriate policy.

Understanding International Interdependence

As a result of the forces of globalization countries are, today, much more interdependent than they had been 20 or 30 years ago. Economic isolation is no longer a viable option for an economy that wishes to benefit from the global flow of goods, services, and ideas. Aided by revolutionary changes in information and communication technology, this flow has undergone tremendous acceleration in recent years. Greater integration with the world economy has opened up new possibilities for the developing countries to move out of economic stagnation by upgrading technology and bringing in qualitatively better products for consumers and better and more sophisticated inputs and managerial skills for entrepreneurs. At the same time, on the flip side, more openness has increased the exposure to global risks. Countries are now much more vulnerable to adverse changes in conditions beyond their control. National governments have lost policy autonomy to a significant extent and their power to insulate their economies against shocks originating abroad has been eroded in consequence.

Greater mobility of financial capital across national boundaries has acted as a very potent source of market disruption and financial crisis, as was made abundantly clear in the Asian Crisis of 1997–8 preceded and followed by similar turmoils in Brazil, Russia, and elsewhere. The experiences of Argentina and Mexico during the 1990s convincingly demonstrate how mismanagement of the exchange rate of the national currency can throw an economy completely out of gear.

How to manage the forces of globalization so that benefits from openness can be maximized while keeping the harmful effects at bay has emerged as perhaps the most complex problem for national policymakers. Macroeconomists, specializing in international affairs, are eminently qualified to offer valuable assistance in this regard.

What Makes an Economy Grow over Time?

Because the aggregate volume of production in an economy is the principal determinant of the economic well-being of its citizens, sustained rise in the general standard of living is possible only if the economy is able to raise the quantum of its production steadily over time. How to achieve this difficult task is the central concern of the analysis of growth. Japan caught up with the affluent industrial countries of the west through sustained growth at a high rate over a quarter-century after the Second World War. A similar experiment was subsequently successfully conducted by four other Asian economies—Hong Kong, South Korea, Singapore, and Taiwan. More recently, high rate of growth has enabled China to launch a successful attack on the problem of pervasive poverty.

Since growth is so important for a nation, economists have devoted considerable effort over the years to identify the conditions that are conducive for sustained long-term growth and to advise governments in the developing countries on policies that will lead to the fulfilment of those conditions.

MACROECONOMIC STABILITY AND BUSINESS ENVIRONMENT

The economic history of the high-performing economies of the world underline, without exception, the crucial importance of good macroeconomic management for economic development. The provision of a stable and predictable macroeconomic environment and getting the key macroeconomic policy variables right induce the private sector to invest successfully in physical and human capital formation. A chaotic economic situation riddled with uncertainty hampers growth by discouraging long-term investment and reducing the incentives for economic agents to strive for improvements in productivity. This happens because the returns from costly investment and productivity enhancement efforts become highly uncertain. The consequences, needless to say, can be extremely damaging for the long-term prospects of an economy.

The symptoms of macroeconomic mismanagement and instability can take many forms. Let us discuss a few major ones that are particularly harmful for sound business decisions.

Excessive and Ill-designed Government Intervention

Since the economic policies pursued by the government (state) and the rules laid down by it, which private players must abide by set the stage on which the individual players act, these policies exert a very powerful influence on a country's performance. Over and above setting the stage, governments often take on a much more active directorial role in the economic drama. This bureaucratic intervention, when carried to excess, has shown an unmistakable tendency to turn counterproductive and harm a nation's interests by reducing the profitability of private business projects. A particularly prominent example is provided by the situation in India before the initiation of economic reforms in the country.

Although comprehensive centralized planning in the post-independence years did create substantial benefits for the economy in several areas (self-reliance in food, a diversified industrial base, to give just two important examples), over time the system tended to degenerate into a maze of bureaucratic mismanagement, inefficiency, and corruption (Licence Raj and Inspector Raj). The public sector, which was placed 'at the commanding heights of the economy', produced a very low return on investment and, after an initial period, began to act as a brake on private sector development. Import competition was restricted to nurture domestic industry, but this also encouraged inefficiency. Participation of foreign firms in the domestic economy was virtually prohibited and this stood in the way of technological upgradation. In short, proliferation of government control, clumsily administered, seriously damaged the competitive strength of the economy.

Economic reforms altered the situation radically by lifting controls and restrictions on private sector operations. Free from state control, prices could begin to play a market-clearing role. Relaxation of controls on foreign collaboration enabled domestic business to go for fruitful partnerships. Although liberalization has created some new problems, there is no doubt that its overall impact on the business environment and the investment climate has been beneficial.

While spectacular performers like Japan in the post-War years, South Korea, Singapore, and Taiwan over the 1960s and 1970s, and China in the 1990s could grow on average at 7 to 8 per cent annually in real terms, India's growth of per capita income averaged a miserable 2 per cent growth from the late 1940s to 1980. As a result of Rajiv Gandhi's (short-lived) liberalization attempt in the mid-1980s, it moved up and settled around 3.8 per cent annually ('Hindu rate of growth'). After the reforms, between 1991 and 1997, it accelerated spectacularly to more than 6 per cent (driven by a strong surge in private investment), which is not a mean achievement in the historical context. Although, owing to a number of factors, growth has slackened off since 1997, India's potential has been substantially unleashed and strong performance over long periods has come within the realms of possibility. This has been made possible because, in the liberalized environment, the more efficient Indian private firms have been able to turn to advantage the new opportunities offered by globalization. In the field of software services and exports a number of Indian firms such as Infosys, Wipro, and Tata Consultancy Services have emerged as important global players. For more on the topic, see the discussion on economic reform and growth in Chapter 10.

High Inflation

In a situation where prices are rising at high and unpredictable rates, cost–benefit analysis becomes difficult and the private sector is led to postpone its investment plans. Production planning in the current period is also thrown off-balance and the disruption of supply adds to the problem of inflation. Therefore, it is not surprising that controlling inflation figures high on the agenda of government action in most countries.

Fiscal Insolvency

If due to persistent budgetary deficits (government expenditure persistently outstripping government revenues at the central as well as regional levels of administration) the public debt keeps piling up, the financial solvency of the government is threatened. This will introduce uncertainty about the government's possible response in the future. Will it raise taxation to service the debt (to pay interest and repay the principal) or resort to inflationary policy to reduce the burden in real terms? Currently, in India, interest payment on public debt is the most important item of central government expenditure and fiscal deficit accounts for a high proportion of national income. Most economists are of the opinion that the situation is not sustainable in the long run.

Fiscal burden inherited from the past causes a cutback in spending on public infrastructure projects. This, coupled with uncertainty about future tax policy of the government, adversely affects business confidence and the incentive of the private sector to undertake long-term investment. Global development agencies such as the World Bank and the International Monetary Fund (IMF) lay great stress on improving the fiscal discipline of governments (both central and state) in the developing world.

Financial Fragility

Development of the financial sector (consisting of commercial banks and other financial intermediaries) is a concomitant of growth. A weak and inefficiently functioning financial sector affects growth adversely by failing to channelize the society's savings to productive investment. In a globalized world, financial fragility tends to magnify macroeconomic business cycles through its mishandling of foreign funds. In Thailand, South Korea, and Malaysia, in the 1990s, poorly supervised banks diverted burgeoning inflow of foreign capital to speculation in real estate. This malpractice was the major factor contributing to the Asian crisis that engulfed these economies in 1998.

The reforms undertaken by the GOI to strengthen the Indian financial sector and the Asian Crisis are discussed in Chapter 6 and Chapter 7, respectively.

Exchange Rate Mismanagement

The exchange rate is the price of a country's currency in terms of that of another. Thus, it is a very important relative price that has important bearing on a country's imports and exports. Improper management can lead to serious disequilibrium in the market for foreign currencies. The resulting distortion in the exchange rate encourages speculation and reduces gainful foreign trade. Speculative movement of 'hot money' (short-term funds looking for quick profits) across national boundaries has repeatedly led to financial crises in a large number of countries in recent years. This type of speculation thrives in a situation of mismanaged exchange rates. Sustaining a healthy business climate in a globalized economy is not possible if a sound exchange rate policy is not in place.

BUSINESS ENVIRONMENT IN INDIA

A business environment survey by the World Bank in 2000 covering a large number of countries revealed that managers spend 5 per cent of their time dealing with government officials in Latin America, twice that in the transition economies of Eastern Europe, and 16 per cent in India. Bad as the situation is, it marks a very significant improvement compared to the pre-reform days of the Licence and Inspector Raj.

According to independent observers, the regulatory and administrative burden on business in India is still fairly high. The current set-up continues to restrict the growth of existing business and the start of new ventures. Excessive regulation in the labour market and reservation for small enterprises (in garments, toys, shoes, and leather products) are often pointed out as the most important reasons for unsatisfactory growth of exports. Barriers to entry and exit in industries have been lowered considerably, but need to be brought down more to improve the mobility of labour and capital. Bankruptcy and liquidation procedures have to be rationalized. According to a study made in 1993, over 60 per cent of liquidation cases before the High Courts have been in process for more than 10 years. The situation continues to be more or less the same today.

Many of the controls and regulations have served useful purpose in the past by protecting the interest of workers and preventing the abuse of monopoly power in product markets. But the majority have outlived their usefulness and should be radically reformed to keep pace with the changing times. Some champions of globalization call for complete elimination of government control on the Indian economy. That will be socially disastrous by encouraging ruthless exploitation of monopoly power by large domestic and multinational corporations. Regulation and vigilance cannot be done away with, but they must be streamlined and much more efficiently administered. Only then can appropriate macroeconomic policies be effectively implemented.

Major Schools of Thought in Macroeconomics

Although macroeconomists fail to agree among themselves on an embarrassingly wide range of issues relating to the proper management of the economy, it will be convenient to organize a differentiation of the major schools in terms of their stance on one central issue, namely, the role of the government in the economy.

The origin of the *classical school* can be traced to the work of the Scottish philosopher–economist, Adam Smith, who, in *The Wealth of Nations* (1776), set forth the famous idea of the invisible hand of the market. He was rebelling against the prevalent practice of excessive government regulation of foreign commerce and industry. This heavy-handed regulation, he rightly pointed out, was acting as a serious barrier to the development of Great Britain at that time. His prescription was to do away with cumbersome intervention in order to clear the field for the free operation of private enterprise. In an economy with smoothly functioning markets, individual agents, while pursuing their self-interest, are led, as if, by an invisible hand to achieve the greatest possible welfare for everyone.

The invisible hand could deliver this desirable outcome only if markets were competitive (not under monopolistic control) and prices responded smoothly and without lag to changes in conditions of demand and supply. In such a situation, market prices will give the right signal to economic agents and their actions will be mutually consistent and compatible with the general welfare. Smith's basic insight about the efficiency and welfare-enhancing properties of unregulated capitalism later came to be enshrined in the *first fundamental theorem of welfare economics.* That pervasive, ill-designed, and excessive governmental regulation can seriously hamper the efficient functioning of an economy is amply attested by the performance of the Indian economy before the reforms of 1991.

Classical followers of Smith assumed that in the absence of outside interference, prices will adjust quickly enough to eliminate any imbalance between demand and supply in any market. In particular, economywide unemployment of labour cannot persist for long because downward adjustment in wages (the remuneration of labour) will quickly induce producers to absorb the unemployed. So if unemployment is observed to persist, the cause can usually be traced to the existence of minimum wage laws, trade union power, and other impediments to wage adjustment in the labour market. More generally, classical economists believe that government policies will be ineffective, if not actually counterproductive, in their attempt to eliminate business cycles or to influence the course of the economy in any other respect.

The faith in the self-correcting properties of free enterprise got rudely jolted in the Great Depression which started in 1929 in the USA and quickly spread to other parts of the world. Unemployment rose to unprecedented levels (afflicting more than one-third of the labour force during the depth of the crisis) and continued for years. The invisible hand was completely ineffective. A new approach to macro policy was clearly needed. John Maynard Keynes' book of 1936, *The General Theory of Employment, Interest and Money*, supplied it.

At the heart of the *Keynesian approach* was the proposition that at least in the short run there is no guarantee that the equilibrium of the economy determined by the volume of planned spending would be consistent with full employment of labour. Prices and wages are not flexible enough to clear the labour market. More importantly, if lack of adequate demand is the chief factor behind the recession, decline in wages is likely to exacerbate the crisis by reducing the purchasing power of workers. The government must step in to boost demand by increasing its own purchase of goods and services and pull the system out of depression by discretionary fiscal/monetary policy. The emphasis is very much on the limitations of the market mechanism and, given the sluggish adjustment of wages and prices, corrective action is fully justified.

The success of Keynesian policies in fighting the Great Depression was spectacular and this approach dominated macrotheory and policy right up to the 1970s. This was the era of 'stabilization optimism'.

In the 1970s the US economy suffered from prolonged stagflation, the simultaneous presence of stagnation and inflation. Since in the Keynesian scheme, inflation cannot be a serious problem in a situation of unemployed resources, this experience led to scepticism about the wisdom of the Keynesian orthodoxy. Also, Keynesians simply asserted that wages and prices are slow to adjust. No sound theoretical logic was provided to justify this very crucial assumption. This was deemed to be a serious flaw. The *monetarists* strongly criticized Keynes for downplaying the importance of money in the economic system and for neglecting the role of expectations in the analysis of inflation. They also expressed serious reservations about the efficacy of discretionary government intervention.

Inspired by monetarism, a new group of economists who came to be known as the *new classicals* emerged on the scene in the late 1970s. Their theoretical apparatus for analysing macroproblems was basically a more sophisticated version of the classical approach. An important new element was the notion of rational expectations, which posited that rational agents use all available information to make forecasts and do not make systematic mistakes in forecast. The classical scheme was adopted because it was consistent with the logic of economic optimization by self-interest seeking agents. Macroeconomics, according to this school, must be grounded in sound microeconomics, and the lack of such microfoundation was adjudged the fundamental flaw of the Keynesian approach.

The new classicals claimed to demonstrate rigorously that no systematic economic policy can influence the real course of the economy even in the short run ('stabilization pessimism'). Keynesians hit back by questioning the validity of the assumptions on which the analysis was based. Admitting the force of several criticisms made by the new classicals, they set about building up a research programme in which wage–price rigidity and activist stabilization policy can be given a solid theoretical foundation. This research programme, popularly known as the *new Keynesian approach,* departs from the classical set-up in making essential use of imperfect information, existence of monopoly power in the product market and the limited ability of even rational economic agents to process and assimilate complex information. The new classicals have retracted (or diluted) some of their revolutionary claims and are trying to improve their explanations of business cycles and unemployment.

As a result of intense debate and cross-fertilization of ideas over the years the two major schools have come closer to each other, but a unified approach to macroeconomics has, unfortunately, not emerged yet. The general consensus seems to be that the Keynesian approach is valid in the short–medium run while in the long run the classical supply side forces come into operation.

WHICH MACROTHEORY FOR INDIA?

Examination of the basic assumptions of the contending schools reveals that the Keynesian approach is best suited for the analysis and design of macro policy of a country like India. The classical or new classical approaches posit perfectly competitive markets and rely critically on the ability of prices to clear all markets completely and continuously. India's reality is radically different. Due to numerous institutional as well as policy induced rigidities, lack of information on the part of buyers and sellers, and fragmentation of markets, prices often fail to play an equilibrating role. Smith's invisible hand is unable to do its work and government intervention becomes essential for stimulating production and promoting social welfare. Existence of substantial excess (unutilized) capacity in the industrial sector, mostly due to lack of demand, also justifies the emphasis on aggregate demand as the major determinant of output and employment.

Even Keynesian economics was developed to address the problems of an advanced capitalist system in depression. Therefore it cannot be expected to fit exactly the enormously complex and essentially different situation of our country. Still, among the alternative frameworks, because of its reliance on price inflexibility and sluggish adjustments, it remains the most useful to our policymakers. Of course, there is no compulsion to stick rigidly to one particular body of thought to the exclusion of others, and Indian economists have productively borrowed from other schools to supplement their own ideas in their analysis of important phenomena when the traditional Keynesian approach failed to provide good insights. For example, the Reserve Bank of India has successfully used elements of the monetarist approach to keep inflation well under control over the past half a century.

Keynes did not foresee the possibility that his ideas might be abused by politicians to serve their own interests. In particular, his advocacy of budgetary deficit to fight unemployment and depression freed governments from the obligation to balance the budget. In the hands of irresponsible and corrupt public administration this inevitably led to fiscal profligacy and unsustainable increases in government debt over the years. In sharp contrast, new classical economics lays stress on the solvency of government operations and advocates fiscal consolidation (reduction of the fiscal deficit of the government). This has had a salutary impact on the conduct of government policy in recent years in many countries including India. This is undoubtedly one area where departure from the traditional Keynesian approach promises to improve the performance of the economy by imposing stricter discipline on governments.

HOW ECONOMISTS EXPLAIN

An economic *model* is a set of relations that describe how variables interact with each other. It is a simplified representation of reality in which the relations usually take the form of mathematical equations. Economists use models to make predictions about the real world. These predictions are then matched with observations to evaluate the models.

Endogenous variables are explained within the model. *Exogenous* variables or *parameters* are given from outside. For example, in trying to explain the level of price in a particular market the tastes and preferences of the buyers, the production technology of the firms, or the rate of commodity taxation set by the government are taken as exogenous. Price of the good and the volume of transactions are endogenous variables. Values of endogenous variables are determined for *given* values of the parameters. As exogenous variables change, endogenous variables change with them. The set of parameters is changed one at a time to isolate the impact of the change on the endogenous variables. Of course, a variable that is exogenous in a given context may be endogenous in another.

OUTLINE OF THE BOOK

In the first chapter, 'Introduction', the major issues addressed by macroeconomists and the major schools of thought in the discipline have been presented. Also, Appendices 1.1 and 1.2 to Chapter 1 concisely present some useful analytical tools, discuss some important elementary concepts of economics, and draw some important distinctions.

In the following chapters these issues with their ramifications are further discussed and dissected in depth. Chapter 2 describes the concepts of national income accounting and their measurement. These measurements supply the data which are used to judge the merits of the rival theories. Good theorization is impossible without good data. India is fortunate to have a system of national accounts of a very high standard.

After prolonged fight over the past three decades, the current consensus among economists seems to be that the Keynesian framework is suitable for the analysis of *short-run* fluctuations in output and employment and the classical (or its more sophisticated version, new classical) approach comes into its own in the *long run* when wages and prices would become flexible, expectational errors would be eliminated, and full employment attained. In our presentation we proceed in natural sequence from the short run to the long, from fixed prices to variable prices and inflation. As explained in the previous section, the Keynesian approach offers the best fit for the Indian reality. Therefore, we start with Keynes and proceed gradually towards the analysis of long-run growth, making close and frequent contact with the monetarist, classical, and new classical doctrines on the way.

Chapter 3 presents the basic Keynesian theory of national income determination in the short-run. The case for corrective government intervention is established. Both closed and open economies are considered. The simple framework of Chapter 3 is broadened in Chapter 4 to include the asset market.

The theoretical aspects of monetary and fiscal intervention are discussed in detail in Chapter 5. The conduct of monetary policy and its interdependence with fiscal action in post-reform India is covered in Chapter 6, which also deals, among other related topics, with the determination of money supply, targets, and instruments of monetary policy under the control of the Central Bank.

Exchange rate management and other macroeconomic problems of an economy engaged in trade in goods with other nations are treated in Chapter 7. The link between India's external balance of payments and domestic money supply are examined. Appendix 7.1 contains a short discussion of the World Trade Organization (WTO), of which India is a member. Monetary and fiscal policy under different exchange regimes in an open economy under capital mobility (trade in financial assets) is the subject of Appendix 7.2.

Chapter 8 presents the analytical determination of the price level using the tools of aggregate demand and supply. The important phenomenon of inflation in all its multifarious aspects gets treated in depth in Chapter 9.

Chapter 10 is devoted to the analysis of long-run growth where the focus is entirely on the supply (productive capacity) side. Along with a detailed discussion of the traditional approach, the modern endogenous growth theory is also introduced. The relation between economic reform and growth in the Indian context is critically examined.

Rational expectations, the policy ineffectiveness proposition of new classical economics, expectation-based derivation of the short-run Lucas supply curve, the new Keynesian research programme, real business cycle theory, and supply-side economics are at the frontier of research of modern macrotheory. The final chapter (Chapter 11) gives an overview of these topics.

Important terms are explained in the Glossary.

Appendix 1.1
Some Elementary Mathematical Concepts and Results

THE Δ SYMBOL

The symbol Δ ('delta') denotes 'change in'. Thus Δx means 'change in x'. If, for example, x changes in value from 5 to 8, $\Delta x = 3$, if the change is from 5 to 1 then $\Delta x = -4$. $\Delta x = 0$ means x is constant (not changing). $\Delta z/\Delta x$ = change in z per unit change in x.

Growth rate of a variable $(\Delta z/z)$ = proportionate change in z, which is the same as the growth rate of z. We shall use the notation g_z to denote the growth rate of z. Multiplying g_z by 100, the percentage growth rate is obtained. Thus if z takes the values 120 in 2000 and 180 in 2003, the (percentage) growth rate of z over the period $= (180 - 120)/120 \times 100 = 50$ per cent.

Suppose there is a linear relation $z = ax_1 + bx_2 + cx_3$, and we want to find out the change in z caused by a unit change in (say) x_2, with x_1, x_3 staying unchanged.

$$z + \Delta z = a(x_1 + \Delta x_1) + b(x_2 + \Delta x_2) + c(x_3 + \Delta x_3)$$

Setting $\Delta x_1 = \Delta x_3 = 0$ (since x_1 and x_3 are not changing) and subtracting z we get, $\Delta z = b\Delta x_2$ or $\Delta z/\Delta x_2 = b$, the coefficient of x_2 in the z function.
$\Delta z/\Delta x_1 = a(x_2, x_3$ unchanged), $\Delta z/\Delta x_3 = c(x_1, x_2$ unchanged).

THE FUNCTION NOTATION

The notation $y = y(x)$ means that the variable y depends on the variable x ('y is a function of x'). x is the independent variable and y, the dependent variable.

If y and x change in the same direction (y rises if x rises, y falls if x falls), y is said to depend *directly* or *positively* on x. If they move in opposite directions (y rises if x falls, y falls as x rises), y depends *inversely* or *negatively* on x. For example, 'consumption spending (C) depends on income (Y)' is mathematically written as, $C = C(Y)$, 'demand for a commodity (D) depends on its price (p)' as, $D = D(p)$. C varies positively with Y, whereas D varies negatively with p.

The nature of dependence can be inferred from the sign of $\Delta y/\Delta x$.

$\Delta y/\Delta x > 0$ implies that Δy and Δx have the same sign, y depends positively on x.
$\Delta y/\Delta x < 0$ implies that Δy and Δx have opposite signs, y depends negatively on x.

IDENTITIES AND EQUATIONS

An identity holds for *all possible values* of a variable. For example, $(x + 1)^2 = x^2 + 2x + 1$ is an identity. An equation holds only for *some particular values* of a variable. $3x - 10 = 17$ is true only for $x = 9$.

SUM OF INFINITE SERIES

If $0 < x < 1$, then $1 + x + x^2 + x^3 + x^4 + \cdots = 1/1 - x$
For example, $1 + 1/3 + (1/3)^2 + (1/3)^3 + \cdots = 3/2$

ALGEBRA OF GROWTH

Two simple results are proved first.

Result 1 For small x, y $(1+x)(1+y) = 1 + x + y$

Proof:

$(1+x)(1+y) = 1 + x + y + xy$. When x and y are small, xy is even smaller and can be ignored. Hence the result.

Result 2 For small x, y $1 + x/1 + y = 1 + x - y$

Proof:

$(1 + x - y)(1 + y) = 1 + x + xy - y^2$. If x and y are small, both xy and y^2 are very small and can be ignored. So, $(1 + x - y)(1 + y) = 1 + x$, or $1 + x/1 + y = 1 + x - y$.

Now we are ready to prove:

Result A If $z = xy$, then $g_z = g_x + g_y$ (If z is the product of x and y, growth rate of z is the sum of the growth rates of x and y).

Proof:

$$z + \Delta z = (x + \Delta x)(y + \Delta y)$$

or $$(z + \Delta z)/z = [(x + \Delta x)/x][(y + \Delta y)/y]$$

or $$1 + \Delta z/z = (1 + \Delta x/x)(1 + \Delta y/y)$$

or $$1 + g_z = (1 + g_x)(1 + g_y) = 1 + g_x + g_y \quad \text{by Result 1,}$$

or $$g_z = g_x + g_y.$$

Since the growth rate of a constant is zero by definition, it follows that if $z = kx$, where k is a constant, $g_z = g_x$.

Result B If $z = x/y$, then $g_z = g_x - g_y$ (If z is the ratio of x and y, growth rate of z is the difference between the growth rates of x and y).

Proof:

$$z + \Delta z = (x + \Delta x)/(y + \Delta y)$$

Dividing both sides by z and using $z = x/y$

$$1 + \Delta z/z = (1 + \Delta x/x)/(1 + \Delta y/y)$$

or $$1 + g_z = (1 + g_x)/(1 + g_y) = 1 + g_x - g_y \quad \text{by Result 2,}$$

or $$g_z = g_x - g_y.$$

Rule of seventy If a variable grows at x per cent per year, its value will double in approximately $70/x$ years. Thus, if it grows at 7 per cent per year, India's national income will double in roughly ten years.

Appendix 1.2
Some Basic Economic Concepts and Distinctions

Cross section and time series data Cross section records values of a variable for different groups at a point in time, for example, unemployment in different states of India in July 2002. Time series lists values of the variable at different points in time, for example: national income of India for the years 1995, 1996, 1999, and 2000.

Stocks and flows Stock variables are measured at a point in time, flows are measured per unit of time. Wealth or value of assets is a stock (Mr Sen's wealth is Rs 50 lakh on 1 January 2002), income is a flow (Mr Sen earned Rs 12,000 per month in 2002). A person's saving is a flow that adds to the stock of his assets. Government's budgetary deficit (excess of spending over revenue) per year makes the stock of government debt grow over time. All national income categories such as GDP, investment, depreciation, consumption spending are flows. Money supply in the Indian economy is a stock that is measured on the last Friday of March.

Equilibrium It is a state where planned (or desired) values and actual values of decision variables are equal, so that no decision-maker has any incentive to change his action. The system is at a state of rest.

Nominal and real Nominal variables are in units of money. Example: income of Rs 1000 per month, wage rate of Rs 15 per hour, price of Rs 50 per kg, assets worth Rs 10 crore. Real variables are in physical units of commodities. Real income is in terms of some commodity (or service) money buys. It is obtained by dividing money income by the corresponding price. If money income is Rs 1000 per month and the price of a shirt is Rs 100, real income is ten shirts per month. Money wage of Rs 15 per hour means real wage of 3 kg of rice per hour if rice sells at Rs 5 per kg. The higher the price of a commodity the lower will be the real income or real wage in terms of that commodity, money (nominal) income or wage remaining unchanged. In macroeconomics a concept of 'average price', P, is used to capture the general purchasing power of money. It is computed as a weighted average of prices of individual commodities, more important goods and services getting greater weights. Higher P implies lower purchasing power and lower real values of all variables whose nominal magnitudes have not increased in the same proportion as P.

Real and nominal rate of interest Real rate of interest = money (nominal) rate of interest – the rate of inflation.

The real rate is the nominal rate corrected for inflation. Savers (lenders) become worse off in real terms if the real rate of interest declines. Suppose that a lender makes a loan for one year at 6 per cent interest, but the general price level rises by 4 per cent over the course of the year. In real terms the return is only 2 (= 6 – 4) per cent at the end of the year, that is, in terms of the goods and services the lender can buy. Real interest would have been (–3) per cent had inflation been 9 per cent over the year. Clearly, it is the real, not the nominal, interest that captures the true cost of borrowing or the true return on lending. Note that real rate of interest may well be negative.

Relative price It is the ratio of two money prices and represents the barter rate of exchange between two commodities. Example: if price per unit of X is Rs 20 and that of Z is Rs 4, the relative price of X in terms of Z is 5. One unit of X will exchange for 5 units of Z without the intermediation of money.

Price index It is the ratio of the monetary cost of a specified bundle of goods and services in a given period to the cost of the same in an earlier period (known as the base period). For example, suppose there are only three goods—apples, shirts, and pens. The base year is 2000 and the current year is 2003.

	Quantities in reference basket	Price in current year (2003)	Price in base year (2000)
Apple	2	3	2
Shirt	3	5	7
Pen	1	4	4

We see that the price index for the current year is $(2 \times 3 + 3 \times 5 + 1 \times 4)/(2 \times 2 + 3 \times 7 + 1 \times 4) = 25/29$.

The index that is usually used to measure the economy-wide price level is the Wholesale Price Index (WPI). It uses the wholesale prices of all the major commodities available in a particular year. A better idea of the change in cost of living caused by price change is given by the Consumer Price Index (CPI). It is computed on the basis of the consumer price (retail price) of a bundle of selected goods and services on which a particular group of people spend most of its income. Price of luxury cars or concrete mixers, for instance, will be included in WPI, but not in CPI.

In computing the CPI the price of each good in the chosen bundle is multiplied by its weight and then the weighted prices are summed. The weight of each good is its share in the budget of the representative consumer. The shares are calculated using data from consumer expenditure surveys. In India the surveys are conducted by the National Sample Survey Organisation (NSSO).

Box A1.2.1 WPI and CPI in India

In India the WPI is calculated on a weekly basis with 1993–4 as the base year. The number of commodities covered is approximately 430. A separate index only for manufactured products is also calculated. It is denoted by WPI (MP). The CPI is constructed on a monthly basis covering 260 items with 1982 as the base year. Three different indices are calculated for three separate groups: industrial workers (IW), agricultural labourers (AL), and urban non-manual employees (UNME). Of these, CPI (IW) is of special significance because changes in the dearness allowance of central government employees are linked to changes in this index.

The weights given to different commodity groups are different under the WPI and the CPI (IW). Food products get 27 per cent weight in the former and 57 per cent in the latter, essential services like housing, transport, health, and education are assigned high weights in CPI but are not considered in the WPI. The share of fuel is much higher in the WPI (14 per cent as against 6 per cent).

In 2000–1 WPI was 155.7 (1993–4 = 100) and All India CPI (IW) stood at 444 (1982 = 100). Values of CPI (IW) are also available for all the major cities.

Rate of inflation Rate of inflation in the economy = rate of growth of some aggregate price index (usually WPI or National Income Deflator [NID], defined in Chapter 2 under the section, 'Real GDP'). Rate of change of CPI indicates the required change in money income that will protect the standard of living of the typical consumer of a particular group. If money income fails to keep pace with CPI, standard of living will decline for that group. When the price index is falling, it is a situation of *deflation*.

Rate of unemployment Rate of unemployment (per cent) = number of unemployed persons/labour force × 100. An unemployed person is one who is looking for work but is unable to find a job during a particular reference period. The *labour force* at any point in time consists of persons who are either working or searching for work (= employed + unemployed). When a person retires or a lady gives up her job to take care of her family after marriage the individuals are getting out of the labour force. The lady may want to re-enter it later. A person may stop looking for work after long period of unemployment. Such a *discouraged worker* is also out of the labour force.

Denoting the number of employed persons by E, the number of unemployed by U, and the labour force by L, we have:

$$L = E + U$$

Unemployment rate (per cent) $u = (U/L) \times 100$.

Labour force participation rate (per cent)

$$= (L/\text{Adult population}) \times 100.$$

In India, in 1999–2000, the labour force was 363 million out of a total population of 1003 million and the unemployment rate was 7.2 per cent in rural areas and 7.6 per cent in urban areas.

Employment in an economy is positively correlated with its GDP. An increase (decrease) in the output of goods and services is usually accompanied by a drop (rise) in unemployment. See Okun's Law in Box 3.1.

Physical and human capital Physical capital consists of factories, machines, school buildings, roads, and other public infrastructure. Human capital is the accumulated skill and knowledge of the people. Addition to human capital improves the quality of the workforce. All factors of production, including physical capital, become more productive as a result.

Box A1.2.2   Measurement of Unemployment in India

On the basis of data collected in surveys conducted by the NSSO unemployment is measured under three criteria.

Usual Status (US): The reference period is one year and a person is classified as unemployed if he could not find work for the major part of the year.

Current Weekly Status (CWS): The reference period is one week. A person is unemployed if he was unable to find work even for one hour during the week.

Current Daily Status (CDS): It measures all the days of unemployment of the unemployed as well as of the underemployed during the reference week.

Of the three, CDS is the most inclusive, covering open as well as partial unemployment. *Economic Surveys*, published annually by the GOI, contain detailed analysis of the employment–unemployment scenario of the country.

Real and financial assets The stock of wealth at any point in time consists of real assets and financial assets. Real assets are tangible, like factories, houses, land, capital equipment. Physical capital is part of the real assets of a community. Financial assets are claims to monetary payments. Corporate shares promise to pay dividend, a bond promises regular interest payment to the holder. These are financial assets. So are bank deposits and currency in circulation.

Investment In ordinary language, investment means purchase of stocks, bonds, national saving certificates, and other financial assets. In economics, investment stands for capital formation which covers purchase of new physical assets such as new machines, construction of new structures like factory buildings or roads or dams or residential houses or additional holding of raw materials and finished goods by firms (inventory investment).

Change along curves and shift of curves Graphs provide a simple yet powerful, device for presenting arguments and results. In handling graphs it is very important to know the distinction between movements along a curve and a shift in the curve itself. To illustrate, let us consider the demand curve for meat.

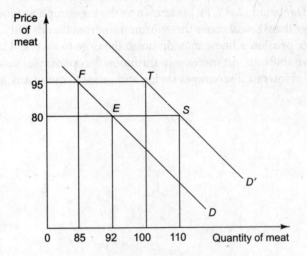

Fig. A1.2.1   Shift of Demand

Demand for meat of a consumer depends on the price of meat (own price), price of fish (related good), income of the buyer, and his taste for meat. The demand curve for meat shows the negative relation between own price and demand, holding the other determinants constant. Thus the curve D in Figure A1.2.1 is drawn for *given* values of the other determinants. At the price of Rs 80, demand equals 92 (point E), if price rises to Rs 95 demand falls to 85 (point F). This is a change *along* the D curve. Now suppose the income of the consumer rises. This may cause him to buy more meat even though the price of meat stays unchanged. That is, he buys more *at each price*. Old demands were 92 at Rs 80 and 85 at Rs 95, now the corresponding demands are 110 and 100 (points S and T). D' is the new demand curve. A rise in income has caused a rightward *shift* of the curve. A fall in the price of fish will induce him to buy less meat at each price of meat. The demand curve shifts to the left in this case. (There will be a movement along the demand curve for fish as more fish is bought caused by a fall in own price.)

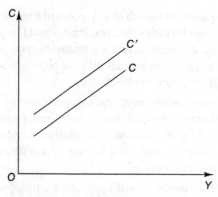

Fig. A1.2.2   Shift of Consumption

In the consumption decision of households, factors like the rate of interest, the wealth of the household, or availability of credit influence C. These are held constant when current C is plotted against current Y. This relation $C = C(Y)$ is known as the consumption function. Any change in one of these variables other than Y will cause the consumption function to shift. An increase in wealth or introduction of a better pension scheme may diminish the urge to save and induce a higher C at each level of Y. The C curve shifts up. An increase in thriftiness (propensity to save) will cause a downward shift. A fall in the rate of interest discourages saving and raises C out of any given level of income and the C curve shifts up.

2. Measuring the Economy's Performance

Understanding and improving the performance of an economy is not possible without a proper quantification of the values of the major macroeconomic variables. This is not an easy task, given the highly aggregative nature of the concepts involved. The standard techniques developed by economists and statisticians for the purpose of measuring the performance of a modern economy are collectively known as methods of national income accounting. Indian statisticians working at the Indian Statistical Institute and the Central Statistical Organisation (CSO) have made important contributions to the development of these methods. The last section of this chapter looks into India's national income accounts in detail.

NATIONAL INCOME ACCOUNTING

Gross Domestic Product (GDP) is the value at current market prices of all *final* goods and services produced within the economy in the current year. Goods are tangible while services are not. Haircuts, economics lectures, performances of actors and singers, activities of lawyers, doctors, bankers, real estate brokers, and transport operators are examples of services.

Only *final* goods and services are included and all intermediate products used up in the production of these goods and services are excluded to avoid double or multiple counting. There would be duplication if, for example, the values of steel, glass, or tyres that are used to build a car are added to the value of the car itself, since the price of the car will cover the prices of all these intermediate inputs. Similarly, the value of the bread finally consumed by the households is included, but not the value of the wheat or flour or any other ingredient that went into it.

But when Mrs Sen purchases flour for baking a cake at home it is a final sale and is included in GDP. Currently produced intermediate goods (steel, glass, rubber, wheat, chemicals and so on) that are held as stocks to be used in future production or to meet sudden spurts in demand are included in current GDP.

Double counting can be avoided by using the concept of *value added*. Value added *(VA)* by any production unit is obtained by subtracting the cost of intermediate inputs (purchased from other business units) from the value of its output. It measures the contribution made by the factors of production (labour, capital, land, and entrepreneur) employed by this particular unit. By summing the value added by different units the value of final output can be obtained.

The general expression for *VA* can be obtained in two steps:

1. Value of output = sales (domestic + exports) + change in stocks (closing – opening).
2. *VA* = value of output – cost of intermediate inputs (domestic + imports).

Consider the following simplified example where there are no exports and imports and no change in stocks. An economy consists of three firms: *J*, *K*, and *M*. *J* supplies an intermediate input to *K* and *M* but does not purchase anything from them. *K* uses *J*'s product as input in production. *M* buys intermediate inputs from both *J* and *K*. The value of *J*'s sales is Rs 100, of which Rs 40 comes from *K* and Rs 60 from M. Value of sales of K is Rs 350, which consists of Rs 200 from sales to M and Rs 150 to final consumers. M sells its output to final consumers for Rs 500. The value of final output in the system is Rs 150 (sold by K) + Rs 500 (sold by M) = Rs 650. VA of J equals Rs 100 (= sales revenue, since it does not purchase any intermediate input), VA of K = Rs 350 – Rs 40 = Rs 310. VA of M = Rs 500 – Rs 60 – Rs 200 = Rs 240. The aggregate VA by all three firms together equals Rs 650, which is the value of final output.

Statisticians of national income usually divide the economy into a few broad sectors and use estimates of value added by them to arrive at a figure for GDP. The major sectors considered by the CSO of India include: agriculture and allied activities, manufacturing, mining and quarrying, electricity, gas and water supply, construction, trade, hotels, transport and communication, insurance, real estate and business services, and community, social, and personal services. National income estimation in India is discussed in more detail in the last section.

Transactions of commodities not produced in the current year are excluded. Thus purchases or sales of existing houses or old furniture or second-hand books and CDs do not contribute to current GDP. However, flow of service from existing assets and durable goods such as houses, cars, and refrigerators should be included.

Payments that are not backed by any current productive activity are called *transfer payments*. Pension (payment for service rendered in the past), unemployment compensation, disability benefits are examples. Such receipts are not included.

Illegal transactions are excluded from GDP.

Non-marketed production (agricultural output retained for consumption by farmers, for example) is evaluated at market prices. Very important unpaid services such as those provided by female members of households are not included because of the difficulty of assigning appropriate values to them. Services of owner-occupied houses are included at the imputed market rent of similar houses.

Government services such as the army, the police force, the bureaucracy, or the judiciary are valued at cost because there is no market in which these services are bought and sold. Wages and salaries (called 'compensation of employees') and other costs of providing their services constitute the contribution of the government administrative departments to national income.

GDP and GNP

Gross National Product (GNP) is the value of final goods and services produced in the current period by *domestically-owned* factors of production at home or abroad. The difference with GDP arises because some production within the domestic economy is done by factors owned by foreigners. For instance, the salary of an American consultant in IBM's office in Bangalore or the profit repatriated from India by the same company belongs to the GNP of the USA. It is part of India's GDP , but not her GNP. Similarly, the earnings of an Indian national working in a bank in Dhaka contributes to Bangladesh's GDP and India's GNP.

GNP = GDP + income earned by domestically owned factors abroad – income earned at home by foreign owned factors = GDP + net factor earning from abroad.

Owing to the relatively poor quality of data on net factor earnings from abroad, India and most other countries publish figures of GDP as the index of the economy's overall performance. Also, GDP is a good indicator of the job-creating potential of an economy. For India the difference between GDP and GNP is not large.

NDP and NNP

Part of a nation's capital stock (plants and equipment, factories and school buildings, warehouses, rail stations and tracks, ports, bridges, etc.) wears out in the process of production. By subtracting the cost of this depreciation (capital consumption allowance or cost of consumption of fixed capital) from GDP or GNP, the values of Net Domestic Product (NDP) and Net National Product (NNP) are obtained. Depreciation is subtracted because this has to be set aside (and hence not available for current consumption) to maintain the stock of capital at its present level.

Real GDP

Nominal GDP is calculated using current prices. This reduces the usefulness of the concept as a tool for comparing the performance of the economy over time if prices are changing. Suppose that between 1995 and 2000 output has stayed unchanged while all prices have doubled in value. In that case, GDP in the latter year will be twice as high as in the former. But this gain in GDP is illusory, created entirely by the change in prices with no change whatsoever in the availability of goods and services to the consumers. The distorting effect of changing prices can be neutralized if production in the two periods are evaluated at the same set of prices. Then changes in value of GDP can be attributed to improvement in real performance of the economy. Current year's output evaluated at the prices of a fixed base year is known as Real GDP (or GDP at Constant Prices). The base year in India used to be 1980–1. Recently it has been changed to 1993–4.

Table 2.1 illustrates the concepts. The current year is 2003 and the base year is 1993.

Table 2.1

	Current quantities	Current year (2003) prices	Base year (1993) prices
Apple	8	6	4
Orange	4	3	7
Pen	10	2	5

$$\text{Current GDP} = 8 \times 6 + 4 \times 3 + 10 \times 2 = 80.$$

$$\text{Real GDP} = 8 \times 4 + 4 \times 7 + 10 \times 5 = 110.$$

(Note that for the base year current and real GDPs are equal by definition.)

It should be clear that there is no unique measure of real GDP, because it depends on the choice of the base year. As a result, GDP for the years 1980–2000, valued at 1980 prices may behave very differently from the same series valued at 1990 prices. Inference and interpretation may be difficult if there is no reason to prefer one base year to the other.

Calculation of real GDP yields one measure of the aggregate price level, called the National Income Deflator (NID).

$$\text{NID} = (\text{Current GDP/Real GDP}) \times 100$$

For the example given above, NID = $(80/110) \times 100 = 72$ per cent (approx).

The rate of change of NID is often used to measure inflation.

$$\text{Per capita GDP} = \text{GDP/population.}$$

Growth rate of per capita GDP = growth rate of GDP – rate of population growth.

Gross Investment (Gross Capital Formation) = production of new capital goods
+ additions to stock (inventory)

Net Investment (Net Capital Formation) = Gross Investment – depreciation.

Box 2.1   PPP National Income for International Comparison

The GDP of India is expressed in rupees while that of the USA in dollars. Comparison is impossible without converting one currency into the other. Usually this is done at the current rate of foreign exchange (say 45 rupees per dollar). But this will fail to reveal the true difference in the standard of living or real income between the two nations because the current rupee–dollar exchange does not accurately reflect the relative purchasing power of the two currencies. In India Rs 45 buys much more than $1 does in the USA. So economists have devised the concept of Purchasing Power Parity (PPP) exchange rate based on the cost of a standard basket of consumption. At PPP rate the rupee equivalent of one dollar will be less than 45 and this will give a boost to India's GDP relative to that of the USA.

The pioneering work in this area was done by Robert Summers and Alan Heston at the University of Pennsylvania, USA. The Penn World Table presents a comprehensive, internationally comparable set of national income figures for a large number of countries of the world. Originally the series ended in 1988, but now it is regularly updated.

Using the market exchange rate the per capita GDP of the USA in 1993 was 97 times that of India. Using PPP numbers it was 'only' 15 times higher. For the year 2000, per capita GDP (PPP dollars) for some countries are given below:

India (2390), China (3940), Mexico (8810), Egypt (3690), South Korea (17,340), Ghana (1940), Pakistan (1960), Brazil (7320), Malaysia (8360), and Kenya (1010).

A nation's capital stock and productive capacity will grow over time only if net investment is positive.

National Income at Factor Cost

Gross domestic product is evaluated at market prices which diverge from the true cost of production, based on payments to factors of production, due to the presence of indirect taxes and subsidies. Suppose that the factor cost of one unit of output (including profit) is Rs 10. If there is a tax of Rs 2 per unit, on the commodity or service, the tax – inclusive market price will be Rs 12. If instead of a tax, there was a subsidy of Rs 2 per unit, the producer could sell at Rs 8 and still incur no loss. Thus indirect taxes push market price above unit cost of production and subsidies do the opposite. So, to obtain the value of aggregate output at factor cost (actual payment to factors for their productive service—which is the true measure of their contribution to national income), indirect taxes are deducted and subsidies added on.

NI at Factor Cost = GDP – (indirect taxes – subsidies)

= GDP – net indirect taxes.

Disposable Income or Disposable Personal Income

Disposable income (DI, or disposable personal income (DPI) is the level of income available to the households for spending and saving. Out of the GDP, personal taxes are collected by the government. This is not available to the households. But the same government also makes transfer payments like pensions, and unemployment compensations which add to the household's ability to spend or save.

Households own the firms and, therefore, are entitled to receive the profits of business. However, owing to a variety of reasons most corporations choose not to distribute the whole of their current profits in the current period. The undistributed part lowers disposable income relative to GDP. Net earnings from abroad are, of course, an addition to disposable income.

$$DI = GDP + \text{net income from abroad} + \text{transfers (TR)} - \text{taxes (TX)}$$
$$- \text{undistributed profits.}$$

Disposable income is either consumed or saved.

$$DI = \text{consumption spending } (C) + \text{personal saving } (S).$$

THREE METHODS OF MEASURING GDP

The three major methods for measuring national income are now discussed.

Product Method Under this method the 'VA' by all the production units (including those producing intermediate goods and services) are summed up to arrive at the value of final production. The problem of multiple counting is avoided thereby.

Income Method Here national income is taken to be the total income earned by all the factors of production in the economy. For each production unit VA is the excess of revenue over cost of intermediate inputs. This surplus gets distributed as payment to factors employed by the firm. Therefore, if we sum VA of all the production units the value of aggregate factor income in the economy will be obtained. Since the actual number of production units in a modern economy runs into tens of thousands, what is usually done is to decompose the system into a small number of aggregative sectors and estimate their VA by various methods. We have already mentioned the classification of sectors used by the CSO in calculating India's national income.

Expenditure Method This method uses the identity that the value of sales equals the expenditure of the buyers. Suppose that the value of final output in the current period is Rs 1000, of which Rs 800 could be sold and unsold goods worth Rs 200 added to inventories or stock. We can at once conclude that the buyers spent Rs 800 on current output. The additional stock of Rs 200 is conventionally taken as investment expenditure by the firms on their own product. It is as if the firms sold the goods to themselves to add to their commodity stocks. Thus total expenditure comes to Rs 1000 (Rs 800 from the households + Rs 200 from the firms on stock holding), exactly equal to the value of output.

Since the number of individual buyers in a modern economy is unmanageably vast, the expenditure method classifies total expenditure in a system under four broad heads according to the source of demand: consumption spending (coming from the households), investment spending by firms, purchase of goods and services by the government (national and regional lumped together) and spending by foreign nationals on our output. The first three are usually denoted by C, I, and G, respectively. What the foreigners spend on our output is the value of our exports. This is denoted by X.

Consumers spend partly on domestic goods and partly on imports from abroad. Similarly, part of total investment spending is on domestically-produced equipment and the rest is on imported capital goods. Government purchases will also, possibly, have two components. We write:

$$C = C_d + C_m, \quad I = I_d + I_m, \quad G = G_d + G_m.$$

The subscript d denotes the portion spent on domestic output and m the portion spent on imports.

GDP $=$ expenditure on domestic production

$$= C_d + I_d + G_d + X$$

$$= C + I + G + X - (C_m + I_m + G_m).$$

But the last term within brackets is nothing but the value of our imports. Denoting this by M we get

$$\text{GDP} = C + I + G + X - M = C + I + G + NX \tag{2.1}$$

where NX is the value of net exports (trade surplus or external surplus) in the current period.

Consumption expenditure C is the largest of the four components of aggregate demand (expenditure) for most economies. In India its share in GDP is about 55 per cent.

Estimates of India's GDP consumption spending, investment (capital formation), and some other important macro variables are presented in Appendix 2.1.

Box 2.2   Can Exports Exceed GDP?

Export ratio is defined to be X/GDP. Can this be greater than unity for a country? At first the answer would seem to be a clear 'no', because no country can sell more abroad than what it produces at home. But then how is one to account for the fact that Singapore, in 1994, had an export ratio of 140 per cent? For Hong Kong also the ratio is above 100 per cent. The clue is to realize that in international trade statistics, exports and imports include exports and imports of both final and intermediate goods. Intermediate goods entering global trade range all the way from unprocessed raw materials to nearly finished products. Inclusion of intermediate goods can make the ratio go beyond unity. Consider a country that imports raw material worth Rs 100 and turns it into final product worth Rs 150 using domestic labour and capital. Suppose it exports final goods valued at Rs 120. Then $X =$ Rs 120, but GDP $=$ domestic value added $=$ Rs 50. In the text, for simplicity, we have considered only final goods and services.

TWO IMPORTANT IDENTITIES

Two important identities follow from the definitions of accounting. Two separate cases are considered.

Economy Without Government and Foreign Trade Let the value of output be Y. Since whatever is produced is either purchased or added to stocks and additions to stock are counted as part of investment by firms, we have the identity:

$$Y = C + I \tag{2.2}$$

There being no government, income and disposable income are the same and disposable income is allocated between consumption and saving. This gives the identity.

$$Y = C + S \tag{2.3}$$

From equations (2.2) and (2.3) we get $S = I$.

In this simple economy investment is identically equal to saving. It is important to note that this identity holds for *actual* or *measured* saving and investment. *Planned* or *intended* magnitudes may well differ in value. In particular, some of inventory investment may be undesired.

Economy with Government and Foreign Trade Let us assume that undistributed profit and net income from abroad are not significant. Then

$$\text{DI} = Y + \text{TR} - \text{TX};$$

$$\text{also}\quad \text{DI} = C + S.$$

So $\quad C + S = Y + TR - TX$

and $\quad Y = C + I + G + NX.$

Combining, $\quad S - I = (G + TR - TX) + NX$ $\hspace{4cm}$ (2.4)

$(G + TR)$ is the total expenditure of the government on goods and services and transfer payments, TX is the tax revenue. So, $(G + TR - TX)$ is the excess of government expenditure over its revenue or the *budget deficit* (BD). This is dissaving (negative saving) by the government. Relation (2.4) can be rewritten as

$$S - I = BD + NX. \hspace{4cm} (2.5)$$

This important equation says that there is a strict association between the excess of private sector's saving over investment, the budget deficit of the government, and the balance in the foreign trade sector. If $S = I$, then budgetary deficit will be reflected in an equal external deficit ($NX < 0$). Another way of looking at equation (2.5) may be instructive. Rewrite it as:

$$S = I + BD + NX.$$

This points to the three uses of domestic household saving. Potential borrowers are on the right-hand side. Part of S may be used by the business sector to finance investment, part may be borrowed by the government to meet its budget deficit and part may be borrowed by foreigners to pay for their trade deficit. ($NX > 0$ for our economy implies that foreigners are indebted to us. Their exports are not sufficient to pay for their imports from us.)

The excess of government revenue over expenditure is the *budget surplus* (negative of BD). This is government saving.

NATIONAL INCOME AND SOCIAL WELFARE

As an index of overall economic performance, GDP or GNP may reasonably be expected to be a good numerical indicator of the (non-measurable) welfare of the citizens of a country. However, due to some serious limitations, the traditional concept of national income fails to serve as an adequate index of welfare. The major deficiencies can be summarized as follows.

- Distribution of income is not reflected at all in GDP. Even a very high GDP may not contribute much to the well-being of a nation if it is not distributed equally. A lower total which is more equitably shared may be better for the society.
- Economic activities that are not marketed are excluded from national income calculations. Important productive services left out of account include the services of womenfolk working at home and self-employed persons. The informal sector plays a very important role in the Indian economy, but most of its activities are unreported and so its contribution eludes proper accounting. At best, partial correction can be attempted through the use of informed 'guesstimates'. Attempts have been made to include the imputed income of housewives (what they could have earned in the labour market) in national income computation. This will add substantially to the GDP of developing countries like India.
- In the course of production, physical capital is not the only social asset that gets depleted. Noise, smoke, carbon dioxide emissions, industrial effluents, chemical fertilizers and pesticides used in agriculture, and other pollutants attendant on production have serious deleterious effects on the 'environmental capital' of a nation. As a result of these harmful side effects, GDP ceases to be a

good measure of *sustainable welfare*, by which we mean the flow of production that can be currently carried on without compromising the well-being of future generations. Also, some expenditures are incurred purely to mitigate environmental damage. Example: cleaning up expenses of firms or money spent by households situated near highways or airports to reduce noise pollution. These protective expenditures do not contribute to welfare in any positive way. Residual pollution, uncorrected by these measures, continues to be a serious menace to the quality of life of the citizens. A downward adjustment to conventional GDP, known as the Index of Sustainable Economic Welfare (ISEW), has been suggested.

ISEW = GDP − (depreciation of physical capital + protective expenditure + depreciation of environmental capital + value of residual pollution)

In spite of the formidable measurement problems associated with environmental depreciation and residual pollution, ISEW is a step in the right direction.

▨ Concentrating, as it does, only on the value of sales (price times quantity), GDP has no direct way of capturing changes in the quality of commodities and services. This is a serious limitation because qualitative improvement has always been a major source of improvement in the general standard of living, particularly so in recent years, after the IT revolution. Over the past decade, the quality of computers has improved dramatically, accompanied by an equally dramatic fall in price. So, the sales revenue or VA by itself is a very imperfect indicator of the contribution of the computer industry to social welfare.

GDP AND THE UNDERGROUND ECONOMY

If the underground or black economy is large, official GDP, based on reported values, will fail to serve as an accurate measure of the volume of activities going on in the system. Inferences drawn from the behaviour of GDP may be erroneous and cause blunders in policymaking. The most commonly used measure of black economy is tax-evaded money, achieved through unreported or underreported income, and overstated tax deductions. Estimates for India range from 15 per cent to more than 50 per cent of GDP. But the problem is far from insignificant even in the more developed countries. By some estimates, as much as 25 per cent of actual transactions in the USA may not make it to measured GDP. 'Irregular' national income exceeds the official figure by more than 30 per cent in Italy. The hidden economy of the UK is estimated between 3 per cent and 15 per cent.

Since black market transactions are almost invariably carried out with cash, a rising trend in cash holding, relative to bank deposits may be an indicator that the hidden economy is expanding.

INDIA'S NATIONAL ACCOUNTS

The CSO classifies production activities in the Indian economy into a number of major groups depending on the type of goods and services produced. These are (i) agriculture, animal husbandry, forestry and fishing; (ii) mining and quarrying; (iii) manufacturing; (iv) electricity, gas, and water supply; (v) construction; (vi) trade, hotel and restaurant; (vii) transport, storage and communication; (viii) finance and real estate; and (ix) community and personal services.

Groups (i) to (v) produce material goods and the rest, services. Groups (i) and (ii) form the *primary sector*, (iii), (iv), and (v) the *secondary sector*, and (vi) to (ix) the *tertiary sector*. 'Manufacturing' is subdivided into r*egistered* and *unregistere*d, and construction into *pucca* and *kutcha*. 'Finance and real estate' is subdivided into banking and insurance, ownership of dwellings, activities of real estate dealers and business services; 'community and personal services' cover activities like defence, public administration, educational, legal and medical services, recreation and personal services.

The CSO defines the *private sector* as consisting of NSSO two subsectors: *private corporate sector* and *household sector*. The *public sector* is divided into government *administrative departments* and *government enterprises*. The latter, in turn, is subdivided into unincorporated *departmental enterprises* (DEs) and *non-departmental enterprises* (NDEs). NDEs (like ONGC, DVC, LIC, nationalized banks, electricity boards, etc.) differ from the DEs, in that they hold and manage the financial assets of their business, and present profit and loss accounts as in the case of the private corporate sector.

Data Collection Systems

Agricultural production statistics are obtained from Agricultural Census and the Landholdings Survey of the 'NSSO'. Crop yields are estimated from systematic crop-cutting experiments carried out all over the country. In the majority of states, there is a system for regularly reporting crop acreages and crop yields by season.

The data on output value, value of inputs, capital expenditure and employment in the registered manufacturing sector are collected through the Annual Survey of Industries (ASI) undertaken by the Department of Statistics, GOI. The field work of the survey is done by the Field Operations Division of the NSSO. The Steering Committee on Industrial Statistics constituted by the NSSO supervises the entire process of data collection, processing, and tabulation.

The estimates for unregistered manufacturing industries are available only once in five years. For other years, the CSO projects the estimates using the indices for industrial production (IIP). This is not quite satisfactory as the IIPs mainly relate to the growth of large industries, which may not be a good indicator of the growth of small industries. The IIP has been revised with 1993–4 as the base year and attempts are being made to improve the representation from the small-scale sector. The system of data reporting for unregistered manufacturing remains unsatisfactory at present.

Private Final Consumption Expenditure

The estimates of private final consumption expenditure (PFCE) are obtained by the commodity flow method. First, the total availability of an item of consumption during a year is estimated by adding up domestic production and import. From the total availability, all other uses of the item (intermediate use in various producing units, change in stocks, government consumption, and export) are subtracted to arrive at final consumption by households. For services, PFCE is calculated from the gross earnings of the agencies providing these services to consumers, after netting out the expenditure of the former, on these services during the period.

Gross Domestic Capital Formation

The CSO's estimate of gross investment or GDCF gives the value of gross additions to stocks (inventories) and fixed assets consisting of construction and machinery and equipment.

- Estimates of inventories are prepared on the basis of stocks held by industries and the total stock of foodgrains held by producers and traders.
- Total expenditure on all construction (new construction, alteration and repair of buildings, streets, railroads, communication networks, etc., improvement of land and development of mining sites, forests and plantations and so on) is estimated as the total value of material inputs used and factor incomes generated in the form of wages, rent, and profits.
- Various items of machinery and equipment are classified into (i) capital goods; (ii) parts of capital goods; (iii) partly capital goods; and (iv) parts of partly capital goods. Capital formation during a

year is estimated to be the domestic availability of items under (i), 50 per cent of the items under (ii), and varying proportions of the items under (iii) and (iv).

SOURCES OF DATA ON THE INDIAN ECONOMY

Macroeconomic data on the Indian economy are regularly published by the following organizations: the GOI (*Economic Surveys*); the RBI Bulletins, RBI Reports on Currency and Finance, the RBI website (www.rbi.org.in); the Annual Survey of Industries (ASI); the Centre for Monitoring the Indian Economy (CMIE); the Economic and Political Weekly Research Foundation (EPWRF); the Directorate General of Foreign Trade (DGFT); the Directorate General of Commercial Intelligence and Statistics (DGCIS); and the Tata Services Limited (*Statistical Outline of India*).

Summary

- Gross domestic product GDP is the value at current prices of all final goods and services produced within the economy in the current year. Gross national product is the value of final goods and services produced by domestically-owned factors at home and abroad.

- Product method, income method, and expenditure method are three ways of calculating GDP.

- Two identities: $S = I$, $S - I = BD + NX$.

- National Income has limitations as a measure of social welfare.

- India has a sophisticated system of national income accounts.

Exercise

1. Suppose GDP is Rs 5000. Domestic residents receive factor payments from abroad of Rs 150. Foreigners receive Rs 90 as factor payment from this country. What is the value of GNP?

2. Which of the following are stocks and which are flows? consumption, capital, investment, transfer payment, depreciation , GDP, budget deficit, net worth (assets minus liabilities) of a company.

3. Why is the imputed rental income of owner-occupied housing included in GDP and not the market value of the house itself? If you give Rs 5 to a beggar should that be included in GDP? What if he sings you a song?

4. What will be the impact on GDP if
   (i) all office bosses marry their secretaries and do not hire new ones until the following year;
   (ii) the government hires an unemployed worker, who had been getting Rs 1000 per month as unemployment benefit, as a government employee doing nothing on Rs 1000 per month;
   (iii) a consumer decides to buy a refrigerator made in South Korea rather than one made in India?

5. What difference would it make to national income accounts if, instead of purchasing a car for the use of its general manager, a company gives her extra salary to buy that car? (Hint: Purchase of durable goods by firms are counted as investment.)

6. Consider the following data for a hypothetical economy:

	Rs
GDP	7000
Gross investment	800
Net investment	550
Consumption	4500
Government purchase of goods	1100
Budget surplus	30

Find: NDP, net exports, government taxes minus transfers, disposable income, and personal saving.

7. Consider the following data:

	Rs (lakh)
Closing stock of Firm A	30
Closing stock of Firm B	20
Opening stock of Firm A	5
Opening stock of Firm B	10
Domestic sales of Firm A	250
Purchase of Firm A from Firm B	100
Purchase of Firm B from Firm A	80
Domestic sales of Firm B	250
Import of raw materials by Firm A	65
Export by Firm B	30

Find the VA of the two firms.

8. Some people argue that government spending on defence or police protection really does not contribute to GDP. What is the logic? (Hint: An increase in the crime rate can change GDP by causing an expansion of the police force.)

9. What, if anything, is wrong with the following data?
In an economy investment exceeds saving by Rs 10,000. Budget deficit is Rs 6000 and net export is Rs 4000.

10. Only two commodities—food and clothing—are used to compute CPI for an economy with respective weights 60 per cent and 40 per cent. If food price rises by 10 per cent and clothing price by 15 per cent what is the impact on CPI?

11. 'A country where the households, investors, and the government together spend more than its income must have an external deficit'. True or False?

12. In an economy, the household buys bread worth Rs 150 from the baker and flour worth Rs 20 from the miller. The baker spends Rs 40 to buy flour from the miller to be used in production. The miller does not purchase any intermediate inputs. Compute GDP by the VA method.

Appendix 2.1
Some Important National Income Aggregates of India

Some important National Income Aggregates of India are presented in the following tables.

Table A2.1 National Income Aggregates at 1993–94 prices

(Rs crore)

Year	GDP at factor cost	GDP at market prices	NNP at market prices	Private final consumption expenditure	Net domestic capital formation
1991–2	701,863	778,289	693,798	536,980	97,782
1992–3	737,792	819,318	729,708	550,828	109,285
1993–4	781,345	859,220	763,787	574,772	115,059
1994–5	838,031	923,349	819,676	601,481	153,424
1995–6	899,563	993,946	882,192	638,938	171,863
1996–7	970,083	1,067,445	949,447	689,566	161,160
1997–8	1,016,594	1,115,247	989,738	707,285	174,198
1998–9	1,082,748	1,182,021	1,047,854	752,440	168,778
1999–2000	1,148,442	1,266,358	1,125,685	797,653	221,088
2000–01	1,198,685	1,316,340	1,167,832	818,636	209,140
2001–02	1,267,833	1,384,011	1,233,460	866,736	204,360
2002–03	1,318,321	1,447,595	1,285,988	897,243	223,302
2003–04	1,424,507	1,560,011	1,389,236	*	*

Note: * information not available
Source: India Development Report, 2004–05.

Table A2.2 GDP and National Savings

(Rs crore)

Year	GDP at current market prices	Household savings savings (gross)	Private corporate savings (gross)	Public sector savings (gross)
1991–2	653,117	110,736	20,304	12,868
1992–3	748,367	131,073	19,968	11,865
1993–4	859,220	158,310	29,866	5,445
1994–5	1,012,770	199,358	35,260	16,845
1995–6	1,188,012	215,588	58,542	24,065
1996–7	1,368,208	233,252	61,092	22,917
1997–8	1,522,547	268,437	63,486	20,255
1998–9	1,740,985	327,074	65,026	−17,169
1999–2000	1,936,925	402,360	84,329	−20,049
2000–01	2,104,298	453,641	86,142	−48,022
2001–02	2,282,143	519,040	78,849	−62,704
2002–03	2,469,564	559,258	84,169	−45,730

Source: India Development Report, 2004–05.

Table A2.3 Private Consumption Expenditure in India in 2000–01

(Rs crore at current prices)

Food beverages, etc. of which:	644,476
	(48.1)
cereals, pulses, etc.	157,568
	(11.8)
sugar and gur	39,701
	(3.0)
oils and oil seeds	29,289
	(2.2)
fruits, vegetables and tubers	136,894
	(10.2)
milk and dairy products	108,775
	(8.1)
beverages, pan, tobacco, etc.	52,350
	(3.9)
clothing and footwear	65,739
	(4.9)
rent, fuel, and power	152,158
	(11.3)
transport and communication	178,885
	(13.3)
Others	299,704
	(22.3)
Total	1,340,962

Source: *Statistical Outline of India*, Tata Services Limited, 2002–3.

Note: Figures in brackets indicate percentages to total.

Table A2.4 Capital Formation in India in 2000–01

(Rs crore at current prices)

Gross fixed capital formation	456,975
Construction	223,431
Machinery and equipment	233,544
Change in stocks	21,217
Total gross capital formation	478,192
Public sector	148,106
Private sector	123,022
Household sector	207,064
Less depreciation	198,447
Public sector	76,655
Private sector	56,350
Household sector	65,442
Total net capital formation	279,745
Public sector	71,451
Private sector	66,672
Household sector	141,622

Source: *Statistical Outline of India*, Tata Services Limited, 2002–03.

3. Theory of Income Determination

If we plot the values of GDP of any modern economy over a period of, say, fifty years, the most prominent feature to strike the eye is the periodic fluctuation around some trend line. The whole graph seems to move in cycles. Systematic fluctuations in the level of aggregate economic activity (known as *business cycles* consisting of booms or expansions and recessions or contractions) have been around for a very long time. Since GDP and employment are strongly correlated, such fluctuations translate directly into instability of employment and income. This has undesirable consequences for the welfare of the citizens of a country.

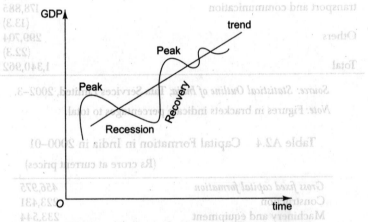

Fig. 3.1   Business Cycle around Trend

Variables that move in the same direction as GDP in the course of a business cycle are called *procyclical*. Those that move in the opposite direction are *countercyclical*. Thus unemployment moves countercyclically. Employment and capacity utilization are procyclical.

If business cycles are to be eliminated (or at least rendered less severe), we need to understand their underlying cause. So, a theory of output determination at the macro level is needed. Chapter 2 gave us methods of measuring GDP, but said nothing about why the value may be low or high or what should be done to pull a system out of a recession and make it grow. For explanation, theory is needed.

Box 3.1   Okun's Law

This is an empirical relationship between the growth of real GDP and the resulting change in the unemployment rate. For the USA the equation is:

$$\Delta u = -0.5(g_Y - 3).$$

This means, if (real) national income is growing at 7 per cent, $\Delta u = -2$, that is, unemployment will decline by two percentage points. 3 per cent is the trend rate of growth of the economy. Actual growth equal to this rate will keep unemployment (and employment) constant.

The general form of the law is:

$$\Delta u = -\beta(g_Y - \hat{g})$$

where $\hat{g}$ is the trend ('normal') growth of output (= sum of the rates of growth of the labour force and of labour productivity) and β is a coefficient that captures the strength of the link between growth and unemployment. A high β implies that any deviation in output from trend translates into large adjustments in employment. The value of β will be influenced by legal and social norms in respect of hiring and firing by firms. Thus β should be low for countries that have restrictions on firing. India, Japan, and most European countries belong to this category. Weakening of governmental regulation under the programme of liberalization will tend to raise the value of β.

DETERMINATION OF EQUILIBRIUM INCOME

The theory of national income (henceforth, 'income') determination to be outlined in this chapter was developed by the British economist, John Maynard Keynes. Therefore, it is known as the *Keynesian approach* to macroeconomics. The basic assumption is that the economy is in a state of recession with resources (labour, raw materials, installed productive capacity) lying underutilized. The implication is that if the level of activity picks up, there would not be any noticeable upward pressure on prices. So all prices (of goods and services as well as of inputs) are taken to be fixed. This will cease to be a good description as the economy approaches the state of full capacity utilization, but the Keynesian analysis is not supposed to be applicable to that case.

The fundamental idea is that output (and therefore employment) in a state of recession is determined by the level of aggregate demand. Income is demand determined in the sense that only that much will be produced that can be sold. In the simplest case, demand is assumed to have only two components—consumption and investment. We deflate consumption spending and investment spending by the aggregate price level (denoted by P) to obtain real consumption and real investment. Since our object of interest is the level of economic activity and not its composition, output is taken to consist of a single homogeneous commodity which is used both for consumption and investment. Supply of this composite commodity will be determined by the real demand for it. Real demand is obtained by deflating monetary expenditure by the constant value of P.

Economy Without Government or Foreign Trade

The fundamental building block is the relationship that states that real consumption in the current period has a strong relationship with current real income. This is written as, $C = C(Y)$. It is very important to recognize that C here stands for *planned* (or *desired*) consumption expenditure by the households. As their income changes in real terms, planned consumption also changes in real terms. The *consumption function* (or consumption demand schedule) shows what the level of planned real consumption would be, if real income assumes various alternative values. Two properties of the consumption function are:

- consumption moves in line with income, it rises as income rises and falls with a fall in income;
- the change in consumption is less than the change in income, because saving also changes. To give an example: if the household gets an additional income of Rs 100, consumption will rise by Rs 75 and Rs 25 will be added to saving. Similarly, if current income falls by Rs 100, consumption may not fall to the same extent. It may fall by Rs 75 and saving will decline by Rs 25. The linear function $C = 10 + 3/4\,Y$ is consistent with our example.

The fraction of extra income that is spent on additional consumption is known as the *marginal propensity to consume* (mpc). For obvious reason, *marginal propensity to save* (mps) is one minus the mpc. For the linear function given above, $mpc = 3/4$ (= the slope) and $mps = 1/4$. The value of mpc is taken to be positive but less than unity.

The ratios C/Y and S/Y are the *average propensity to consume* (apc) and the *average propensity to save* (aps) respectively. For the linear consumption function $C = a + cY$, mpc (= c) is constant, but apc = $C/Y = a/Y + c$ declines as Y rises.

Since consumption plus saving always equals disposable income and, in the present context, due to the absence of government taxes and transfers, disposable income and income are the same, the saving function can be obtained as $S = Y - C = Y - (10 + 3/4\,Y) = -10 + 1/4\,Y$. (Note that saving is negative for low values of income.) Mps (= $1/4$) is the slope of the saving function.

A part of consumption spending will be independent of current income. This is *autonomous* consumption. For the C function given above, autonomous C is 10. The other part (= $3/4\,Y$) is *induced* by income. Similarly, autonomous investment is the level that does not change with current Y. When we take I to be constant, we are assuming that the whole of I is autonomous. This is done purely for convenience and will be relaxed later.

For simplicity let us assume that planned investment by firms is positive and constant. We have the following central proposition.

Equilibrium Income Determination

Given the household's consumption demand schedule and the planned investment of firms, there is one and only one level of income at which there can be equilibrium.

Let us demonstrate with the help of a numerical example. The consumption function is $C = 10 + 3/4\,Y$ and investment $I = 20$. The aggregate demand (AD) function is $C + I = 30 + 3/4\,Y$. Aggregate supply is nothing but Y, the value of income. So equality between AD and AS will occur at the level of Y which satisfies

$$Y = C(Y) + I = 30 + 3/4\,Y.$$

The solution is $Y^* = 120$. Only at this value of income, there will be no unintended change in stocks held by firms.

Suppose, for some reason, $Y = 180$. Then $C = 10 + 3/4(180) = 145$, and $I = 20$, so that AD = 165. In other words, if 180 units of output are produced, households and firms together will buy only 165 units. Unsold 15 units will be an unplanned addition to the inventory of firms. Actual investment (planned plus unplanned) including inventory investment is 35 (= 20 + 15), whereas the firm's desired investment is only 20. So next period firms will want to reduce output. Hence, 180 is not the equilibrium level of production. Similarly, it can be checked that at any level of Y below 120, AD will exceed

AS $(= Y)$ and firms will be forced to draw down their stocks to meet demand. This unplanned disinvestment will be a signal to raise production in the next period. Only at $Y = 120$ there will be no tendency to change on the part of firms.

Box 3.2   The Algebra of Income Determination

Suppose, the consumption function is $C = a + cY$ and investment is $I = I_0$. Here mpc $= c$, $0 < c < 1$. The condition for macro equilibrium is:

$$Y = C + I = a + cY + I_0$$

Solving, $Y^* = (a + I_0)/(1 - c)$ (3.1)

The numerator on the right-hand side is the sum of autonomous consumption (a) and autonomous investment I_0, which may be called autonomous AD. Two results follow:

- Other factors being equal, the greater the autonomous consumption or investment, the higher is the equilibrium output;
- Given the level of autonomous AD, the higher the mpc (c), the higher is the equilibrium output. A higher c makes the denominator $(1 - c)$ lower.

Since c is the mpc, $(1 - c)$ equals mps. Denoting mps by s, we can alternatively write:

$$Y^* = (a + I_0)/s$$ (3.2)

The maximum output that an economy is capable of producing, given its productive capacity (built up through past investments), and the existing labour force is called the *potential* or *full employment* output. Let us denote it by Y_f. If AD is low, the equilibrium Y^* will be less than Y_f, implying loss of potential output due to underutilization of available resources.

It is very important to understand the distinction between $Y = C + I$ as an equilibrium *equation* and $Y = C + I$ as an *identity* in national income accounting. In the determination of equilibrium C and I refer to *planned* magnitudes, whereas the national income statistician deals with *realized or actual* figures. In our numerical example, for $Y = 180$, planned $(C + I)$ was less than Y and, therefore, 180 was not the equilibrium output. But if we take actual or realized values, we have $C = 145$ and $I = 35$,

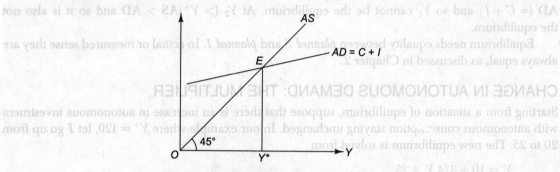

Fig. 3.2   Income Determination ($Y = C + I$)

of which 20 is planned and 15 unplanned in the form of unintended inventory change. So in actual values, $Y = C + I$ even for $Y = 180$. In actual or realized terms, $Y = C + I$ holds for each and every value of Y. That is why the relation is an identity. The equilibrium equation, on the other hand, holds only at $Y = 120$.

Geometrically, the value of Y^* is obtained at the point of intersection between the AD curve and the 45° line. The 45° line has a property, that at any point on it the values of the two coordinates will be equal. Since AS = output = Y, the AS line coincides with the 45° line. Macro balance $(AD = AS)$ holds at E in Figure 3.2.

An Alternative Representation

Since in this economy, $Y - C = S$, the equilibrium condition can also be written as $S(Y) = I_0$. For $C = a + cY$, $S = Y - a - cY = -a + sY$. Graphically, the S function is an upward sloping straight line with slope s and a negative intercept. $I = I_0$ is a horizontal line. Equilibrium is shown at E in Figure 3.3.

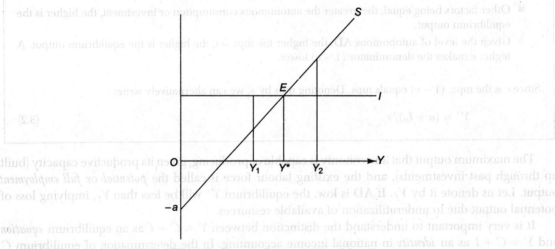

Fig. 3.3   Income Determination $(S = I)$

At the level of income Y_1 $(< Y^*)$ planned $S < I$, which is the same as $AS (= C + S) < AD (= C + I)$ and so Y_1 cannot be the equilibrium. At Y_2 $(> Y^*)$ AS > AD and so it is also not the equilibrium.

Equilibrium needs equality between *planned* S and *planned* I. In actual or measured sense they are always equal, as discussed in Chapter 2.

CHANGE IN AUTONOMOUS DEMAND: THE MULTIPLIER

Starting from a situation of equilibrium, suppose that there is an increase in autonomous investment with autonomous consumption staying unchanged. In our example where $Y^* = 120$, let I go up from 20 to 25. The new equilibrium is solved from

$$Y = 10 + 3/4\, Y + 25$$

or $Y^* = 140$.

Thus an increase in investment of 5 units has caused Y^* to increase by 20, a multiple of the rise in autonomous investment.

The multiplier is the change in income caused by a unit change in *autonomous* demand (here investment). In this case, the value of the multiplier is $20/5 = 4$. For the general linear function $C = a + cY$, the equations 3.1 and 3.2 give the multiplier as:

$$\Delta Y/\Delta I = 1/1 - c = 1/s.$$

Figures 3.4a and 3.4b show the multiplier.

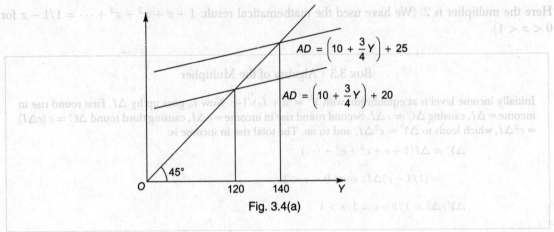

Fig. 3.4(a)

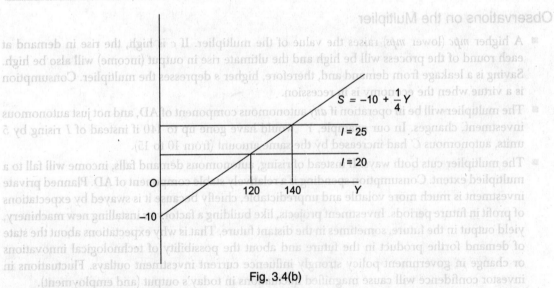

Fig. 3.4(b)

Let us enquire why the multiplier works. Let $mpc = 1/2$. Suppose investment demand rises by 100. This leads to extra output of 100 units to meet this demand. So income rises by 100 (first round). But this will lead to an increase in consumption spending $= 1/2 (100) = 50$. This will cause output to rise by 50 (second round). This rise in income will lead to extra consumption of 1/2 (50) = 25, which will be met by extra output of the same value (third round). The recipients of this income will spend 1/2 (25) on additional consumption causing income to rise to the same extent. Although theoretically this process continues for ever, the ultimate rise in income is obtained by summing the infinite series:

$$100 + 50 + 25 + 12.5 + 6.25 + \cdots$$

$$= 100(1 + (1/2) + (1/2)^2 + (1/2)^3 + (1/2)^4 + \cdots)$$

$$= 100(1/1 - 1/2) = 200.$$

Here the multiplier is 2. (We have used the mathematical result: $1 + x + x^2 + x^3 + \cdots = 1/1 - x$ for $0 < x < 1$).

Box 3.3   Algebra of the Multiplier

Initially income level is at equilibrium with $Y^* = (a + I_0)/1-c$. Now I_0 goes up by ΔI. First round rise in income $= \Delta I$, causing $\Delta C = c\Delta I$. Second round rise in income $= c\Delta I$, causing third round $\Delta C = c(c\Delta I)$ $= c^2\Delta I$, which leads to $\Delta Y = c^2\Delta I$, and so on. The total rise in income is:

$$\Delta Y = \Delta I(1 + c + c^2 + c^3 + \cdots)$$

$$= (1/1 - c)\Delta I, \text{ since } 0 < c < 1.$$

$$\Delta Y/\Delta I = 1/1 - c = 1/s > 1$$

Observations on the Multiplier

- A higher *mpc* (lower *mps*) raises the value of the multiplier. If *c* is high, the rise in demand at each round of the process will be high and the ultimate rise in output (income) will also be high. Saving is a leakage from demand and, therefore, higher *s* depresses the multiplier. Consumption is a virtue when the economy is in recession.

- The multiplier will be in operation if *any* autonomous component of AD, and not just autonomous investment, changes. In our example, Y^* would have gone up to 140 if instead of *I* rising by 5 units, autonomous *C* had increased by the same amount (from 10 to 15).

- The multiplier cuts both ways. If instead of rising, autonomous demand falls, income will fall to a multiplied extent. Consumption spending is a relatively stable component of AD. Planned private investment is much more volatile and unpredictable, chiefly because it is swayed by expectations of profit in future periods. Investment projects, like building a factory or installing new machinery, yield output in the future, sometimes in the distant future. That is why expectations about the state of demand for the product in the future and about the possibility of technological innovations or change in government policy strongly influence current investment outlays. Fluctuations in investor confidence will cause magnified fluctuations in today's output (and employment).

- The operation of the multiplier is crucially dependent on the assumption that unutilized resources are available in abundance, so that output can smoothly increase in response to rise in demand without any upward push on the price level. If, however, some crucial input is in limited supply then the process of income expansion will come to a halt as soon as that supply is exhausted. Further increase in demand will lead only to a rise in price. Unable to raise *real* income and employment, the multiplier process will work itself out in nominal terms. This will also be the outcome, if, in the initial situation the economy was at or close to its potential output Y_f. A rise in AD in this case will cause prices to rise.

■ If $mpc > 1$, then income will rise (fall) without limit following a rise (fall) in autonomous demand and the expression $(1/1 - c)$ cannot be used as the value of the multiplier. The value $(1/1 - c)$ is valid only for $0 < c < 1$.

Induced Investment

We now relax the assumption that investment is entirely autonomous and allow it to be influenced by current income. It may reasonably be assumed that as the level of activity picks up and output expands, business will be induced to step up planned investment spending to boost their productive capacity. We capture this through a new investment function $I = b + dY$, with $b > 0, d > 0$. Autonomous investment is b, dY is the induced part.

The change in investment caused by a unit change in Y is the *marginal propensity to invest* (*mpi*). Here mpi is d. The sum of mpc and mpi ($= c + d$) is assumed to be less than one.

Equilibrium holds at the value of Y at which

$$Y = C + I = a + cY + b + dY$$

or $\quad Y^* = (a + b)/[1 - (c + d)].$

In Figure 3.5, Y^* is the equilibrium income. The gap between the C line and the $C + I$ line widens because I rises with income.

The multiplier in this case has the value $1/[1-(c + d)]$, under the assumption $(c + d) < 1$.

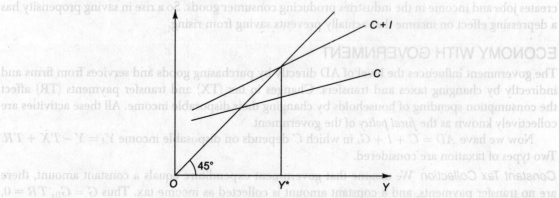

Fig. 3.5 Equilibrium with Induced Investment

The Paradox of Thrift

In the economy we are considering, output is determined by the level of AD. This has the implication that if the households, for some reason, want to change their consumption behaviour and become more thrifty (inclined to save more), the effect on output will be adverse and saving may actually fail to increase. Consider once again the case $C = 10 + 3/4\,Y$ (or $S = -10 + 1/4Y$) and $I = 20$. Equilibrium output is 120 where $S = I = 20$. A rise in the propensity to save (an upward shift of the S curve) can be represented by a new S function with a higher vertical intercept. Let the new function be $S = -8 + 1/4\,Y$. With I staying constant at 20, the new equilibrium $Y = 112$. Attempt to save more has led to a decline in income. Actually, income has declined enough to make the value of S (calculated from the new S function) equal to the constant investment level of 20 once again. There has been no change in S despite an increase in thriftiness. Figure 3.6 illustrates.

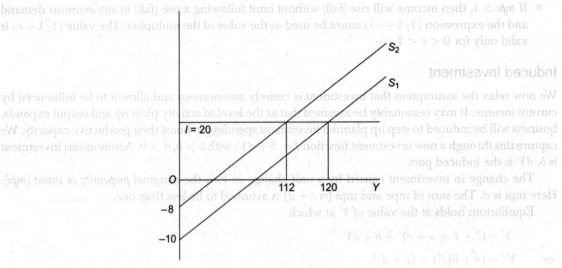

Fig. 3.6   Paradox of Thrift

The reason behind the paradox is that in a situation of widespread unemployment of resources, a cutback in consumption is a bad thing, because it reduces aggregate demand. Consumption spending creates jobs and income in the industries producing consumer goods. So a rise in saving propensity has a depressing effect on income that actually prevents saving from rising.

ECONOMY WITH GOVERNMENT

The government influences the level of AD directly by purchasing goods and services from firms and indirectly by changing taxes and transfers. Changes in tax (TX) and transfer payments (TR) affect the consumption spending of households by changing their disposable income. All these activities are collectively known as the *fiscal policy* of the government.

Now we have $AD = C + I + G$, in which C depends on disposable income $Y_d = Y - TX + TR$. Two types of taxation are considered.

Constant Tax Collection   We assume that government expenditure equals a constant amount, there are no transfer payments, and a constant amount is collected as income tax. Thus $G = G_0$, $TR = 0$, and $TX = T_0$. Investment also is constant at I_0.

The consumption function is $C = a + cY_d = a + c(Y - T)$. The macro balance condition is:

$$Y = a + c(Y - T) + I_0 + G_0 = a - cT_0 + I_0 + G_0 + cY.$$

Autonomous AD now has an extra component $(-cT_0)$.

Solving, $Y = (a - cT_0 + I_0 + G_0)/1 - c.$

Changes in autonomous consumption a, I_0, and G_0 have magnified impact on income. The investment and government expenditure multipliers are:

$$\Delta Y/\Delta I_0 = \Delta Y/\Delta G_0 = 1/1 - c$$

A change in T_0 causes autonomous demand to change by cT_0 in the opposite direction. A rise in tax collection by Re 1 reduces consumption by 75 paisa, if $mpc = 3/4$. Saving falls by 25 paisa. So far as the effect on Y is concerned, it is the change in consumption that matters. The tax multiplier is:

$$\Delta Y / \Delta T_0 = -c/1 - c < 0.$$

The negative sign implies that income will fall (rise) if tax collection is raised (reduced).

Proportional Income Tax Let a constant fraction t of income be collected as tax. Thus $G = G_0$, TR = 0, TX = tY, $0 < t < 1$. Investment is still assumed to be constant at I_0. The consumption function is:

$$C = a + cY_d = a + c(Y - tY) = a + c(1 - t)Y. \tag{3.3}$$

This differs from the C function in the absence of government in one important respect. Proportional taxation has reduced mpc out of Y from c to c (1- t). To illustrate, let $C = 10 + 3/4Y_d$, $t = 0.1$. Then C as a function of Y is $C = 10 + (3/4)(9/10)Y = 10 + 27/40\, Y$. Without government $(Y_d = Y)$, $mpc = 3/4$. Now it has the lower value 27/40.

Using equation (3.3), the macrobalance condition $AS = AD$ is:

$$Y = a + c(1 - t)Y + I_0 + G_0$$

or $\qquad Y^* = (a + I_0 + G_0)/[1 - c(1 - t)]. \tag{3.4}$

Autonomous demand now has three components: a (autonomous C), I_0, and G_0. Income will change to a multiplied extent if *any* of these components changes. The value of the multiplier is $1/[1 - c(1 - t)]$. This is lower than the value $(1/1 - c)$ in the non-government case due to proportional taxation. The multipliers (investment and government expenditure) are:

$$\Delta Y / \Delta I = \Delta Y / \Delta G = 1/[1 - c(1 - t)].$$

With $c = 0.8$ and $t = 0.5$, the multiplier is 2.5. If I_0 or G_0 rises by Re 1, equilibrium income will rise by Rs 2.50. The results are summarized by the following proposition.

Multiplier with Taxation

If autonomous private investment or government spending changes by one unit, income changes by:
   $1/1 - c$ *(constant tax collection)*;
   $1/[1 - c(1 - t)]$ *(proportional taxation)*.

Box 3.4   An alternative statement

In the present, context income is either consumed or saved or paid in taxes $Y = C + S + $ TX. Using this the equilibrium condition $Y = C + I + G$ can be restated as $S + $ TX $= I + G$.

Saving and taxes are leakages (outflows) from the income stream, investment and government purchases are injections (inflows). The system is in balance when the inflows and outflows cancel each other.

An increase in t, the rate of income taxation, will have an adverse impact on Y, through a reduction in mpc $(= c(1 - t))$.

Equation (3.4) has one very important implication. For given values of a, c, and t, output depends only on $(I_0 + G_0)$. So if private I falls for some reason, the possible negative effect on Y can be countered by raising G_0 by the same amount, so that $(I_0 + G_0)$ remains unchanged. A cut in t at the same time will help matters by boosting consumption. Thus, expansionary fiscal action (increase in government spending and cut in taxation) can help maintain output and employment in the face of falling business investment.

The deliberate use of fiscal instruments to neutralize fluctuations in output is known as *stabilization policy*.

The *budget deficit* (BD) is the excess of the government's expenditure on goods and services and transfer payments over its revenue consisting of taxes. (A negative budget deficit is a budget surplus.)

$$BD = G + TR - TX \text{ (or } BS = TX - (G + TR))$$

$$= G + TR - tY, \text{ under proportional taxation.}$$

Raising TX, cutting G and TR are known as *fiscal consolidation* as they cause BD to fall.

Fiscal Policy and Budget Deficit

Let us examine how fiscal policy affects the budget deficit. For simplicity we ignore transfer payments. An increase in G by itself adds to BD, but it also raises income to a multiplied extent. This will bring in additional tax revenue through proportional taxation. What is the net impact on BD? Is it possible that the increase in TX caused by the multiplier may actually outweigh the increase in G?

$$\Delta T = t\Delta Y = t/[1 - c(1 - t)]\Delta G$$

$$\Delta BD = \Delta G - \Delta T = [1 - t/1 - c(1 - t)]\Delta G$$

$$= (1 - c)(1 - t)/[1 - c(1 - t)]\Delta G > 0.$$

The positive sign means that the net effect is to raise the budget deficit. For instance if $c = 0.8$, $t = 0.1$, Re 1 increase in G will create Re 0.64 increase in BD.

A rise in the tax rate t, with G unchanged, raises tax revenue (at unchanged Y) but reduces equilibrium Y^* by making *mpc* ($c(1 - t)$) smaller. However, the net effect is a reduction in BD.

Any mechanism that reduces the response of GDP to fluctuations in AD is known as an *automatic stabilizer*. It is automatic (as opposed to discretionary) because nobody has to decide when they should go into operation. Income tax acts as an automatic stabilizer by reducing the multiplier from $(1/1 - c)$ to $1/[1 - c(1 - t)]$. Effects of shifts in autonomous components of AD are dampened thereby. This dampening is stronger, the higher is the tax rate t. Even if the government does not do anything, business cycles are likely to be less severe in economies with higher rates of income taxation.

OBSERVATIONS ON FISCAL POLICY

The effectiveness of fiscal action is subject to several qualifications.

Response Lag and Imperfect Information Although our simplified analysis suggests that discretionary fiscal action can be relied on to neutralize adverse changes in AD, in practice no government is able to achieve perfect stabilization of income and employment. This is due to the existence of various *lags and imperfection of information*. In particular, the value of mpc is not precisely known. Economic data at best give a rough estimate. Hence, in the event of a fall in I, it is not easy to figure out quickly the required compensating changes in G and taxation. Also, raising G and TR or cutting t may take considerable time. There will be a time lag between tax cuts and improvement in consumption spending and a further lag before firms can raise production in response to the rise in C. As a result of all these factors, fiscal policy cannot be counted on to maintain Y continuously at a high level. It can, nonetheless, be a powerful tool for mitigating the severity of business cycles.

Mode of Financing and Crowding out Our theory calls for an increase in G to fight a recession. But how is this extra expenditure to be financed? Raising taxes is ruled out (in fact taxes should preferably be cut to stimulate AD). This leaves borrowing as the only means of finance. The government may borrow from three sources: domestic citizens, foreign nationals, or the domestic Central Bank. Borrowing from the Central Bank adds to the supply of money in the economy. (The exact mechanism is explained in Chapter 6.) So this mode is equivalent to printing of money to finance the deficit caused by expansionary fiscal action.

Borrowing from abroad involves a drain on foreign exchange reserves, because interest payment will have to be made in foreign currency. Even domestically-held debt adds to the government's interest burden. In fact, interest payment on public debt is the largest component of current expenditure of the GOI and it is growing. Chapter 9 treats the issue of domestically-held debt.

Some economists contend that as the government steps up its borrowing in the domestic market, the savings left for lending to firms go down by the same amount, so that the rise in debt-financed G is exactly offset by a fall in I. Since AD stays unchanged, there is no expansionary effect. Government borrowing *crowds out* private investment. While complete crowding out is unlikely, we shall see (in Chapter 4) that if government borrowing pushes up interest rates, it may indeed have contractionary effects through a fall in investment. Borrowing from the Central Bank (*money-financed deficit* or *monetized deficit*) adds to the supply of money and may cause inflationary pressure to build up.

Since each of the modes of financing a deficit carries some burden with it, our conclusion is: although BD plays a useful role in fighting recessions, large and persistent deficits may end up imposing serious costs on the economy in the long run.

Supply-side Effects In Keynesian analysis fiscal policy affects Y solely by affecting AD. The *supply-side* does not enter the picture because production is assumed to respond passively to demand. Equilibrium output is low because AD is low. Complete neglect of the supply side has been criticized on the ground that fiscal action, change in taxation in particular, may have important *incentive effects* on producers and workers. Higher income tax rates depress production by discouraging people from earning activities. According to *supply-side economics*, tax cuts work not because consumption is stimulated but because people are induced to put in more effort and to work more productively (see Chapter 11). If such supply-side effects are significantly strong and pervasive, the simple demand-oriented Keynesian framework will cease to be a good guide to government policy.

Cyclical versus Structural (Cyclically Adjusted) Deficit The value of actual BD by itself is not a good indicator of the fiscal stance of the government in any period. This is because the value of BD depends, in part, on the state of the economy. A fall in output and income tends to raise BD as tax collection declines but committed expenditures do not fall. Similarly, a boom automatically improves BD by raising tax revenue. Cyclical deficit is the part of deficit that is explained by the level of economic activity. Structural or cyclically-adjusted deficit is the discretionary part for which the policy-makers are directly responsible. The *fiscal stance* of the government is captured by this discretionary part. The structural deficit is taken to be the deficit that would exist, even if the economy were at the level of potential or full employment output. For its measurement, the value of potential output has to be estimated. This is not an easy task.

Denoting by Y_f the full employment level of income, structural deficit can be written as $BD_f = G + TR - tY_f$. The difference between the structural deficit and the actual deficit is the cyclical component of the deficit. It is given by

$$BD_f - BD = t(Y - Y_f).$$

Fiscal Expansion and Corruption Historical experience shows that increases in government spending are often associated with extension of political patronage and additional scope for corruption. Keynes broke with tradition and boldly advocated budgetary deficit to pull the system out of the depths of recession and downplayed the importance of balanced budgets. Unfortunately, politicians were not slow to exploit this legitimization of fiscal deficits.

Fiscal consolidation may help in bringing down the level of corruption in a system and improve its health by reducing unproductive government expenditure. After years of lax discipline, the Indian government at present is making bold attempts to achieve fiscal consolidation. Results are not up to the expectation yet.

AN OPEN ECONOMY

Here, we consider the effects of opening up our economy to foreign trade. Only trade in final goods will be considered. Now exports will constitute an additional source of demand for the nation's product and imports a leakage from the domestic income stream. Total available supply in the economy consists of domestic output (Y) and imports (M), so that $AS = Y + M$. Total demand or AD consists of planned spending by the households, the firms, the government, and the foreign country that buys our exports. The equilibrium condition $AS = AD$ takes the form:

$$Y + M = C + I + G + X$$

or $\quad Y = C + I + G + (X - M) = C + I + G + \text{NX}.$ \hfill (3.5)

NX is net export (export minus import). All terms on the right-hand side of equation (3.5) are *planned* magnitudes. If we take actual or measured values, it is an identity, as explained in Chapter 2.

Another way of looking at equation (3.5) is that since spending on imports M is included in C, I, and G we must subtract it out of $C + I + G + X$ to arrive at AD for domestic production.

To determine the equilibrium value of Y, we take I, G, and X to be exogenously given. Since in this section, we are interested in issues raised by foreign trade, taxes and transfers are assumed to be absent, so that income equals disposable income. The demand for imports is taken to vary positively with the level of domestic Y. Our exports being the same as the imports of the foreign countries that trade with us, our exports depend on *their* income. From the point of view of the home country foreign income, and, hence, home exports, can be taken to be exogenous as a first approximation.

Let the consumption function and the import function be

$$C = a + cY \quad \text{and} \quad M = u + mY, \ 0 < c < 1, m > 0$$

The increase in M caused by Re 1 increase in income is the *marginal propensity to import* (*mpm*). Here *mpm* = *m*. The autonomous component of import is u.

Box 3.5   Alternative representation

Since an open economy has exports as an extra source of injection into the domestic income stream and an extra leakage, imports, the balance condition (3.5) can be restated as:

$$S + \text{TX} + M = I + G + X$$

or $\quad S - I = (G - \text{TX}) + (X - M) = \text{BD} + \text{NX}.$

BD is budget deficit.

At equilibrium

$$Y = (a + cY) + I_0 + G_0 + X_0 - (u + mY)$$

or $\quad Y = (a + I_0 + G_0 + X_0 - u)/(1 - c + m).$ $\qquad$ (3.6)

From this equation the multipliers for an open economy can be calculated.

$$\Delta Y/\Delta I = \Delta Y/\Delta G = \Delta Y/\Delta X = 1/1 - c + m$$

The value of the multiplier now is smaller than that for a closed economy, For example, if $c = 0.8$ and $m = 0.3$, $1/(1 - c + m) = 2$ while $1/(1 - c) = 5$. This reduction is due to the presence of imports, which is a leakage from the flow of domestic income.

Compared to a closed economy, the open system has an additional source of demand, namely, exports to foreign countries. An increase in exports will raise income through the multiplier, just as an increase would in G or I. A rise in the autonomous component of imports (the u term in the M function), on the other hand, will cause a multiplied contraction of income.

Change in Demand and Trade Surplus

The *trade surplus* or *trade balance* is the excess of the value of exports over that of imports. This is the same as net exports, NX.

$$\text{TS} = X - M = X - u - mY \qquad (3.7)$$

It follows that, given the exogenously fixed X_0, an increase in I_0 or G_0 will worsen trade balance by pushing up Y. The gain in output and employment is at the cost of a reduction in trade balance.

What will be the impact of a rise in X? We use equation (3.7) to obtain

$$\Delta \text{TS}/\Delta X = 1 - m(\Delta Y/\Delta X) = 1 - (m/1 - c + m)$$

$$= (1 - c)/(1 - c + m) > 0.$$

So, although a rise in X_0 causes M to rise by raising Y, the net impact is positive. Greater exports improve trade balance after all.

FISCAL OPERATIONS OF THE GOVERNMENT OF INDIA

Basics of the Government Budget The budget consists of two parts: the revenue budget and the capital budget. The revenue budget is concerned with the current, regular operational receipts and expenditure of the government. The major items of expenditure are civil administration, grants to the states and union territories, subsidies, defence, pension, and interest on public debt (National Saving Certificates and other government bonds, for example).

The capital budget is concerned with (i) expenditure relating to creation of assets for the nation (for example, airports, post offices, railway stations) and loan repayment and (ii) loans and advances made by the GOI.

Revenue receipts are of two types: *tax revenue* and *non-tax revenue*. The former can be broken up into revenue from direct taxes (personal income tax, corporation tax, wealth tax, etc.) and that from indirect or commodity taxes (customs, sales and excise duties, etc.). Major items of non-tax revenue are earnings from public property—forests, irrigation works, etc., earnings from PSUs and departmental undertakings such as the railways, posts and telegraphs, and interest on loans advanced. *Capital receipts* consist of borrowing from the public (domestic and foreign), small savings, provident funds, recovery of past loans, and revenue from sale of equities (disinvestments) in public sector units (PSU). The interest charge on public borrowing goes into expenditure in the revenue account.

Different Concepts of Budget Deficit

- Overall budget deficit = total expenditure (revenue + capital) – total receipts (revenue + capital).
- Revenue deficit (RD) = revenue expenditure – revenue receipts.
- Primary deficit (PD) = non-interest expenditure – receipts (revenue + capital). (Thus, interest payment on public debt is excluded in calculating PD.)
- Fiscal deficit (FD) = expenditure (including loan repayment) – non-debt creating receipts (revenue + non-debt creating capital receipts). (In calculating FD, government borrowing, which is a debt-creating capital receipt, is excluded. For obvious reason, FD is also known as Public Sector Borrowing Requirement, (PSBR).)

Budgetary figures are available in India for the central and the state governments separately and also for the consolidated government sector (centre plus states).

Table 3.1   Receipts and Expenditures of the Central Government

(per cent of GDP)

	1998–9	1999–00	2000–1	2001–2
1. Revenue receipts $(a + b)$	8.6	9.4	9.2	10.1
(a) tax revenue (net of states' share)	6.0	6.6	6.5	7.1
(b) non-tax revenue revenue	2.6	2.7	2.7	3.0
2. Revenue expenditure $(a + b + c)$	12.4	12.9	13.2	13.5
(a) interest payment	4.5	4.7	4.7	4.9
(b) major subsidies	1.2	1.2	1.2	1.2
(c) defence	1.7	1.8	1.8	1.8
3. Revenue deficit $(2 - 1)$	3.8	3.5	4.1	3.4
4. Capital receipts $(a + b + c)$	6.1	6.0	6.2	6.3
(a) loan recovery	0.6	0.5	0.6	0.7
(b) disinvestments	0.3	0.1	0.1	0.5
(c) borrowing	5.2	5.4	5.6	5.1
5. Capital expenditure	2.2	2.5	2.3	2.8
6. Total expenditure $(2 + 5)$	14.7	15.4	15.5	16.3
7. Fiscal deficit $(6 - 1 - 4(a) - 4(b))$	5.1	5.4	5.6	5.1
8. Primary deficit $(7 - 2(a))$	0.7	0.7	0.9	0.2

Source: Economic Survey, GOI, 2002–3.

Over the past decade, at the behest of the IMF, the GOI has been trying to impose strict discipline on its fiscal operations. Achievement, however, has not been up to the mark. Fiscal deficit relative to GDP has continued to rise, albeit at a slower rate. This is largely attributable to unbridled growth in revenue deficit, which is expenditure for current unproductive consumption activities. The consolidated (central plus state governments) RD in 1999–2000 was 6.3 per cent of GDP, considerably higher than the level of 4.2 per cent in 1990–1. In 2000–1 revenue expenditure accounted for 85 per cent of total central government expenditure. Although successive pay revisions (following the recommendation of Pay Commissions) have contributed towards this situation, the two major culprits are (i) uncontrolled expansion of subsidies and (ii) ever-growing interest payment on public debt.

Table 3.2   Fiscal Parameters of the GOI

			(per cent of GDP)
	1970–9	1980–91	1992–2000
Total expenditure	14.4	17.7	15.7
Revenue expenditure	8.4	11.7	12.3
Interest payments	1.5	2.8	4.4
Subsidies	0.8	1.7	1.3
Capital expenditure	6.0	6.0	3.4
Direct tax	2.3	2.0	2.8
Indirect tax	6.4	7.9	6.3
Non-tax revenue	2.0	2.4	2.5
Fiscal deficit	3.8	6.8	5.7
Primary deficit	2.3	3.9	1.3
Revenue deficit	−0.3	1.9	3.2

Source: India Development Report, 2002.

For political reasons it has been impossible to reduce even non-merit subsidies (see Box 3.6). In democratic India, subsidies have provided the chief means of keeping different pressure groups happy. It is still a major instrument of redistributive politics. Interest burden on debt increased from 4.3 per cent of GDP in 1991–2 to 4.7 per cent in 1997–8. At above 4 per cent of GDP, interest burden currently exceeds the share of defence and accounts for about two-thirds of the tax revenue of the central government, net of the states' share. Value of total outstanding debt (of which only one-sixth is foreign or external) relative to GDP came down from 60 per cent in 1990–1 to 56 per cent in 1997–8. The interest burden has not lessened in proportion because the government now pays higher interest on domestic borrowing.

External debt, as a percentage of GDP, currently stands at 23 per cent, which is quite low by the standards of other developing countries. The average for the developing world is about 40 per cent.

Box 3.6   Subsidies in India

Subsidies are transfer payments to producers that enable them to charge a price below the average cost. The objective is to improve the welfare of particular groups of deserving consumers who will otherwise be hurt by high prices. There are subsidies on food, fertilizer, exports, power, irrigation water, credit subsidies that lower the interest charged, procurement subsidies (purchase of foodgrains at higher than market price to help the seller), in-kind transfers in the form of free provision of medical services or food, subsidy on urban transport, and transfers in diverse other forms.

An important distinction is between *merit* and *non-merit* subsidies. The former cover cases like basic health, sanitation, primary education, roads and bridges and other social infrastructure, and defence. The major non-merit subsidies are on food, fertilizers, power, and higher education. In their attempt to rein in revenue deficit, the central and the state governments have in recent years, raised the price or user charge on a wide variety of non-merit items. This is a step in the right direction that was long overdue.

The ballooning of revenue expenditure has caused a cutback in the capital expenditure of the government. This, in turn, has adversely affected the growth prospects of the country by retarding the development of its social infrastructure (roads, health, education, power, and irrigation projects).

Private investment, at best, plays a complementary role in this vital area. Without substantial public investment one can hardly hope for private initiative in social capital formation.

Tax revenue of the government has grown at a disappointingly slow rate. Direct taxes (mainly income and corporation tax) account for only about 25 per cent of total revenue. This is chiefly due to the absence of agricultural income tax, the narrow tax base, and substantial tax evasion. Non-tax revenues have stagnated as a proportion of GDP.

One area in which notable success has been achieved is the control of monetized deficit (deficit financed by borrowing from the Reserve Bank of India [RBI], which is equivalent to printing money). Chapter 6 treats this topic in more depth. Since the freedom to borrow unlimited amounts from the RBI has been substantially curtailed, it is likely that the government will, henceforth, be compelled to raise more resources through taxation. This will require stricter vigilance to combat tax evasion. Lessening of tax evasion will contribute towards greater economic equality.

Box 3.7   Legislative Mandate for Fiscal Responsibility

In 2000, the Fiscal Responsibility and Budget Management (FRBM) Bill was introduced in Parliament. The major features are:

- Complete elimination of RD by March 2006;
- Reduction of FD to 2 per cent of GDP by March 2006;
- Quarterly review of fiscal trends to be placed before Parliament;
- Proportionate cuts in expenditure in case of shortfall of revenue or excess of expenditure over budget targets.

The majority of economists are sceptical that this will just be another piece of legislation that exists only on paper and is never honoured in practice. The difficulty of enforcing constitutional constraints on government spending is illustrated by the experience of the USA. The Gramm–Rudman–Hollings Bill, passed in 1986, called for specific budget deficit targets with the hope of achieving a balanced budget by 1991. If actual expenditure exceeded targets, a preset formula cut back expenditure on each programme. But the Bill became inoperative after the Supreme Court declared the procedure unconstitutional.

Summary

- Aggregate demand is the sum of planned spending by house- holds on consumption, by firms on investment, by government on its purchase of goods and services, and by foreigners on the economy's output (economy's net exports).
- Macroequilibrium is attained when output (aggregate supply) equals aggregate demand. In equilibrium, all plans are fulfilled and there are no unintended changes in inventories.
- The consumption function is the relation between planned consumption spending and current income, net of taxation (disposable income). The marginal propensity to consume is the additional consumption caused by a Re 1 rise in disposable income. The saving function can be obtained from the consumption function.
- The multiplier is the amount by which a Re 1 change in autonomous aggregate demand changes national income.

- Fiscal policy consists of changes in government spending and/or revenues (mostly taxes). Budget deficit is the gap between government expenditure and taxes. Rise in budget deficit (fiscal expansion) stimulates output by stimulating aggregate demand. A rise in net exports has a similar effect because net export is a component of aggregate demand in an open economy.
- Overall budget deficit, revenue deficit, primary deficit and fiscal deficit are the major categories of deficit in India's budget.

Exercise

1. (i) If $C = 10 + 0.9\ Y$, $I_0 = 60$, what is the level of unplanned inventory accumulation at $Y = 850$? (Hint: inventory accumulation is the excess of production over demand.)

    (ii) If $C = 12 + 4/5\ Y$, $I_0 = 20$, what are the values of autonomous saving and the marginal propensity to save? What is the equilibrium level of Y?

    Find the impact on Y if I falls to 15.

2. Show that the impact of the aforementioned fall in I (see last question of Problem 1(ii)) can be neutralized by an appropriate rise in autonomous C.

3. Will aggregate output rise or fall if an increase in autonomous consumption spending is matched by an equal increase in T? Explain your answer.

4. Suppose that government transfer is at a constant level Z, irrespective of the value of income. There is no tax on income. Show that autonomous AD will now have an extra term (cZ). What is the multiplier if Z changes? Why is the value lower than the case when I or G goes up?

5. Suppose $C = 10 + 3/4\ Y_d$, $t = 10$ per cent, $I_0 = G_0 = 10$. Calculate the impact on equilibrium output if (i) the tax rate is raised to 20 per cent and (ii) autonomous C falls to 5 due to an increase in the propensity to save.

6. Investment tax credit allows a firm to deduct a portion of investment spending from its corporate tax liability. Examine the impact of the introduction of such a scheme in the simple Keynesian model for a closed economy.

7. What is the value of budget deficit (BD) at the initial equilibrium Y of Problem 5 (when $t = 10$ per cent)? What is BD when t increases to 20 per cent?

8. Consider an economy in which $C = 10 + 3/4\ Y$, $I_0 = 30$ and initially $G_0 = TX = 0$. Let $Y_f = 200$ be the full employment level of income. By how much should G be raised to attain full employment?

9. For the economy of Problem 8, suppose there is income tax with $t = 10$ per cent. Recalculate the required change in G to attain Y_f. What was the initial value of BD? What is the value of structural deficit?

10. Obtain the equilibrium values, of Y and S for $C = 25 + 0.7Y$, $I = 5 + 0.2Y$. There is no

government. Show that the equilibrium S falls if autonomous C falls to 20. (This is the Paradox of Thrift in a severe form. Any attempt to save more causes an actual decline in S.)

11. Consider an open economy without government with $C = 20 + 0.8Y$, $I = 15$, $X = 8$, and $M = 5 + 0.3Y$. Compute the changes in Y and in the trade surplus if (i) X becomes 10 and (ii) autonomous import rises from 5 to 7.

12. Use equation (3.6) to obtain the change in Y when autonomous import rises by 1 unit.

Appendix 3.1
International Business Cycle Transmission

We relax the assumption of exogenously given exports and show that nations involved in trade are interdependent in the sense that the equilibrium levels of income are simultaneously determined and disturbances in one economy are transmitted to its trading partners. For each country imports depend positively on its own income. The import functions of two countries (country 1 and country 2) are, respectively:

$$M_1 = u_1 + m_1 Y_1 \text{ and } M_2 = u_2 + m_2 Y_2, \, m_1 > 0, \, m_2 > 0.$$

But by definition import of country 1 is the export of country 2 and vice versa $(M_1 = X_2, M_2 = X_1)$. The balance conditions (setting $G = TX = 0$, and taking investment to be given in each country for simplicity) are:

$$Y_1 = C_1 + I_1 + X_1 - M_1$$
$$= a_1 + c_1 Y + I_1 + u_2 + m_2 Y_2 - u_1 - m_1 Y_1;$$
$$Y_2 = C_2 + I_2 + X_2 - M_2$$
$$= a_2 + c_2 Y + I_2 + u_1 + m_1 Y_1 - u_2 - m_2 Y_2.$$

Writing $s_1 = 1-c_1$ and $s_2 = 1-c_2$, these can be rearranged as

$$Y_1(s_1 + m_1) = a_1 + I_1 + u_2 - u_1 + m_2 Y_2;$$
$$Y_2(s_2 + m_2) = a_2 + I_2 + u_1 - u_2 + m_1 Y_1.$$

Note that in the first equation, Y_1 depends positively on Y_2. This is because a rise in its income leads country 2 to import more from country 1, this rise in export stimulates output and income in country 1. Similarly, from the second equation, Y_2 depends positively on Y_1. The two equilibrium relations are

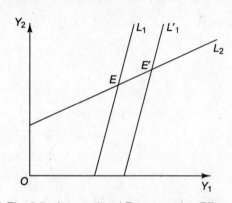

Fig. 3.7   International Repercussion Effect

plotted as two straight lines in Figure 3.7. The slopes are $(m_2/s_1 + m_1)$ and $(m_1/s_2 + m_2)$, respectively. The equilibrium values of Y_1 and Y_2 are simultaneously determined at the point of intersection E.

Suppose autonomous investment I_1 rises in country 1. At each level of Y_2 now Y_1 is higher than before. The line L_1 shifts to the right and the new equilibrium is at E', with both Y_1 and Y_2 higher. Income of country 2 is stimulated by the rise in investment in country 1. The reason is simple. Improvement in I_1 raises Y_1 through the operation of the multiplier. This causes M_1 $(= X_2)$ to rise and Y_2 gets a boost through the rise in exports. Country 2, sitting passively, reaps the benefit of an increase in investment in its trade partner.

Unfortunately, the process is equally operational for a decline in I_1. The resultant fall in Y_1 reduces M_1 $(= X_2)$ and this has a contractionary impact on Y_2. This time country 2 has to share the misfortune of its partner.

Such repercussion effects act as a potent mechanism for transmitting business cycles originating in one country (caused by fluctuations in domestic investment or other components of AD) to its partners in trade. Fortunes of countries linked through exchange of goods and services rise and fall together.

Appendix 3.2
The Microeconomics of Consumption and Saving

In the foregoing chapter, consumption (and saving) were taken to be increasing functions of income. The relationships were simply assumed and not derived from any economic logic. Critics of the Keynesian approach consider this procedure unacceptable. Consumption and saving decisions, according to them, must be consistent with microeconomic optimization by rational economic agents. In this section we analyse the consumption and saving decision of Mr Sen, a typical income earner. The decision problem is intertemporal because in deciding how much to consume and how much to save, Mr Sen will have to consider the present as well as the future. The whole point of saving is that, by sacrificing consumption today, one is enabled to raise one's consumption in the future or to leave a bequest for one's children. This particular theoretical approach is known as the Fisher model in honour of the economist, Irving Fisher, who first presented it.

To keep the analysis simple, we assume:

- Mr Sen lives only for two periods. The current period might represent his working years and the future period, his retirement years.
- Mr Sen does not want to leave any bequest for his children.
- The price level is constant. Absence of inflation means that all nominal and real magnitudes are equal. In particular, nominal and real interest rates are the same.
- Unlimited borrowing and lending are possible at a constant interest rate of r. Constraints on borrowing or lending are absent. This is the most important feature of a perfect capital (credit) market.

Mr Sen earns income Y_1 in the current period (period 1) and expects to earn Y_2 in period 2. He also has an initial stock of wealth W. Consumption in the two periods are C_1 and C_2. Unlimited lending and borrowing are possible at interest rate r. Let saving be denoted by S.

The relevant equations are:

$$S = Y_1 + W - C_1;$$

$$C_2 = Y_2 + (1+r)S.$$

Since life ends after period 2 and there is no bequest, Mr Sen saves only in period 1. That saving S plus the interest on it (rS) is available for consumption in period 2. The two equations can be combined to yield the lifetime budget constraint:

$$C_1 + C_2/1 + r = Y_1 + (Y_2/1 + r) + W.$$

The left-hand side is the present value of lifetime consumption and the right-hand side is the present value of lifetime income (LTI). Geometrically, the lifetime budget constraint is a straight line with slope $(-(1 + r))$. The slope has this particular value because if current consumption is reduced by one unit (S goes up by one unit), next period's consumption will go up by $(1 + r)$.

The preferences of Mr Sen over current and future consumption are summarized by his utility function $U(C_1, C_2)$. Graphically, this function is assumed to generate a map of convex to the origin indifference curves. The slope of an indifference curve at any point is the marginal rate of intertemporal substitution in consumption. Mr Sen's problem is to choose consumption levels in the two periods so as to maximize utility, subject to the budget constraint.

The most preferred point is given by E_1 in Figure 3.8.

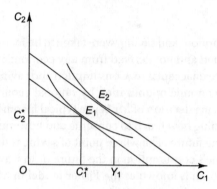

Fig. 3.8   Consumption and Saving

The optimal consumption levels are given by C_1^* and C_2^*. The amount of saving is the gap between Y_1 and C_1^*. Let us now examine how consumption in different periods and saving respond to changes in income or wealth.

Consumption in each period depends on r and LTI. This is in contrast with the Keynesian view of the consumption function where current consumption depends primarily on current income. An increase in Y_1 or Y_2 or W raises LTI. Graphically, the budget line shifts to the right and the new equilibrium at E_2 shows an increase in both C_1 and C_2 (Figure 3.8).

The most important conclusion of the model is that change in current income affects consumption (both current and future) only by affecting LTI. Rise in Y_1 will have no effect on C_1 if there are offsetting changes in Y_2 or W that leave LTI unchanged.

Transitory versus Permanent Change in Income

In terms of our model, a permanent increase in income is an increase in *both* current and future income, whereas a transitory or temporary increase is an increase in current income alone with no change in future income. Clearly, a permanent one-unit increase in income has a greater impact on LTI than a temporary increase of the same amount. Since consumption, according to our theory, depends only on LTI, a permanent change in income will have greater impact on consumption expenditure than a temporary income change of equal magnitude. A new job with a higher salary is a permanent addition to income, whereas extra earning in a particular year through overtime work is a transitory change. The former will have stronger impact on lifetime consumption than the latter. The distinction between transitory and permanent changes in income was first made by Milton Friedman, who made it the basis of his Permanent Income Theory of Consumption.

The new classical economists use the Fisher model to criticize Keynesian policy. Low responsiveness of C to current income reduces the force of stabilization policy. A temporary cut in taxation or an increase in transfer payments during recession may fail to boost C, because the rise in the disposable income of the households will be transitory in nature. Also, if C is basically geared to long-term income or income averaged over a number of periods including the current one, mpc out of current Y will be lowered simply because this Y contributes only one term to the average.

However, the validity of the intertemporal optimization model or of the permanent income theory is crucially dependent on the existence of perfect capital markets. Unfortunately, plans of households are often frustrated by serious *borrowing constraints* or *liquidity constraints* they have to face. It is very difficult to borrow for current consumption without adequate collateral even if future income prospects are good. Lenders insist on collateral because they do not have adequate mechanisms to monitor borrowers and ensure repayment. Another symptom of credit market imperfection is that borrowing rates of interest are higher than lending rates. Presence of borrowing constraints and high borrowing rates brings the Keynesian consumption function back into reckoning by raising the sensitivity of current C to current Y. If borrowing against future income is impossible or difficult, current income, rather than LTI, becomes the principal determinant of current consumption and to that extent the power of Keynesian macropolicies is restored.

Efficacy of Fiscal Action (Ricardian equivalence)

We have already noted that there will be no change in Mr Sen's consumption if his LTI remains unchanged (assuming perfect capital market). Under certain conditions it implies that a reduction in current taxes, financed by borrowing, will fail to stimulate consumption. Let us see why.

The basic logic is that rational and forward-looking Mr Sen realizes that today's tax cut (financed by public debt) means higher taxes in the future because the government will have to pay off that debt and it will resort to higher taxation for that purpose. Therefore, Mr Sen's LTI will be unchanged and his consumption will remain the same. The extra disposable income generated by today's tax cut will be saved to meet the future tax liability that the tax cut implies. From the rational saver's point of view, government debt and taxation are equivalent because debt today merely reschedules taxation to a future period. This proposition is known as *Ricardian Equivalence*, after the classical economist, David Ricardo.

Suppose the government cuts taxes in period 1 by Rs 100, but keeps its expenditures in the two periods unchanged. With expenditure unchanged, the reduction in taxes will force the government to borrow Rs 100 from Mr Sen. Other things equal, the fall in taxation raises LTI and causes Mr Sen to raise C_1 and C_2. This is in accordance with the prediction of the traditional theory that increase in disposable income boosts C and AD in the current period.

However, if the government has to balance its budget over the two periods, other things will not stay equal. Let the interest be 10 per cent. In period 2, the government will have to repay Rs 110 as debt plus interest. In order to do it, taxes in period 2 must be raised by Rs 110, so Mr Sen's future income falls by the same amount. Overall, the government's action has raised his current income by Rs 100, but reduced his future income by Rs 110. At interest of 10 per cent, the two changes cancel out leaving his LTI unchanged. His current (or future) consumption should not change.

This conclusion has been challenged by the Keynesians on two grounds. First, the analysis of intertemporal choice assigns a degree of foresight to Mr Sen which he is unlikely to possess. Due to short-sightedness, he may fail to grasp the full budgetary implications of a tax cut in the current period. This may induce him to consume a large part of the rise in current disposable income, ignoring the lifetime consequences.

Second, if Mr Sen is currently facing a borrowing constraint, the result will be different. As discussed earlier, a person who cannot obtain a loan (possibly because the lender has doubts about his ability to repay) is forced to consume his current income. For such a person, current, rather than LTI, is the principal determinant of current consumption. Hence, consumption will rise sharply following the reduction in taxation and the equivalence will fail to hold.

In developing countries, such as India, the capital market is far from perfect and the number of persons facing borrowing constraints is high. As a result, the traditional view of fiscal action is likely to be much more relevant. Even in the developed economies, empirical studies support the view that changes in current income have significant effect on current consumption expenditure.

4. Money, Interest, and Income

Monetary factors played no role in the determination of output and employment discussed in Chapter 3. The analysis was deliberately kept simple to bring out clearly the importance of aggregate demand. But monetary factors such as changes in the supply of money or the rates of return on financial assets do exert considerable influence on the behaviour of households and firms in an economy. Therefore, our basic framework must be expanded to incorporate monetary variables. In this chapter, the rate of interest will be included as an additional determinant of planned investment. Monetary policy will affect output through the interest route.

The central result is that the rate of interest (return on financial assets) and the level of income will be jointly determined, in simultaneous equilibrium, in two markets: one for commodities and one for financial assets. (Assets are classified as *physical* and *financial*. The machinery, buildings, and stocks of commodities owned by firms are examples of the former. Bank deposits or equity shares or bonds issued by firms to raise finance belong to the latter. We concentrate on transactions in financial assets only.) The aggregate price level P is still taken to be fixed.

Prior to economic reforms, the rates of return on almost all major financial assets in India were subject to strict control by the RBI. This was known as a system of administered interest rates. There were also numerous restrictions on lending and borrowing. By preventing interest rates from varying freely in response to changes in market conditions, this regime of *financial repression* considerably reduced their relevance as important macroeconomic variables. However, most of the rates have been deregulated and are free to respond to market forces of demand and supply. Consequently, the analysis of this chapter is much more relevant today than it had been a decade ago.

INTEREST RATE AND AGGREGATE DEMAND—THE INVESTMENT FUNCTION

The components of AD may be responsive to the rate of interest. Planned business investment may be particularly sensitive. The relationship is an inverse one, that is, as the rate of interest rises, planned investment spending is curtailed. The reason is that most investment projects are financed by borrowing funds from banks and other financial intermediaries. Higher interest cost of borrowing has a dampening effect on the incentive to invest. Even if the firm is using its own internal funds and not borrowing from external sources to finance investment, higher interest makes putting money in physical capital less attractive because it will earn more if lent out at the higher r. Higher return on financial assets discourages investment in plant or machinery.

A more subtle reason operates through the concept of *net present value* (NPV). We take up this very important concept now.

Present Value of an Income Stream

Suppose that the annual rate of interest is r, which means that if you lend Re 1 today you will get back Rs $(1+r)$ next year. The yield will be Rs $(1+r)(1+r) =$ Rs $(1+r)^2$ in 2 years' time, Rs $(1+r)(1+r)^2$ = Rs $(1+r)^3$ in 3 years' time, and Rs $(1+r)^n$ in n years' time. Another way of looking at it is: I need to lend only Rs $1/1 + r$ today (which is less than Re 1) to obtain Re 1 $(= (1/1 + r)(1 + r))$ next year, or only Rs $1/(1+r)^2$ today to get Re 1 after 2 years, or only Re $1/(1+r)^n$ today to get Re 1 in n years. Money received in the future is worth less, because if received today, it can be invested to generate a larger sum at compound interest at that future date.

The present value (PV) of Re 1 available in n years' time = Rs $1/(1+r)^n$. *(The PV of Rs X in n years is Rs $X/(1+r)^n$.) The expression $1/(1+r)^n$ is the discount factor for period n.*

For example, suppose the rate of interest is 10 per cent per year $(r = 0.1)$ and you are promised Re 1 after 2 years. The PV of this promise to you is Rs $1/(1+0.1)^2 =$ Re 0.826. The prospect of Re 1 in 2 years improves your *current* wealth by Re 0.826. If the rate of interest is 10 per cent, $1/(1+0.1)^{10}$ = 0.386 implying that Rs 1000 in ten years is worth Rs 386 now. Since $1/(1+0.1)^{30} = 0.057$, the same amount (Rs 1000) in thirty years is worth only Rs 57 now.

The *PV* of an income stream of (Rs) R_1 in period 1, R_2 in period 2, $\cdots R_n$ in period n is:

$$PV = R_1/(1+r) + R_2/(1+r)^2 + \cdots + R_n/(1+r)^n.$$

Clearly, PV varies inversely with r. If r goes up (down), each term on the right-hand side gets smaller (bigger) and the sum goes down (up).

Consider an investment project that generates cash flows per period over a known and fixed lifetime. The cost, however, has to be incurred in the current period. In deciding whether to accept or reject a particular project, the firm will weigh its cost against its benefit. Since the cash flows are spread over several years, the value of benefit is the PV of the cash flow (or return) stream. Subtracting the cost from the PV, we arrive at the NPV of the project. It is worthwhile to undertake the project if NPV > 0.

To illustrate, consider a project that costs Rs 100 today (period 0), and yields Rs 50 in period 1 and Rs 70 in period 2. The rate of interest is 10 per cent $(r = 0.1)$.

$$NPV = 50/(1+0.1) + 70/(1+0.1)^2 - 100 = 3.3$$

So this investment should be accepted. At any point in time, total investment of a firm is the value of all projects that pass the positive NPV test. If the rate of interest goes down NPV increases and the set of acceptable projects expands, because some projects that had NPV < 0 before, now have NPV > 0 at the lower r. (Exercise: recalculate NPV for $r = 15$ per cent.) Thus a fall in r boosts investment, I.

Planned investment varies inversely with the rate of interest because:

- *rise in r makes investment in plants or machinery less attractive by pushing up the cost of borrowed funds and, if internal funds are used, pushing up the return on competing financial investment (lending);*
- *a rise in r causes the number of eligible (NPV > 0) investment projects to decrease.*

Like business investment, planned consumption spending of households too may be influenced by the rate of interest. Purchase of houses, cars, refrigerators, airconditioners, and other durable goods are usually financed by loans. A fall in interest cost stimulates such purchase. Similarly, even government agencies (central or state) may be encouraged to spend more if a reduction in r makes borrowing less costly. Thus, it may reasonably be assumed that AD $(= C + I + G)$ is inversely related to r.

In addition to r, planned business investment may be influenced by several other factors such as the expected change in demand or stock market conditions. These are discussed in Appendix 4.1.

We have assumed an unchanged price level. If there is inflation, then the *real* interest rate should be used to calculate NPV and planned investment will be a function of the real interest. Real interest rate is obtained by subtracting the rate of inflation from the nominal rate of interest.

THE *IS* CURVE

It shows the combinations of r and Y at which equilibrium prevails in the market for commodities. Consider Figure 4.1(a) and (b). Initially the interest rate is r_1 and income is at level Y_1. A decline in

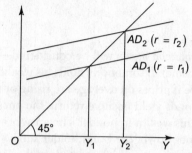

Fig. 4.1(a)   AD under Change in Interest Rate

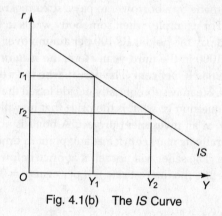

Fig. 4.1(b)   The *IS* Curve

r to r_2 shifts the AD_1 curve up to AD_2 and the new equilibrium has a higher $Y = Y_2$. Thus the *IS* curve is downward sloping. To establish the inverse relationship algebraically in a simple manner, let us assume that C depends only on Y and not on r, while I depends only on r and not on Y. There is no government.

$$C = a + cY, \ I = f - gr, f > 0, \ g > 0.$$

For equilibrium we need

$$Y = C + I \text{ or } Y = a + cY + f - gr$$

or $\qquad r = (f + a)/g - [(1 - c)/g]Y.$

This is the equation of the *IS* curve. It is a negatively sloped straight line with slope $[-(1 - c)/g]$ and intercept $(f + a)/g$. The slope can alternatively be written as $(-s/g)$, where s is the marginal propensity to save (mps).

OBSERVATIONS ON THE *IS* CURVE

- The *IS* Curve is negatively sloped.
- The larger g (the interest elasticity of I) or the smaller s (the marginal propensity to save), the flatter will be the *IS* curve (the absolute value of its slope, (s/g), becomes smaller). This is because the rise in I and, hence, the upward shift of AD following a decline in r will be larger if g is higher. The upward shift will bring about a larger rise in Y if the multiplier is higher (smaller mps).
- The position of the *IS* curve depends on the level of autonomous AD $(= a + f)$. An increase in $(a + f)$ causes Y to rise for any given level of r. The curve shifts to the right. Fall in autonomous AD causes a leftward shift.

THE ASSET MARKET

For simplicity only two types of financial assets will be considered—money (which bears no interest) and bonds (which yield interest income). If somebody holds his wealth in the form of money, the return is zero. (The return will be negative if prices on average are rising or positive if they are falling, but we assume P to be constant.) Since bonds yield positive return, the question is: why should anyone hold money at all instead of putting all his wealth in bonds? The answer is: the price of a bond is subject to fluctuations, so that, if the price goes down, the bond holder suffers a capital loss (fall in the value of his asset). Fluctuation in bond price is caused by fluctuation in the rate of interest, because the two are intimately related.

A bond is simply a promise made by a borrower to pay a stream of returns, over a specified period, in exchange for payment, now. For example, when somebody wants to borrow Rs 1000, he may issue a 3-year bond which promises to pay the holder Rs 100 per annum over the next two years and Rs 100 plus the original amount of Rs 1000 in the third year. Here, the *maturity period* is three years and the interest rate (called the *coupon rate*) is 10 per cent. The person who buys the bond for Rs 1000 is lending Rs 1000 to the issuer of the bond. He may subsequently decide to sell the bond in the secondary market for financial assets. The crucial question is: what is the price that he will get?

Recall our discussion of PV of an investment project. A bond is nothing but a stream of income over a specified period. So naturally its market price at any point in time is the PV of its returns at the currently prevailing interest rate. The seller will not sell it at price below the PV and no buyer will pay more than the PV. Thus, if currently the interest rate is 8 per cent $(r = 0.08)$, the bond in our example will fetch the price (in Rs):

$$P = 100/1.08 + 100/(1.08)^2 + 1100/(1.08)^3 = 1051.54.$$

If the current interest rate falls to 6 per cent, the *PV* and, hence, the price will go up. The new price is:

$$P = 100/1.06 + 100/(1.06)^2 + 1100/(1.06)^3 = 1106.92.$$

Thus bond price and r are inversely related. A fall in bond price (a rise in r) implies capital loss for the bond-holder. A drop in r causes capital gain.

In an actual economy there is a multiplicity of interest rates at any point in time depending on the maturity periods of bonds and the degree of risk attached to them. Risks are of two types: *default risk* (the possibility that the borrower may fail to repay on maturity) and *risk of capital loss* (fall in the market price after purchase). Our analysis assumes away both default risk and difference in maturity periods. However, the chance of capital loss or gain is very much there. Since there is only one type of bond, we can talk of 'the' rate of interest. In India, before financial liberalization, capital loss risk (also called 'interest rate risk') was largely absent because interest rates were not allowed to change beyond a very narrow band. Secondary market for bond trading was in a rudimentary state of development. Conditions are markedly different now.

Box 4.1   Bonds and Bond Markets

Bonds issued by the government to raise money (usually to finance deficits) are called *government bonds* or *securities* and those issued by the firms to finance investment are called *corporate bonds*. *Nominal bonds* pay a series of fixed nominal returns, while *indexed bonds* pay returns adjusted for expected inflation. Almost all Indian bonds are nominal. Bonds that yield exactly one cash flow in future (for example, Rs 2000 ten years from now) are *zero coupon bonds*, those paying multiple returns over a number of periods are *coupon bearing bonds*. A bond is *short term* if its maturity period is less than one year, it is *long term* if its maturity is ten years or more.

Instead of issuing a bond, a borrower may take an ordinary loan from a financial institution. The basic difference between the two modes is that a bond is tradable while a loan agreement is not. If Mr Dasgupta sells off his corporate bond to Mrs Verma, she will continue to get the returns promised by the bond. Existence of well-functioning markets for bonds and government securities is an important aspect of the financial maturity of an economy. There is no such market for loan agreements. Therefore, loans are often called *non-marketable debt.*

A *primary market* is a financial market in which new issues of bonds or securities are sold to initial buyers by the government agency or corporation borrowing the funds. Bonds already issued are traded in the secondary market. In India, the primary issue of GOI bonds (with maturities spanning all the way to twenty-five years) is done through auctions by the public debt office (PDO) of the RBI. The secondary market features bilaterally negotiated trades between agents of banks, mutual funds, and other financial intermediaries. There are proposals to move the PDO outside the RBI to improve the efficiency of its functioning. Securities Trading Corporation of India Ltd (STCI) is now the leading primary dealer in government securities. It also deals in corporate bonds.

Some major reforms were introduced in India's government securities market in the 1990s. They include (i) adoption of the auction system for selling of government securities; (ii) introduction of treasury bills (T-bills) of various maturities; (iii) establishment of the STCI; (iv) prescription of standard valuation norms for bond issue. In the non-government debt market also significant changes were made to improve its functioning. National and local stock exchanges have been granted facilities for trading in government and corporate debt through screen-based system. The Securities and Exchange Board of India acts as the overall regulator.

Source: Reddy (2000).

The variety of interest rates prevailing in an actual economy covers mortgage rates, house-loan rates, car-loan rates and rates on different types of bonds and other financial assets. Luckily, all the rates have a tendency to move in unison, enabling analysts to lump them together under 'the interest rate'. One indicator that is widely used is the Prime Lending Rate (PLR) of a major financial institution.

PLR is the lower limit to the rates charged by a financial institution. It is the rate charged to the best customer. The PLR of the State Bank of India (SBI) or the Industrial Development Bank of India (IDBI) is often used to represent the interest rate for the Indian economy. The IDBI-PLR dropped from 14 per cent to 11.5 per cent over 2000–2.

Motives for Holding Money (Liquidity Preference)

The *liquidity* of an asset is the ease with which it can be exchanged for cash. By definition, money is the most liquid of all assets. Demand for money is the demand for liquidity or 'Liquidity Preference' in Keynesian terminology.

Each household and firm requires a certain stock of money (in the form of either cash or current account deposits in banks on which cheques can be drawn) to carry out current transactions. This is known as the *transactions demand for money*. The required volume of transactions balance of an economic agent depends on the volume of its receipts and expenditures, and their time distribution. Since the level of national income is a good index of the total volume of transactions in an economy, the transaction demand for money is assumed to be proportional to national income (in money terms).

$$M^d = kPY, \ k > o$$

Money is useful because it enables one to carry out transactions (purchase and sale of goods and services). So what is really important is the command over commodities, rather than the value of cash as such. If all prices get doubled, the same quantities of goods can be transacted only if one carries twice as much cash. Therefore, demand for money is really demand for purchasing power or *real balances*, denoted by M^d/P. Transaction demand for real balances is proportional to real income Y.

In addition to transactions demand, households keep a portion of their wealth in the form of real balance for speculative purposes. 'Speculation' refers not to speculative hoarding of goods, but to expectations regarding the price of bonds. Changes in these expectations induce shifting of wealth between bonds and real balances. Expectations are influenced by the level of the current rate of interest.

If r is high, most people would expect it to fall (bond price to rise) and bond holders will want to hold more bonds in order to reap the benefit of capital gain, so that demand for money (real balance) will be low. A low r, on the other hand, raises the demand for real balances (lowers the demand for bonds) by creating the expectation of a rise in r (capital loss on bonds). Thus speculative demand for real balances is inversely related to r.

A high r means that one is sacrificing a lot of interest income by holding money instead of interest earning assets. Even if the speculative element is absent, on this ground alone an inverse relation between money demand and r can be expected.

Combining the two motives, transactions and speculative, demand for real balances can be given a simple linear form:

$$M^d/P = kY - hr, \ k > 0, \ h > 0$$

Liquidity Preference Theory of Interest

Let us take money demand to depend only on the interest rate (only the speculative motive, ignoring the transaction motive for the moment). Supply of money is fixed by the monetary authorities. Let us take that as given. (Determinants of money supply will be discussed in depth in Chapter 6.)

In Figure 4.2 the downward sloping line is the money demand or liquidity preference function and the vertical line is the exogenously given money supply. The equilibrium interest rate is r^*.

If for some reason the supply of money goes up in the economy, the M^s line shifts to the right and r goes down in the new equilibrium. An exogenous rise in demand for money (caused, perhaps, by an increase in the perceived riskiness of bonds making bond-holding a less attractive prospect, although r has not changed) will give the demand curve an outward push and r will increase.

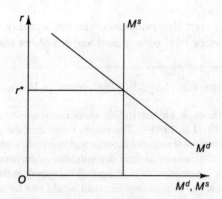

Fig. 4.2   Liquidity Preference and Interest Rate

Note that here we have ignored the influence of Y on money demand. For a complete theory, the role of Y will have to be recognized and Figure 4.2 will not be an accurate picture of asset equilibrium. In the complete theory, both Y and r will be simultaneously solved for, as is shown below in the text.

Another partial theory of interest is the loanable funds theory.

Loanable Funds Theory of Interest

Here interest rate, which is the price of loans (loanable funds), is taken to be determined by the demand and supply of loans. Demand comes from investment which is inversely related to r, and supply of loans is generated by the flow of savings in the economy. As interest is the return on loans provided, savings is assumed to be stimulated by a rise in r.

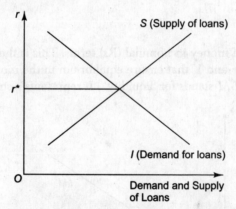

Fig. 4.3   Loanable Funds Theory of Interest

Demand for loans (I) is equal to its supply (S) at $r = r^*$. Like any other price, r will respond to changes in demand and supply conditions. If investment becomes more attractive, demand for loans will improve shifting the I curve to the right. The equilibrium r will go up. Similarly, an increase in saving will lead to a fall in r.

Note that this approach to interest determination, like the liquidity preference approach outlined above, is also partial, as the influence of Y on demand and supply of loans is ignored.

Box 4.2   Liquidity Preference in India

The short-run money demand function for the Indian economy was estimated by Manohar Rao using quarterly data over the period 1970–1 to 1980–1. The results confirmed the predictions of theory that real money demand varies positively with real national income and inversely with the interest rate. The interest rate used was the three-year term deposit rate as term deposits with maturities of three-year and above were the most popular financial assets (alternative to holding real balances). It turned out that for every 1 per cent increase in real income, short-run real money demand would rise by about 0.44 per cent and a rise in r of 1 per cent would drive money demand down by 0.2 per cent. Long-run responses (when variables had time to adjust fully to their equilibrium values) were much stronger, exceeding the short-run values by a factor of nearly 3.2.

Source: Rao (1997).

The general integrated theory of interest includes the roles of all four factors—investment, savings, money demand, and money supply. Investment–saving relation is captured by the *IS* Curve, while the demand–supply conditions in the money (assets) market is encapsulated in the *LM* curve. We now turn to this aspect.

THE *LM* CURVE

The supply of money (M^s), fixed by the monetary authorities, is given from outside. Dividing by P, we get money supply in real terms or the supply of real balances. Equilibrium in the money market needs:

$$M^s/P = kY - hr \tag{4.1}$$

Here M^s is the fixed supply of money in nominal (Rs) terms. This is the equation of the *LM* curve, which shows combinations of r and Y that ensure equilibrium in the money market for given values of M^s and P. (The letter L of *LM* stands for 'liquidity'.) It represents a straight line with slope (k/h).

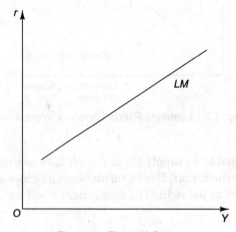

Fig. 4.4   The *LM* Curve

OBSERVATIONS ON THE *LM* CURVE AND MONEY (ASSET) MARKET EQUILIBRIUM

- The *LM* curve is positively sloped.
- It will be relatively flat if the income elasticity of money demand (k) is low and/or the interest elasticity of money demand (h) is high. It will be steep if h is low. If money demand does not depend on interest rate ($h = 0$), *LM* is vertical.
- The position of the *LM* curve depends on the supply of money in the system. A rise in M^s (with P unchanged) causes Y to rise for any given value of r. The curve shifts to the right. Fall in M^s causes a leftward shift.
- There are only two forms in which wealth can be held—either money or bonds. So if the money market is in equilibrium (households are satisfied with their holding of real balances), the bond market must also be in equilibrium (households cannot be dissatisfied with their bond holding).

Box 4.3   Liquidity Trap

It is a situation in which the interest rate r is so low (bond price so high) that nobody wants to hold bonds. Households hold their wealth in the form of money as bond price is almost certain to fall from its high level causing capital loss. Additional money supply will simply be absorbed in the people's portfolio at the prevailing value of r. The elasticity of money demand (demand for real balance) is infinite. The coefficient h is infinitely large and *LM* becomes horizontal. This is a theoretical possibility, rarely observed in reality.

DETERMINATION OF INCOME AND INTEREST RATE: INTEGRATED MODEL

The *IS* and *LM* schedules are combined in Figure 4.5. The downward sloping *IS* shows all the points of equilibrium in the product market and the upward sloping *LM* shows all the points of equilibrium in the money or asset market. The point of intersection is the point of simultaneous balance in the two markets. Also, as noted above, money-market equilibrium implies bond-market equilibrium, so that the values r^* and Y^* actually ensure balance in three markets—product, money, and bonds.

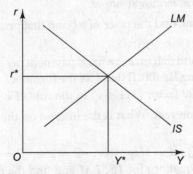

Fig. 4.5   Determination of Y and r

To repeat the central conclusion:

The propensity to consume, the propensity to invest, the demand for money, and the supply of money jointly determine the rate of interest r and the level of income Y. Change in any of these factors will cause the equilibrium values of both Y and r to change.

Let us illustrate with an example. Suppose that due to some institutional change or change in the public's preference real money demand increases. This means that more real balances will be held at each value of Y and r. Let us capture this by introducing a new constant term z in the equation for money demand, which becomes

$$M/P = z + kY - hr.$$

A new term z is added to the right-hand side of the original equation 4.2. Now for any value of Y, the value of r has to be higher to satisfy this equation. Graphically, this implies an upward shift of the LM Curve. With an unchanged IS, this will cause Y to fall and r to rise.

Summary

■ The components C and I of AD are responsive to the rate of interest. Planned investment depends inversely on r because (i) r is the cost of finance for investment and (ii) present value of investment projects varies inversely with r.

■ The IS Curve gives the equilibrium relation between r and Y in the commodity market. It is negatively sloped.

■ Demand for money (real balances) varies positively with Y and inversely with r.

■ The LM Curve gives the equilibrium relation between r and Y in the money (asset) market. It is positively sloped.

■ Output and rate of interest are jointly determined through interaction of IS and LM.

Exercise

1. Suppose that (i) in addition to r, investment also depends positively on Y and (ii) in addition to Y, consumption also depends negatively on r. Using linear forms obtain the equations of IS, LM. Is IS invariably downward sloping and LM invariably upward sloping? Write the conditions for the curves to have their conventional slopes.

2. If the interest rate is 10 per cent, find the price of a bond that promises to make just one payment of Rs 200 after two years.

3. A consol is a special type of bond that makes a fixed payment per period for ever. At interest rate r, find the price of a consol paying Rs 100. (Hint: Use the formula $1 + x + x^2 + x^3 + \cdots = 1/1 - x$, for $0 < x < 1$, with the discount factor $(1/1 + r)$ in the role of x.)

4. A bond will pay Rs 1000 in one year. What is the interest on the bond if the price today is (i) Rs 700 and (ii) Rs 900?

5. Suppose that $C = 60 + 0.8Y_d$, $I = 150 - 10r$, $G = 250$, $T = 200$, $M^d = 40 + 0.1\,Y - 10\,r$, $M^s = 100$, $P = 1$. Write the equations for IS, LM and find the equilibrium values of Y and r.

6. Use the loanable funds theory to find the impact on r of
   (i) an increase in the propensity to save (thriftiness);
   (ii) discovery of a profitable investment opportunity.

Appendix 4.1
More on Business Investment

Here we explain the influence of changes in output on the decision to invest. The role of the stock market will also be discussed.

THE ACCELERATOR THEORY

Net investment measures the addition to the stock of capital. Capital is needed to produce output to be sold for profit. Naturally enough, the planned production (sales) of business firms will be an important factor in determining the desired level of the capital stock. Once the desired capital stock is known, investment is undertaken to close the gap between the actual stock and the desired stock. There will be no investment if the actual exceeds the desired.

In the accelerator hypothesis a simple proportional relation is posited between the desired capital stock and the level of output in any period t.

$$K_t^* = \alpha Y_t, \quad \alpha > 0 \tag{4.3}$$

Thus α is the desired capital output ratio $(= K^*/Y)$.

In the simplest version, costs of adjusting the stock of capital are absent and, therefore, the entire gap between the desired stock and the actual stock inherited from the preceding period can be instantly closed through investment. In other words, the capital stock jumps immediately to the desired level. (Note that we are *not* assuming that there are no costs of investment, in which case the desired stock will be infinitely large. Adjustment costs are the internal costs of implementing the investment projects in the firm. These are separate from the cost of raising the finance for investment.)

For simplicity let us assume zero depreciation, so that net and gross investment are the same.

$$I_t = K_t^* - K_{t-1} \tag{4.4}$$

Since the gap between the desired and actual is closed in each period, the actual stock at the end of the previous period equals the desired stock of that period.

$$K_{t-1} = K_{t-1}^* = \alpha Y_{t-1}$$

Therefore equation (4.4) can be rewritten as

$$I_t = \alpha Y_t - \alpha Y_{t-1} = \alpha(Y_t - Y_{t-1}) = \alpha \Delta Y \tag{4.5}$$

Planned investment is proportional to the rate of change of output. To illustrate, suppose the desired capital output ratio to be $\alpha = 3$. Then if Y changes by 1 unit, investment will change by 3 units.

The simple accelerator analysis will be modified in the presence of *capital stock adjustment costs*. New investment, which calls for installation of new machines or additions to existing plants or construction of new buildings, entails additional costs as the normal production schedule is hampered or temporarily altered to accommodate these activities. If such costs rise steeply as the rate of investment is stepped up, it may be optimal for the firm to close the gap between the actual and the desired stock gradually over time. This contrasts with the previous case of costless adjustment where the gap was closed without any lag. Equation (4.4) now has the modified form:

$$I_t = \theta(K_t^* - K_{t-1}), 0 < \theta < 1 \tag{4.6}$$

Equation 4.6 captures partial (or lagged) adjustment where a fraction θ of the gap between desired and actual capital stock is filled by new investment each period. Using (4.3) we have

$$I_t = \theta(\alpha Y_t - K_{t-1}) \tag{4.7}$$

This relation is called the *flexible accelerator* model of business investment. This version gets greater support from empirical studies of actual investment behaviour (see Box 4.4 for the Indian experience). Several points are to be noted in this context:

- Due to incomplete adjustment within each period, we can no longer set $K_{t-1} = K_{t-1}^*$ and, therefore, an expression similar to equation (4.5) is not obtained.
- Since only a fraction of the desired change in K is achieved within any period, investment in any period will be responding to changes in income in many previous periods. Changes during more recent periods will carry greater weight.
- Instead of being fixed, as assumed, the adjustment parameter may actually be a choice variable of the firm. The value of θ may be affected by the rate of interest, tax treatment of capital expenditure or other variables. It is plausible that, other factors being equal, rate of investment may be slowed down (θ lowered) during any period when the interest rate (cost of funds) goes up. Thus, the flexible accelerator hypothesis is consistent with an inverse relation between I and r.
- In addition to investment in fixed (physical) capital, firms also invest in inventories which consist of raw materials, goods in the process of production, and finished goods held in anticipation of future sales. Empirical studies show that the accelerator hypothesis provides a good explanation of such *inventory investment*.

THE STOCK MARKET AND INVESTMENT (THE q THEORY)

Modern theories of investment emphasize a link between stock prices and firms' investment in physical capital. Empirically it has been found that investment does tend to go up when share prices are on the rise and to fall when the market is down and share prices are declining. The central theoretical concept in this context is the q-ratio of a firm (called Tobin's q), defined as:

$$q = V/P_k K$$

V is the value the stock marketplaces on the firm's assets (basically its stock of capital) and $P_k K$ is the 'replacement cost of capital', which is the cost of purchasing the existing capital stock at current prices. When $q > 1$, it is profitable to create additional capital because the return from doing so (captured by V) exceeds the cost of acquiring it. So investment should rise. When $q < 1$, the value of additional capital falls short of the cost of acquiring it and investment will not be profitable. Since in an efficient stock market share prices reflect V accurately, share prices and investment should display a strong positive correlation.

CREDIT RATIONING AND INVESTMENT

Both the accelerator theories (simple or flexible) and the q-theory assume that the credit market is perfect, in the sense that firms can borrow as much as they like for investment, at the going rate of interest. However, when lenders are not certain about the ability of the borrower to repay, they will resort to credit rationing (putting upper limit to the amount they will lend to a particular borrower, even though the borrower is willing to pay the going rate of interest), in order to minimize the probability of loss. This is particularly likely if regulatory authorities put banks and other financial intermediaries under stricter supervision to improve the quality of their portfolios.

Box A4.1.1   Investment Behaviour of Indian Firms

The first comprehensive study by Krishnamurthy and Sastry (1975) used data provided by the RBI and the Stock Exchange Official Directory. Their results suggested that the accelerator theory was important for cotton textiles, jute, and chemical and engineering industries. They also found existence of competition for funds between fixed and inventory investment. On the basis of aggregate time series data for the period 1960–1 to 1982–3 Sharma (1998) found that cost considerations played an important role in Indian investment decisions. Agarwal (1990) obtained good estimates of investment by using Tobin's q. Athey and Reeser (2000) included both Tobin's q and cash flow in their equation and also used net sales as a proxy of expected demand. Using a panel of 142 firms from 7 industrial groups over the period 1981–96, they found cash flow to be more significant for firms with limited access to capital markets. Using annual data for the period 1954–96, Athukorala and Sen (see Jha 2003) investigated the pattern of corporate investment in India. They found that (i) investment is negatively affected by the initial captial stock and the rental cost, (ii) the accelerator is valid for India (1 per cent rise in real GDP leads to 6 per cent rise in investment in the long run) and (iii) availability of bank credit and public investment have significant positive short run effects on investment.

Sources: Athey and Reeser (2000) and Goldar (1997).

Large firms with established reputation usually get all the credit they want but small and medium firms with higher perceived risk of default are denied access to funds. They face a borrowing or liquidity constraint in the market for finance.

Under credit rationing, the borrowing-constrained firms will have to fall back on their own internal resources for investment. (Remember Mr Sen of Appendix 3.2 who had to finance his current consumption out of his current income when he faced a borrowing constraint.) The implication is that the volume of retained earnings (undistributed past profits) should have a positive link with investment. Also, a larger cash flow (excess of receipts over costs) in the current period is interpreted by lenders as a signal of health and quality and makes it easier to obtain credit. Thus, under credit rationing, investment is affected by the volume of retained earnings and by current cash flows, as well as by the cost of funds, as in traditional theory.

5. Fiscal and Monetary Policy

In the analysis in Chapter 4, the government was absent. However, we now turn to the $IS - LM$ apparatus which, suitably modified, can be used to trace the impact of fiscal and monetary intervention by the government. The focus will be mostly on the theoretical aspects. The practice of monetary and fiscal policy, in general, and the Indian context, in particular, will be treated at length in Chapter 6.

To start with the simplest case, suppose that both government expenditure and tax collection take constant values, G_0 and T_0, respectively. Consumption C depends on disposable income $(Y - T_0)$. Product market balance needs

$$Y = C + I + G_0 = a + c(Y - T_0) + f - gr + G_0;$$

or $\quad Y = [(a + f + G_0 - cT_0)/1 - c] - (g/1 - c)r.$ \hfill (5.1)

This is the equation of the new IS Curve. A rise (fall) in autonomous AD $(= a + f + G_0 - cT_0)$ will make Y higher (lower) for any given value of r. Graphically, IS shifts to the right (left).

Denoting the given supply of money by M, the LM curve is given by:

$$M/P = kY - hr.$$ \hfill (5.2)

FISCAL POLICY

Fiscal policy involves changes in G and T. Suppose the government steps up its spending (G) on goods and services, keeping T unchanged. In Figure 5.1, IS_1 shifts to IS_2. Compared to the old equilibrium, both Y and r are higher in the new equilibrium, E_2. Expansionary fiscal action stimulates output and employment, as in the simple Keynesian model of Chapter 3.

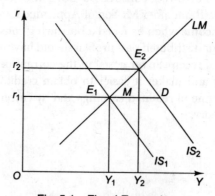

Fig. 5.1   Fiscal Expansion

The rate of interest goes up after the rise in G for the following reason. As Y goes up, the transactions demand for money also rises. With money supply unchanged, this rise in demand will cause r to go up. Another way of looking at it is: people will have to sell bonds to get the extra money needed to meet the higher transactions demand. This causes bond price to decline, which is the same as a rise in r. At the new equilibrium r must rise sufficiently to keep money demand unchanged even though income is higher.

Crowding out Effect

The rise in r dampens the impact of fiscal action by reducing private investment. In Figure 5.1, if r had not risen from the old level r_1, income would have expanded all the way up to the point D on the new IS. But the rise in r to r_2 has choked off the part MD. Presence of the assets market reduces the force of fiscal action. This offsetting (partial) of expansionary fiscal action through a rise in the rate of interest is called the *crowding out effect*. It is clear that higher the g (which measures the sensitivity of I to changes in r), the higher will be the shortfall from the maximum impact. It will also vary directly with k (the income elasticity of money demand). A high value of k implies a large increase in money demand when Y rises. This will need a large increase in r to maintain money market balance. Thus, a combination of high g and high k will strengthen the crowding out effect. In other words, low g and low k make fiscal policy more effective. Low k implies a relatively flat LM.

In Figure 5.2a, LM is steeper than in Figure 5.2b. Rightward shift of IS is more effective in raising Y in the latter because crowding out is weaker.

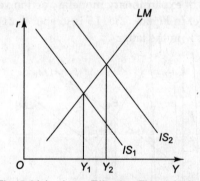

Fig. 5.2(a)   Less Effective Fiscal Action

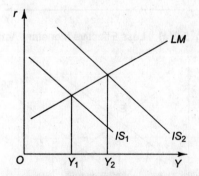

Fig. 5.2(b)   More Effective Fiscal Action

An expansionary fiscal policy may take the form of a cutback in tax collections, T. This leads to a rightward shift in IS by raising the first term on the right-hand side of (5.1.) Thus, other factors being equal, tax cut raises Y (and r), whereas increase in taxes lowers Y (and r). The rise in r would partially offset the stimulating effect of a reduction in taxation.

Fiscal consolidation or budget deficit reduction (cutback in G and/or rise in T) leads to a decrease in output and interest rate. In India, the blame for inflation is often laid squarely at the door of budgetary deficit of the central government and deficit reduction is strongly recommended for containing inflationary pressures. In our present analysis, there is no room for inflation as the price level P is held constant. So, the link between deficit and price rise cannot be addressed. That is done in Chapter 9. In the context of widespread underutilization of labour and other resources, the constancy of prices may not be an inappropriate assumption, and our analysis is applicable to such an economy.

MONETARY POLICY

Consider an increase in the supply of money M, other factors remaining unchanged. This pushes the LM_1 curve out to LM_2 in Figure 5.3. In the new equilibrium at E_2, income Y is higher but interest rate r is lower. The effect of a decrease in money supply—contractionary or tight monetary policy—is to raise r and reduce Y.

When money supply expands, the increase in Y is brought about by a rise in I induced by the fall in r. The higher is g (the interest elasticity of investment), the larger will be the boost to I following a drop in r. Thus the effectiveness of expansionary monetary action varies positively with g. Recall that a high g implies a flatter IS curve. In Figure 5.3a, IS is steeper than in Figure 5.3b. Rightward shift in LM is more successful in raising Y in the latter.

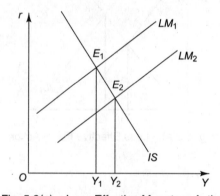

Fig. 5.3(a)   Less Effective Monetary Action

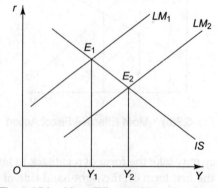

Fig. 5.3(b)   More Effective Monetary Action

In the $IS - LM$ model, it is easy to verify that fiscal policy cannot affect output if the LM curve is vertical and monetary policy is powerless to affect output if the IS curve is vertical. LM will be vertical if money demand does not depend on $r(h = 0)$. IS will be vertical if investment does not depend on $r(g = 0)$. Keynesian economists believe that the value of g is not high (particularly in depressions) and, hence, they do not have much faith in the efficacy of monetary action. The Monetarists, on the other hand, are sceptical about fiscal action, because they do not think that r has any significant influence on money demand. The Monetarist view is treated in Chapter 9.

Table 5.1   Effects of Fiscal and Monetary Policy

	Shift in IS	Shift in LM	Y	r
Increase in T	left	none	falls	falls
Decrease in T	right	none	rises	rises
Increase in G	right	none	rises	rises
Increase in M	none	right	rises	falls
Decrease in M	none	left	falls	rises

Monetary and fiscal policy may be used in combination. In Figure 5.4, a rise in G shifts IS. By itself this fiscal action would push r up to r_2. Due to crowding out, Y would rise only to Y_2. If the move were accompanied by an increase in the supply of money, LM would shift to the right. If the new LM passes through E_3, output will rise to Y_3 without any rise in r. Here the crowding out effect is neutralized by appropriate monetary action.

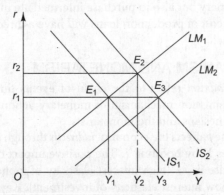

Fig. 5.4   Neutralization of Crowding Out

Consider another policy action. Taxes are raised to reduce the budget deficit. But the authorities do not want income to fall. Without any monetary intervention the tax increase shifts IS down and Y will fall from Y_1 to Y_2 in Figure 5.5. The downward pressure on Y can be neutralized by increasing the supply of money in an appropriate manner. The final equilibrium after adjustment in M is at E_3, where the level of output is unchanged at Y_1.

The important point to bear in mind is that fiscal and monetary actions may interact with each other and the impact of any policy change will depend crucially on the interdependence.

Although Y can be raised either by fiscal or monetary expansion, the effect on the *composition of national income* is different in the two cases. Fiscal expansion reduces I by raising r, whereas I is stimulated under monetary expansion through the fall in r. Note that if I is also positively influenced

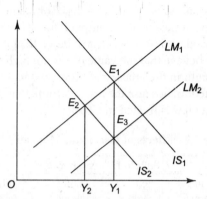

Fig. 5.5 Combined Fiscal and Monetary Action
to Maintain Output

by Y, then the ultimate impact of fiscal policy on I will depend on the strength of the income elasticity of I relative to its elasticity with respect to r. We have not considered the possible influence of Y on I. Since monetary expansion raises Y and reduces r, the impact on I is unambiguously positive.

As in the case of fiscal policy (recall the observations made in Chapter 3), our analysis of monetary policy has concentrated only on the demand side of the economy. A fall in money supply pushes up r. The rise in the interest cost of loans (credit) induces a cutback in planned I. Output Y falls because I is a component of aggregate demand. However, loans are taken by business not only to finance long-term investment in plant and machinery but also to purchase intermediate inputs and maintain inventories for current production. Rising cost of production loans will have a direct contractionary impact on Y through this supply-side channel.

TRANSMISSION MECHANISM AND MONETARISM

Transmission or propagation mechanism refers to the chain of events through which a policy change affects the economy. The transmission mechanism of monetary action is a very prominent point of disagreement between the Keynesians and the monetarists.

In the $IS-LM$ model, money affects the economy *indirectly* through the interest rate (asset market). A rise in M lowers r, this raises Y by boosting I. The positive impact on Y will be small if (i) r does not fall significantly after the rise in M (high interest elasticity of money demand) or (ii) I does not respond much to the fall in r (low interest elasticity of investment). Keynesians generally believe that both (i) and (ii) are likely to hold, particularly in a situation of recession, and are, therefore, sceptical about the effectiveness of monetary action in fighting a recession.

Monetarism, originally championed by Milton Friedman, is a counter-attack designed to reassert the importance of money as an instrument of macropolicy. The monetarists reject the Keynesian transmission mechanism because, in their view, money has a *direct* (and not via the interest route alone) impact on total spending on goods and services in an economy.

The major conclusions of monetarism may be summed up as:

(i) *Money supply is the dominant influence on nominal GDP (PY)*;

(ii) *In the long run, money supply affects only nominal variables such as the price level P or nominal wages. Real output, employment, and other real variables are unaffected. They are determined by real forces of demand and supply.*

To establish (i), the Equation of Exchange of traditional monetary theory is invoked.

$$MV = PY \qquad (5.3)$$

where V is income velocity of circulation of money (or velocity, for short). It is the number of times per year that the money stock M turns over to finance national income. For example, if $M = \text{Rs } 2000$ and $V = 10$, then GNP $= \text{Rs } 20{,}000$.

Monetarists believe that V is a stable constant determined by the degree of financial development of an economy and the payment habits of its citizens. Equation (5.3) then posits proportionality between PY and M. A change in M will cause an equal proportionate change in PY.

In the long run, Y attains the full employment value Y_f, so that, with both V and Y given, equation (5.3) yields a proportional relation between M and P. (This leads to the Quantity Theory hypothesis about inflation, which is discussed in Chapter 9.) In the short-run, Y is not at full employment and change in PY, following change in M, will partly be a change in P and partly a change in Y. Thus, fluctuations in money supply will cause short-run fluctuations in both prices and income.

Box 5.1   Monetarism and $IS - LM$

Although the monetarists do not use the $IS - LM$ model, it can be conveniently used to illustrate their approach. Monetarism denies any role to interest rate in money demand. The basic equation $MV = PY$ can be restated as: $M/P = kY$, where $k = 1/V$ is constant because V is constant. This may be interpreted as the money market equilibrium condition where demand for real balances (the right-hand side) is independent of r and depends only on Y. The equation yields a unique value for Y. Graphically this implies a vertical LM curve.

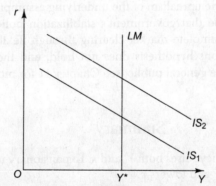

Fig. 5.6   Monetarism and Ineffective Fiscal Policy

Fiscal expansion that shifts IS_1 to IS_2 fails to change the level of Y. It is completely crowded out by the rise in r. A rise in M, on the other hand, shifts the vertical LM to the right and Y goes up. Thus, in stark contrast to the Keynesian view, *only* monetary policy matters.

Monetarism and the Conduct of Monetary Policy

The major policy conclusion of monetarism is that stability in money supply is crucial for stability in the economic system. And stability in money supply can be ensured by adopting a rule for the growth of M. The best possible thing that the monetary authorities can do is to announce a fixed rate of growth of the money stock and stick to that irrespective of short-run fluctuations in prices or output.

Discretionary action (raising M to fight a recession or lowering it to combat inflation) will actually be a destabilizing force.

The money supply rule—*Announce a rate of growth of money stock and do not deviate from it*—is known as *money stock targeting* by Central Banks. Although the RBI has now officially given up this type of targeting, in practice it continues to do so for the sake of price stability. Chapter 9 treats the issue in more detail.

NEW CLASSICAL ECONOMICS AND ECONOMIC POLICY

New classical economists appeared on the scene in the 1970s. They have a very strong faith in the equilibrating power of prices and assert that fully flexible prices, including wages, will keep all markets in equilibrium all the time. Keynes' basic assumption that prices and wages will be inflexible, in a situation of depression, is rejected on the ground that prices are never rigid and falling wages and prices can always be relied on to lead the system out of depression.

Also, it is maintained that Keynesian policy analysis is seriously flawed because it does not take the public's possible response to policy into account. In particular, it ignores the role played by people's expectations about economic variables and government policy. Intelligent and informed (rational) agents, according to the new classicals, have *rational expectations* in the sense that they can anticipate the type of policy the government will initiate in any particular phase of a business cycle. They will internalize that knowledge into their decision-making, change their behaviour accordingly, and this reaction of rational agents will nullify the attempt by the government to alter the course of the economy. This very striking result came to be known as the *policy ineffectiveness proposition* and created quite a stir among macroeconomists in the 1970s. Most economists, however, found the result unconvincing because of the stringency and the unrealism of the underlying assumptions.

The consensus seems to be that government's stabilization policy is effective for all practical purposes, as continuous and complete market clearing through flexible wages and prices does not happen, the rational expectations hypothesis does not hold, and the authorities have information superior to that possessed by the general public (see Chapter 11 for more detailed discussion).

Summary

- Expansionary fiscal policy raises both Y and r. Expansionary monetary policy (increase in money supply) raises Y and lowers r.
- Monetarists emphasize the direct role of money in influencing aggregate spending and are against discretionary policy action. They advocate strict adherence to pre-announced growth of money supply. The RBI follows this principle of money stock targeting.
- New classical economists hold that due to rational expectations government policy (monetary or fiscal) will be powerless to affect the values of economic variables. The majority of economists do not accept this because of the unrealism of the underlying assumptions.

Exercise

1. Suppose that $C = 400 + 0.75Y_d$, $I = 400 - 20r$, $G = 300$, $T = 400$, $M^a/P = 0.25Y - 10r$, $M = 1000$, $P = 2$.

   (i) Calculate the equilibrium values of Y and r.

   (ii) Suppose the government decides to remove the budget surplus, either by raising G to 400 or cutting T to 300. Is the effect on Y the same? Explain your answer.

2. Using the IS–LM analysis discuss the policy mix required to reduce the interest rate, keeping output unchanged.

3. Obtain the equilibrium values of Y and r for the following economy:

   $C = 60 + 0.8Y_d$, $I = 150 - 10r$, $G = 250$, $T = 200$,

   $P = 1$, $M = 100$,

   $M^d/P = 40 + 0.1Y - 10r$.

4. Explain the shape of the LM curve if money demand is independent of r. In this case fiscal policy is powerless to influence output. Do you agree?

5. Trace the impact of financial innovations like the introduction of credit cards on Y and r. (Hint: Credit cards reduce the need to hold cash balances for transaction purposes.)

6. 'A combination of tight monetary policy and expansionary fiscal policy leads to a high rate of interest, but the effect on output is uncertain.' True or False? Explain your answer.

7. Use the IS–LM analysis to trace the impact of an autonomous export boom on the economy. (Hint: exports are part of AD in an economy.)

8. Suppose that taxes are raised to reduce the budget deficit, but for some reason the central bank does not want the interest rate to change. What policy should it adopt? What will be the effect on the level of income? Use IS–LM graph to explain.

9. In an economy recession (falling output) is observed with falling interest rate. Show the situation in IS–LM diagram using shift of one of the curves. How will the graph change if the interest was rising instead?

10. Suppose that the monetary authority can follow two alternative policies—either keeping the money supply constant or keeping the interest rate constant by adjusting the money supply. Now consider two situations:

    (i) an exogenous (autonomous) fall in demand for goods and services, and

    (ii) an exogenous rise in demand for real balances.

    Compare the effect on output in each case under the two policies.

Appendix 5.1
Algebra of IS–LM

Solving the two $IS–LM$ equations (5.1) and (5.2), we get the equilibrium value of income:

$$Y = (a + f + G_0 - cT_0 + g/hM)/(1 - c + gk/h). \qquad (5.4)$$

The impact on Y per unit increase in G is given by:

$$\Delta Y/\Delta G = 1/(1 - c + gk/h) > 0.$$

The denominator is greater than $(1 - c)$ owing to the term $gk/h > 0$. The existence of financial assets has reduced the value of the government expenditure multiplier. This is the crowding out effect. The effect will be absent and the maximum value of the multiplier $(1/1 - c)$ regained if $g = 0$ or $k = 0$. A low value of h makes (gk/h) in the denominator large and a large denominator makes the whole expression smaller. Low h makes the LM steep and diminishes the impact of fiscal action. In the extreme case $(h = 0)$ fiscal policy will fail to affect Y. LM is vertical. In the other extreme of the liquidity trap (h infinitely large), LM is horizontal and the maximum multiplier prevails.

From equation (5.4) the money supply multiplier is:

$$\Delta Y/\Delta M = (g/h)/(1 - c + gk/h) = g/[(1 - c)h + gk] > 0.$$

Monetary expansion will fail to change Y if $g = 0$ (vertical IS). A large h (flat LM) reduces the multiplier by enlarging the denominator. When h is infinitely high (liquidity trap), the money multiplier drops to zero.

6. The Banking System, Supply of Money, and the Conduct of Monetary Policy

In Chapters 4 and 5, we assumed the supply of money to be exogenously given from outside. In this chapter we look into the money supply process in more detail. The crucial role played by the commercial banking system under the guidance of the Central Bank (the RBI) is highlighted. It is shown that by a judicious use of several instruments the Central Bank can exercise control over the supply of money in the economy.

DEFINITION AND FUNCTIONS OF MONEY, MEASURES OF MONEY SUPPLY

Money is a financial asset that is universally accepted as a means of payment in transactions and settlement of debt. It represents general purchasing power in the most *liquid* form, in the sense that it does not need to be converted into something else before it can be used for transactions.

The most important function of money is to act as a *means of payment*. Without money, exchange will have to be in the extremely inconvenient and limited form of barter–direct exchange of goods and services for other goods and services. Money also acts as a *unit of account* (values of goods and services are expressed in units of money) and a *store of value* (wealth can be held in the form of money for future use). All these functions, however, are derived from the primary one of medium of exchange.

In a modern economy, money usually consists of coins, currency notes, and current/savings account (demand) deposits of commercial banks. The last item is included because cheques drawn on such deposits are readily accepted in the settlement of transactions and debt.

Demand deposits are deposits payable on demand through cheques or otherwise. All other deposits have a fixed term to maturity and cannot be withdrawn on demand. They are called time deposits or term deposits.

There is a distinction between *legal tender* and *non-legal tender* or credit money. Coins and currency notes are legal tender. They cannot be refused in settlement of payments of any type. This is not true of non-legal tender money like demand deposits of banks. A payee can choose not to accept a cheque drawn on a demand deposit in a commercial bank.

Measures of Money Supply (Monetary Aggregates)

Supply of money is a stock variable whose value can be measured on a particular date. The RBI publishes figures for four measures of money supply. Also known as monetary aggregates, they are:

$M1 = CU + D$;

$M2 = M1 +$ savings deposits with post office savings banks;

$M3 = M1 +$ net time deposits of banks (interbank deposits are netted out); and

$M4 = M3 +$ total deposits with the post office savings organizations.

In the above definitions, $CU =$ currency (coins plus notes) held by the public, $D =$ demand deposits of the public in banks (interbank deposits are not included).

$M1$ is called *narrow money*, $M3$ is also known as *broad money* or *aggregate monetary resources* (AMR). $M2$ and $M4$ have been devised to accommodate post office deposits.

Table 6.1   Money Supply in India

(Rs crore)

Year	$M1$	$M3$
1989–0	81,060	230,950
1990–1	92,892	265,828
1991–2	114,406	317,049
1992–3	124,066	364,016
1993–4	150,778	431,084
1994–5	192,257	527,496
1995–6	214,844	599,191
1996–7	240,615	696,012
1997–8	267,844	821,332
1998–9	309,128	981,020
1999–2000	341,796	1,124,174
2000–01	379,450	1,313,220
2001–02	422,843	1,498,355
2002–03	472,827	1,725,222

Source: India Development Report, 2002, 2004–05.

Commercial banks are financial intermediaries who collect deposits from households and firms and use these funds to make financial investments (loans and purchase of bonds). The difference between the lending rate of interest (charged on loans and earned on bonds) and the borrowing rate (paid on deposits) is the source of their profit. Although, banks typically offer a wide variety of deposits, for simplicity, we shall assume that all deposits are demand deposits. Demand deposits are the liabilities of banks. On the asset side are loans and bonds and cash reserves.

Cash reserves include cash in hand and balance with the RBI. Cash in hand is used to meet the day to day withdrawal of cash by the public. Banks hold reserves at the RBI because they are required to do so under *cash reserve requirements*. This provides an important instrument of monetary control to the Central Bank, as will be shown below. No interest is earned on the balance held at the RBI.

Assets	Liabilities
Cash reserves (cash in hand plus reserves at RBI) Loans Bonds	Deposits (Demand deposits plus Time deposits)

Fig. 6.1   Balance Sheet of Commercial Bank

Just as deposits of ... ...iabilities of banks, the reserves of banks are the liabilities of the RBI. Its other ... ...ncy in circulation. Actually, they are the direct monetary liability of the ... ...ulation by the RBI on behalf of the government and counted a... ...ent bonds held by the RBI appear on the asset side. Non-b... ...its at the RBI.

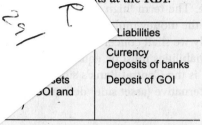

	Liabilities
	Currency
	Deposits of banks
...ets	Deposit of GOI
...OI and	

6.2   Balance Sheet of RBI (Central Bank)

... Bank domestic assets is called *domestic credit*. This consists of the RBI's loan ...nus loan to the private sector—usually to banks.

M... ...REATION BY THE BANKING SYSTEM

Let us ...ke a close look at the process of money creation by the banking system. First the algebra will be presented and then the process will be illustrated with an example. An important definition first:

Box 6.1   The Reserve Bank of India

The RBI, the apex institution of our financial system, was established on 1 April 1935, under the Reserve Bank of India Act. It was nationalized on 1 January 1949. The Bank has a central board of directors headed by the Governor who is assisted by deputy governors and other executive officers. The head office is in Mumbai with four local boards at Delhi, Kolkata, Chennai, and Mumbai.

The RBI performs four major functions as:

Currency authority: It is the sole authority for the issue of currency other than one rupee notes and coins and other small coins (which are issued by the GOI). Control of the supply of money and credit in the economy is its responsibility.

Banker to government: It is in charge of all banking business of the central as well as state governments. The governments maintain accounts at the Bank which makes loans and advances to them. The Bank is also the manager of the public debt, both internal and external, of the country. Currently, GOI bonds are auctioned through the public debt office (PDO) of the Bank.

Banker's bank and supervisor: The RBI holds part of the cash reserves of commercial banks, lends funds to them in times of need, provides them clearing facilities, and keeps a close watch on their activities. To banks, it is the lender of last resort. In India the demand for funds increases steeply during the months of November to April to finance the marketing of major kharif crops. The RBI lends to banks generously to help them meet this need. Credit provided by the RBI, in its role as lender of last resort, is known as *refinance*. By varying the amount and cost of refinance of different types of loans, the Bank can use it as a flexible instrument for influencing liquidity in the system.

Custodian of foreign exchange: It is entrusted with managing the country's foreign exchange reserves and maintaining the external value of the rupee. In the days before economic reform, the exchange rate of the rupee was rigidly controlled. Now the RBI intervenes in the foreign exchange market only to keep the market-determined rate within reasonable bounds.

The liabilities of the RBI are variously known as *base money* or *reserve money* or *monetary base* or *high powered money*. It consists of currency in circulation and reserves held by banks at the Bank.

$$B = CU + R$$

B stands for the monetary base. The term 'high powered' refers to the fact that an increase in base money by Re 1 creates, through the money multiplier, an increase of more than Re 1 in money supply. As our measure of money supply we shall concentrate on $M1$ only.

Since the RBI's assets and liabilities must be equal by balance sheet identity, it also must be true that $B = FA + DC$, where FA is the Central Bank's stock of foreign assets (including gold) and DC is domestic credit. This is an alternative (asset side) definition of the monetary base or high powered money.

$$B = CU + R = FA + DC$$

DC consists of the RBI's credit to the GOI and to the commercial sector (including commercial banks).
Initially, purely for simplicity, we also assume:

(i)   the public hold no currency ($CU = 0$) and use only cheques for payment;
(ii) there is no dearth of demand for bank loans. In other words, if a bank wants to give a loan, it can always find a willing borrower; and
(iii) assets of banks consist of only commercial loans.

Let the cash reserve ratio (CRR) set by the RBI be α, which means that a fraction α of total deposits will have to be kept as reserve at the RBI. So we have three equations:

$$B = R;$$

$$M^s = D; \text{ and}$$

$$R = \alpha D$$

which gives $M^s = (1/\alpha)B$.   (6.1)

The money supply is equal to the money multiplier $(1/\alpha)$ times the monetary base. The money multiplier is greater than one, because it is the inverse of the fractional CRR.

If, for example, $\alpha = 10$ per cent, money supply is ten times the monetary base. If B rises by Re 1, M^s will go up by Rs 10 through the deposit creation operation of the banking system as a whole.

Let us illustrate the multiplier process using an example. Let $\alpha = 10$ per cent. Suppose the government purchases goods worth Rs 100 from Mr A_1 and pays him by drawing a cheque on its account at the RBI. This starts the process.

A_1, by assumption, does not want to hold any currency. He deposits the cheque in his account at Bank B_1. This raises the value of D and money supply by Rs 100. Bank B_1 presents the cheque for clearance at the RBI, which transfers the amount from the government's account to that of B_1. Thus R (B_1's reserve) also goes up by Rs 100.

B_1 keeps (0.1) Rs 100 = Rs 10 to meet reserve requirement and lends out the rest, Rs 90, to Mr A_2 by opening a new account in his favour. This is an addition to D, as A_2 can draw cheques on it.

A_2 buys goods from A_3 and pays by cheque. A_3 deposits it in his bank, Bank B_3. B_3 keeps (0.1) Rs 90 = Rs 9 as reserve and lends out Rs 81 to Mr A_4 by opening an account in his favour. This adds to D by Rs 81.

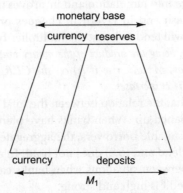

Fig. 6.3   Money Stock Pyramid

A_4 spends the money to buy goods from A_5 and pays by writing a cheque. A_5 deposits in his bank, Bank B_5, which keeps (0.1) Rs 81 = Rs 8.1 and lends the remainder.

And so the process goes on and on. The total rise in D, taking all the rounds together, comes to:

$$Rs\ 100\ +\ Rs\ 90\ +\ Rs\ 81\ +\cdots$$
$$=\ Rs\ 100(1 + 0.9 + (0.9)^2 + (0.9)^3 +\cdots)$$
$$=\ (1/1 - 0.9)\ Rs\ 100$$
$$=\ Rs\ 10,000.$$

The multiple expansion of D (and, hence, M^s) is taking place due to the lending (deposit-creating) activities of the banking system *as a whole*. At every step of the process each bank is strictly maintaining its reserve requirement. No single bank can grant loans exceeding Re 1 when it receives a fresh deposit of Re 1, but all the banks collectively can generate extra D of Rs 10,000 out of an initial injection of Rs 100, if the reserve ratio is 10 per cent.

The possibility of multiple expansion depends critically on the assumption that banks can always find borrowers for their loans. If at any stage, a bank is unable to lend, the process of deposit expansion comes to a halt right there.

We now relax the assumption that people do not hold any currency. Let us assume that desired currency holding is proportional to demand deposits, $CU = cD, 0 < c < 1$.

$$B = CU + R = cD + R = (c + \alpha)D$$
$$D = (1/c + \alpha)B$$
$$M^s = CU + D = (1 + c)D = (1 + c/c + \alpha)B \qquad (6.2)$$

The money multiplier (denoted by m) now has the value $1 + c/c + \alpha$. The value is lower compared to the previous case $(1/\alpha)$ because now the recipient of a cheque withdraws a fraction c from his demand deposit to hold in the form of cash. This leakage into currency at each step reduces the power of the banking system to extend credit and create money. The portion of the increase in the monetary base (high powered money) that finds its way into currency at any stage does not contribute to further deposit expansion. The multiplier of (6.1) is a special case of (6.2) with $c = 0$.

A smaller c implies less leakage into circulation and improves the multiplier. Change in payment habits of the public, away from cash and in favour of cheques or introduction of credit cards and automated teller machines (ATM) will tend to boost the multiplier by reducing the need to carry cash.

Money supply, as shown by (6.2), being the product of the money multiplier m and B, will change if either or both m and B change. In particular, M^s will rise if (i) α, *the CRR, decreases; (ii)* c, *the public's desired currency–deposit ratio, decreases; or (iii) B increases.*

It is very important to realize that the relation between the total money supply and base money B holds only when banks are fully loaned up. When banks have plenty of excess reserves (excess over required reserves) but cannot find suitable borrowers, the aggregate bank deposits are determined by the actual amount they are able to lend and (6.2) does not hold. In analysing the behaviour of money supply, it is crucial to distinguish between situations when banks cannot find enough outlets for their funds and when the demand for credit is high and strong.

In the light of our discussion, the equation for the LM curve can be written as:

$$(1 + c/c + \alpha)B/P = kY - hr.$$

Changes in c, α, and B (with P unchanged) will cause LM to shift by changing the left-hand side.

TARGETS OF MONETARY POLICY

The RBI conducts its monetary policy to attain the following major goals:

High and stable employment: Unemployment causes intense suffering and entails loss of potential output to the economy. Therefore, reducing unemployment and maintaining it at a tolerably low level is an important policy goal of all Central Banks.

Economic growth: Steady rise in national income over time is absolutely essential for improving the standard of living of a country. When income and output are rising, firms are stimulated to undertake new investment in plant and equipment and this keeps the economy on its path of growth. Since productive activities cannot be sustained without the availability of adequate credit, sound management of monetary and credit policy is absolutely vital for supporting the process of growth in an economy.

Price stability: Inflation has strong negative impact on social welfare. The poorer sections of the population, in particular, are hit especially hard in a situation of rising prices (see Chapter 10 for a discussion of the costs of inflation). It is, therefore, not surprising that all Central Banks have adopted price stability as a major, if not the supreme, goal of economic policy. Growth in output, with price stability, is the ideal towards which a society can be steered with the help of efficient economic policy of which monetary management forms a very important part.

Financial stability: A strong and stable financial system contributes to growth by smoothly channelling funds from savers to business firms with profitable investment opportunities. Financial crises cause sharp setbacks in economic activity and lower economic welfare significantly. Promotion of a stable financial system which can avert crisis by absorbing shocks is thus an important goal of a Central Bank. In fact, the financial panic of 1907 was a prominent factor behind the creation of the Federal Reserve System of the USA.

Stability in the foreign exchange market: With the increasing importance of international trade and investment ('globalization') to national economies, the exchange rate (the value of the national currency in terms of other currencies) has become a crucial macroeconomic variable. A rise in the value of the rupee (appreciation) makes Indian exports less competitive abroad, whereas a decline in the value (depreciation) tends to stimulate inflationary pressures (see Chapter 7 for a detailed analysis of these important issues). Fluctuating exchange rate makes planning difficult for traders. As a result, in the post-reform period, preventing sharp fluctuations in the value of the rupee so as to maintain orderly conditions in the foreign exchange market is rightly counted as a major goal of the RBI.

Although many of the goals mentioned are consistent with each other—growth and high employment, low inflation, and financial stability—this need not always be the case. Control of inflation, for example, may call for restrictions on aggregate demand and this may cause unemployment to rise. Conflicting goals confront the monetary authorities with hard choices which have to be adroitly handled with a proper balancing of the various trade-offs involved. That is what makes central banking a highly intricate art.

Ultimate versus Intermediate Targets

The ultimate targets that the monetary authority attempts to control are major macro variables such as unemployment, inflation and growth of real GDP. However, due to imperfect monitoring under imperfect information about the operation of the economy, it is not possible for the RBI to act on the ultimate targets directly. Therefore, it often chooses to control *intermediate targets* which are not important in their own right, but help in influencing the ultimate goals in a predictable way. Important intermediate targets are the monetary aggregates ($M1$, $M2$, or $M3$) or the interest rate. Regulating money supply is an effective way of regulating the rate of inflation and changes in the structure of interest rates affect growth by altering the incentives for investment in physical capital and other financial assets (liquidity preference).

Intermediate targeting on a monetary aggregate by the RBI typically proceeds as follows. At the beginning of each quarter, the Bank determines the money growth rate that it deems consistent with the ultimate goals of price stability and growth. The decision is made in light of the data on past performance and forecasts about the next quarter or year made by its team of analysts. Policy actions during the quarter are chosen to hit this chosen target. At the beginning of the next quarter, the money supply target is reviewed and adjusted on the basis of the experience within the quarter.

In 1998, the RBI formally switched from exclusive money supply targeting to a broad-based list of policy indicators. Nevertheless, monetary aggregates such as $M3$ continue to be the most important indicator of its policy stance. There are two reasons for this:

- In India, over a period of 3–5 years, $M3$ remains a reasonably accurate predictor of inflation (as measured by the WPI).
- Money stock targeting is well understood by the public at large. With money stock targeting, the policy stance is unambiguous and gives a clear signal to the economy. The RBI believes that a strong commitment to keep money growth within a target range enhances its anti-inflationary *credibility* and keeps inflationary expectations at a low level. Other modes of intermediate targeting—targeting interest rates, for example—do not have such anti-inflationary guarantee.

INSTRUMENTS OF MONETARY POLICY

The RBI can affect money supply by changing the monetary base B, or the value of the multiplier. The three major instruments are:

Variation in CRR: If the Bank raises the CRR, the loanable funds at the disposal of commercial banks get reduced at one stroke and the money supply contracts. To meet higher reserve requirements the banks will have to recall loans. The opposite effect occurs if the CRR is reduced. This enhances the ability of the banks to create deposit money. Since it is a rather drastic way of changing the money multiplier , CRR variation is not used very frequently. Frequent use will destabilize the system.

Over the last decade, central banks all over the world have been reducing the reserve requirements of their commercial banks. Switzerland, New Zealand, and Australia have eliminated it entirely. This action is motivated by the desire to make banks more efficient and competitive. Since no interest is paid on reserves, the system of required reserves acts as a heavy tax on banks, which puts them at a disadvantage vis-à-vis financial intermediaries not subject to such requirements. In India, CRR has been gradually reduced from 15 per cent in 1992 to 5 per cent in 2002.

Variation in the Bank Rate: Commercial banks may approach the RBI for loans to add to their reserves. The bank rate is the interest charged by the Bank for such loans. If the bank rate is low, the banks are encouraged to borrow reserves against which they can advance loans. This facilitates credit creation. An upward revision in the rate discourages borrowing and exerts a contractionary effect on money stock. A rise in the bank rate is usually followed by a rise in the rates the banks charge on their loans. This diminishes the demand for credit by firms and households.

Open Market Operations (OMOs): The RBI's open market policy consists of purchase and sale of bonds (mostly government bonds) in the open market. An open market sale contracts B and a purchase enhances it. OMOs are usually classified into two broad types: (i) dynamic: deliberately planned to change the level of bank reserves and the monetary base and (ii) defensive: intended to offset undesirable changes in reserves brought about by exogenous factors.

Suppose the RBI buys bonds worth Rs 1000 from Mr A by writing a cheque on itself. When A deposits it in his bank account, that bank's reserve at RBI goes up by Rs 1000. This will lead to a rise in the aggregate money stock through the multiplier process outlined above. Sale of bond will have the opposite effect. A part of B is now withdrawn from circulation and the resulting fall in money supply will be a multiple of the amount withdrawn. Instead of government securities, OMOs may involve buying and selling of foreign exchange. Clearly, the ability of the RBI to reduce reserve money by selling bonds or foreign exchange is limited by its stock of such assets.

Is there any way for commercial banks to protect themselves against the loss of reserves resulting from a contractionary open market policy? If payment habits of the public are unchanged they cannot get additional cash from that source, nor can they acquire it by selling bonds to one another because one bank's gain will be offset by the loss of another. The only way is to approach the RBI for loans, but the Bank is unlikely to oblige as this will tend to neutralize the contractionary policy.

The chief advantage of OMOs over other instruments of control available to a Central Bank is that they are flexible, precise (in the sense that they can be undertaken to any desired extent), and can be implemented quickly. They are easily reversed. If a mistake is made and detected, a correction in policy can be made immediately without administrative delay or cost. However, the use of OMO presupposes the existence of a well-developed market for government bonds. In India that market, in spite of some growth in recent times, is still very shallow. OMOs were insignificant in the pre-liberalization period as government debt could not be traded at market-determined rates. But over 1995–2002, net sales of GOI securities and treasury bills climbed up to attain average annual value of approximately 6 per cent of reserve money.

One major disadvantage of OMO is that the sale of government bonds imposes a cost on the government as interest will have to be paid to the purchaser of the bonds. Since changing the CRR has no such cost, it used to be the favoured method in India.

Intervention in the Foreign Exchange Market

The RBI, like most other central banks, regularly engages in international financial transactions in order to influence the exchange rate. (For comprehensive discussion on exchange rates see Chapter 7.) Attempts by a Central Bank to influence the exchange rate of its home currency through buying and selling domestic or foreign currencies is known as a *managed exchange regime* or *managed float*.

> **Box 6.2 Repos and Reverse Repos**
>
> A repo is a repurchase agreement in which the Central Bank buys bonds with the agreement that the seller will repurchase them within a short period ranging from 1 to 15 days. In a reverse repo, the Bank sells bonds and the buyer agrees to sell them back within a short period. Since the effect on reserves of the banking system of the initial purchase or sale is reversed on the date of repurchase or resale, these are very flexible instruments of short-term defensive OMO.
>
> In recent years, repos and reverse repos are being increasingly used by the RBI, as part of its discretionary monetary policy.

Suppose that the RBI decides to sell \$100 of its foreign assets (FA) to Mrs Sen in exchange for \$100 of the home currency (= Rs 5000, assuming an exchange rate of Rs 50 per dollar). Mrs Sen pays Rs 5000 in cash. The transaction has two effects. First, it reduces the RBI's FA by \$100. Second, currency in circulation (CU) falls by \$100 (= Rs 5000).

Since the monetary base $B = CU + R$, the result is that the base falls by Rs 5000.

If, instead of paying cash, Mrs Sen pays for her purchase of \$100 by writing a cheque for Rs 5000 on her account at the SBI, then the RBI reduces the SBI's reserves by the same amount. The effect on the monetary base is the same as, this time, R rather than CU falls by Rs 5000. Thus *the RBI's sale of foreign currency (purchase of rupee) in the foreign currency market leads to an equal decline in the monetary base. Purchase of foreign currency (sale of rupee) leads to an equal expansion of the monetary base.* It should be clear that the RBI's sale (purchase) of foreign exchange is no different from an OMO sale (purchase) of government bonds in its impact on the monetary base.

The type of intervention just described in which the RBI's purchase or sale of foreign assets causes equivalent changes in base money (and, hence, in money supply) is called *unsterilized foreign exchange intervention.*

Often Central Banks do not want the domestic monetary base (and, hence, domestic money supply) to change as a result of its transactions in foreign assets. Then, it has to undertake appropriate offsetting OMO in government bonds. For example, the monetary impact of the RBI's sale of \$100 to Mrs Sen (which caused the monetary base to contract) can be neutralized by conducting an open market purchase of government bonds worth Rs 5000. This will leave the monetary base unchanged.

A foreign exchange transaction coupled with an offsetting OMO that leaves monetary base and, hence, money supply unchanged is called *sterilized foreign exchange intervention.*

Deficit Financing

A government can finance its budget deficit (BD), that is, excess of spending over revenue, by borrowing. It may borrow either from the public, the banks, or the RBI. Borrowing from the RBI is special because it leads directly to an increase in the stock of base money in the economy and, hence, in money supply. By borrowing from the Central Bank, the government effectively finances itself by printing money. The process is very simple. If the government wants to step up its expenditure by Rs 5000 without raising additional revenue through taxation or other means, it issues a bond and asks the Bank to buy it. The Bank buys the bond and makes the money available to the government, who then proceeds to spend the same. The recipients of this expenditure put the money in their banks and the resulting rise in reserves triggers off the money multiplier. Therefore, this method of deficit financing is called *debt monetization* or *monetization of deficit.* Actually, the word 'deficit financing' in India is most of the time taken to mean 'deficit financed by borrowing from the RBI'.

It may be instructive to note the difference between borrowing from the public and borrowing from the RBI as ways of deficit financing. Suppose Mr Sen lends Rs 5000 to the government by buying a newly-issued government bond. The RBI clears his cheque drawn on his bank, Bank B, by transferring Rs 5000 from Bank B's account to the government's. B's reserve at the RBI goes down by Rs 5000. The government spends Rs 5000 to buy goods from Mr Das, who has an account at Bank C. When Mr Das deposits the government's cheque in his account, the RBI clears it this time by transferring Rs 5000 from the government's account to Bank C's. Total reserve of the banking system stays unchanged, as Bank B's loss is exactly offset by Bank C's gain. So borrowing from the public (and banks) does not have an expansionary impact on money supply.

FINANCIAL SECTOR REFORM, CHANGES IN FISCAL AND MONETARY POLICY IN INDIA

Banking reform is a very vital component of the ongoing process of economic reform in India. In the pre-reform days, interest rates and returns on all types of financial investments were strictly regulated and banks had to operate under numerous restrictions imposed by the GOI. Competition in the field was virtually absent and the nationalized banks were required to perform many 'social duties', like lending to priority sectors at subsidized rates of interest. Heavy regulation, lack of competition and accountability plus emphasis on social responsibility, at the cost of profitability, led to cumulative rise in inefficiency and non-performing assets (NPA) over the decades.

Prior to economic reform, the RBI lacked autonomy in the sense that monetary policy played a largely accommodative role to fiscal policy. The central government could borrow without limit from the RBI through ad hoc treasury bills (which were basically overdrafts on the Bank). In addition to CRR, commercial banks were statutorily required to hold a specified percentage of their assets (statutory liquidity ratio, SLR) in the form of government bonds. These bonds had zero risk of default, but yielded very low returns. SLR was the mechanism that forced the banks to lend to the GOI at interest rates that were kept artificially low. In the early 1990s more than 60 per cent of incremental bank deposits were getting allocated to meet the CRR and SLR requirements.

To minimize its cost of borrowing, the GOI maintained interest rates on government bonds at levels much lower than those on other assets. As a result, these bonds never figured prominently in the portfolio of households. They were held, under compulsion, mostly by banks, provident funds, and nationalized insurance companies.

On the recommendations of the Narasimham Committee on Financial System (1991), the GOI has adopted measures to restructure the banking system. The major steps include:

- lifting of regulations on interest rates on deposits and advances;
- reduction of barriers to entry of private banks;
- liberalization of branching regulations for both public and private sector banks;
- introduction of capital adequacy, income recognition, and provisioning norms; and
- reduction of the appropriation of loanable funds by the GOI through gradual decrease in CRR and SLR. Banks have now more funds at their disposal for lending on commercial terms.

A major feature of monetary reform is the move from *direct* instruments (such as administered interest rates, reserve requirements, selective credit control) to *indirect* instruments (such as open market operations, purchase and repurchase of government securities) for the conduct of monetary policy.

The GOI no longer has the power to control interest rates on government bonds and the SLR has been progressively reduced. It was 38.5 per cent in 1992, but only 25 per cent in 2005. A secondary market for government securities has begun to develop. Attracted by their low risk and high liquidity, banks still hold a large portion of their portfolio in the form of such securities, but they are no longer compelled to do so.

Through the use of ad hoc treasury bills the GOI used to enjoy unlimited access to the RBI credit. On an average, throughout the 1980s, deficit financing or the RBI credit to the central government accounted for more than 90 per cent of the variations in reserve money. Automatic monetization of deficit severely hampered the ability of the monetary authorities (RBI and the Ministry of Finance) to pursue independent monetary policy. As part of fiscal consolidation, issue of ad hoc treasury bills has been abolished and a system of Ways and Means Advances (WMA), with a mutually agreed prior limit, introduced to meet temporary mismatch between receipts and expenditures of the GOI. Significantly, greater autonomy of the RBI has been one of the major positive results of financial reform in India. The enactment of the FRBM Act has strengthened this further. From 2006, the RBI will no longer be permitted to subscribe to government securities in the primary market.

Monetized deficit as a proportion of GDP has declined from 2 per cent over the decade 1980–91 to 0.5 per cent over 1992–2004. By restricting the growth of money supply, this has undoubtedly helped to keep inflation down to moderate levels.

Since budget deficits are not automatically monetized any more, reserve money is no longer passively determined by fiscal policy. On the contrary, it is 'increasingly reflecting the RBI's assessment of market liquidity and absorptive capacity' (RBI Annual Report, 2000–1). The role of active open market operations is also growing in the new environment where monetary authorities have much more discretionary control over the stock of reserve money. In the pre-reform days, the yield on government bonds was kept at such a low level that there was not much demand for it. In sharp contrast to the situation, in the developed economies, the market for government debt was very narrow and undeveloped. This blunted the edge of OMOs as an instrument of credit control. Conditions are changing at a relatively fast pace.

FOREIGN CAPITAL INFLOW, MONEY SUPPLY AND STERILIZATION IN INDIA

Liberalization has significantly increased the degree of openness of the Indian economy. Lifting of restrictions has stimulated considerable inflow of foreign capital, particularly of the portfolio type. This has exerted an upward pressure on the money stock. An American investor planning to invest in India sells dollars to the RBI to obtain the money needed for investment. When he deposits the amount in a bank, the monetary base (reserve money) goes up, triggering a possible multiple expansion. If this is deemed undesirable, the central bank will have to take measures to *sterilize* the inflow (= net addition to its foreign exchange assets). There was a surge in capital inflow in 1993–4 and the RBI responded by selling government securities worth more than Rs 9000 crore in the open market. Once again, in 2000, in response to volatile capital flows, it had to temporarily raise the bank rate and the CRR. The CRR was subsequently reduced in May 2001.

We know that the monetary base can be expressed as $B = DC + FA$, where DC is domestic credit extended by the RBI and FA is its stock of foreign assets. DC is the sum of the RBI's credit to the GOI and its credit to the commercial sector (including commercial banks). Because of continuous inflow of foreign capital into the Indian economy (mostly portfolio funds) and the RBI's policy of not letting the rupee to appreciate, the Bank's stock of FA has been continuously on the rise, pulling up the share of FA in the monetary base, over time. From 9.1 per cent at end-March 1991, the share of FA in reserve money had reached 78.1 per cent by the end of 2001–2. This substantial rise was partly neutralized by the negative growth of the RBI's domestic credit (sterilization).

Table 6.2   Sources of Changes in the Monetary Base

(per cent of change in monetary base)

Year	Δ RBICG	Δ RBICC	ΔFA
1984/5–1989/90	105.50	13.60	7.60
1991–2	44.00	-34.00	92.50
1992–3	38.80	32.72	33.30
1993–4	3.10	14.90	103.90
1994–5	7.10	26.30	76.10
1995–6	79.30	34.90	−2.50
1996–7	50.10	−275.40	366.90
1997–8	41.80	7.70	80.30
1998–9	52.40	30.80	66.60
1999–2000	−20.20	31.00	131.80
2000–1	24.70	−25.50	137.50
2001–2	1.70	−27.70	193.50

Source: Kohli (2005).

Notes: RBICG: RBI's credit to government, RBICC: RBI's credit to commercial sector; FA: foreign assets of the RBI.

Decreasing numbers in the first two columns indicate that the authorities have been tightening DC as part of sterilization exercise to counter the expansionary impact of rising FA on money supply.

The share of the RBI's credit to the GOI in reserve money has declined steadily from 1991 to reach 31 per cent in 2003. This is chiefly due to the discontinuation of the practice of issuing ad hoc treasury bills and automatic monetization of budget deficit.

Table 6.2 displays the behaviour of the monetary base broken down into its major components.

Summary

- The most important monetary aggregates are $M1$, $M2$, $M3$, $M4$.
- The banking system as a whole can create money through multiple expansion of deposits. The value of the money multiplier depends inversely on the CRR and the public's desired currency deposit ratio and positively on the monetary base.
- High and stable employment, economic growth, price stability, financial stability, and stability, in the foreign exchange market constitute the major goals of monetary policy. These ultimate targets are sought to be achieved through the intermediate targets: $M1$, $M2$, $M3$, $M4$ and the rate of interest.
- The major instruments of monetary control are: CRR, Bank Rate, OMO.
- The RBI's intervention in the foreign exchange market leads to equal change in the monetary base.
- Deficit financing (monetization of government deficit) adds to the supply of money by expanding the monetary base.

- Economic reform introduced substantial changes in the conduct of fiscal and monetary policy in India. The RBI has become much more independent. Automatic monetization of government deficit has stopped.
- Huge inflow of foreign capital has been followed by sterilized intervention by the RBI in recent years.

Exercise

1. Bankers often say that they are only lenders and borrowers of funds, not creators of money. Is this view correct? Why or why not?

2. Determine the maximum increase in money supply that can result from a Re 100 increase in reserve money, if the CRR is 10 per cent? Give some reasons why the actual increase may fall short of the maximum possible.

3. Use the IS–LM model to trace the impact of the following policy actions:
   (i) an open-market sale of securities by the RBI;
   (ii) a decrease in CRR;
   (iii) an increase in the public's preferred currency–deposit ratio.

4. What are the advantages of OMO over other methods of credit control? What are its limitations?

5. 'The discontinuance of automatic deficit monetization has restored the autonomy of the RBI.' Discuss.

6. Explain why money supply is unaffected when budget deficit is met by borrowing from the public.

7. Explain the concept of the money multiplier. What factors determine its size?

8. Suppose that a country's stock of FA decreases for some reason. What will be the effect in the absence of sterilization? If the Central Bank decides to sterilize, what kind of action should it take?

7. Foreign Trade and Exchange Rate

ECONOMIC OPENNESS

In this chapter the problem of macroeconomic balance in an economy that interacts with the rest of the world through international trade is considered. We have seen in Chapter 3, that net exports (NX) constitute an important element of aggregate demand (AD) in an economy. An autonomous rise in NX (caused by an autonomous rise in exports X or a fall in imports M) will stimulate output, just like an autonomous rise in investment I or government spending G. But the exchange rate between the domestic currency and the foreign currency was not brought into the picture. The assumption of constant prices included the exchange rate. Now we shall allow the exchange rate (denoted by e) to vary, retaining the assumption of unchanged commodity prices for the most part.

Openness of an economy covers three important aspects:

- *Goods market openness*: This refers to free exchange of commodities across national boundaries. The share of trade as a proportion of world GDP has been steadily growing over the post-war decades. In recent years, it has really accelerated in growth. A major factor has been the decision of the less developed countries (LDCs) to move towards a policy of greater integration with global markets.

- *Capital market openness*: This relates to international trade in financial assets. (Capital refers to financial, not physical, capital.) Investors today have more freedom to choose between domestic and foreign assets. It is much easier now for a foreign investor to acquire assets in India (share of an Indian company, a GOI bond, for example). Also, Indian firms have greater ability to raise finance abroad to meet their investment needs. This is due to relaxation of *capital controls* under the reform programme. Progressive elimination of capital controls is a crucial feature of the ongoing process of globalization the world over.

- *Factor market openness*: If the major factors of production—labour and capital—have more freedom to choose their location of work, the factor market becomes more open. Multinational companies (MNCs) are moving their operations with greater ease around the world in search of lower costs and workers can move from one country of the European Union to another without facing serious restrictions.

Leaving the factor market aside, we shall focus on trade in goods and trade in financial assets (international lending and borrowing).

Openness of the Indian Economy

The system of centralized planning in India was based on a policy of industrialization through import substitution. Participation in foreign trade was heavily regulated, with the result that, by 1991, India was the most autarkic (closed to foreign commerce) non-communist country in the world. The situation changed dramatically after the initiation of reforms, of which external liberalization was the most prominent feature.

Table 7.1   India's Foreign Trade Ratios

Year	Export/GDP	Import/GDP	(Export+Import)/GDP
1980–1	4.6	8.9	13.5
1990–1	5.8	8.8	14.6
1992–3	7.3	9.6	16.9
1993–4	8.3	9.8	18.1
1994–5	8.4	11.2	19.6
1995–6	9.2	12.4	21.6
1996–7	8.9	12.8	21.7
1997–8	8.7	12.5	21.2
1998–9	8.2	11.4	19.6
1999–2000	8.3	12.3	20.6
2000–1	9.4	12.4	21.8

Source: *Statistical Outline of India*, Tata Services Limited, 2002–3.

Total foreign trade (export + import) as a proportion of GDP is a widely used measure of the *degree of openness* of an economy. It is clear from Table 7.1 that openness of the economy has improved steadily in the post-reform period. In 1970 the index was as low as 8 per cent. Another measure of openness is the value of import duties as a proportion of the value of imports. A reduction implies greater openness (lower import restrictions). From a peak of 53 per cent in 1987 and a value of around 46 per cent in 1991, it has come down to approximately 24 per cent in recent years. This is still fairly high by international standards.

Trade liberalization in India has involved the following major steps:

- Removal of restrictions on a wide range of imports.
- A change from a regime of rigidly controlled exchange rate to flexible exchange. (Fixed and flexible rates are discussed below.)
- Making the rupee fully *convertible on current account*. This means that there are virtually no restrictions now on the purchase and sale of foreign exchange for trade in goods and services. However, trade in assets (international lending and borrowing), particularly by residents, is still very carefully regulated by exchange controls. This means the rupee is not convertible on capital account. Since international integration of capital markets is one of the pillars of globalization, the GOI has adopted a policy of gradually moving towards full capital account convertibility in the near future.

The country's external sector policy since the 1990s has evolved around the following major elements:

- keeping the current account deficit and external debt–GDP ratio at reasonably low (sustainable) levels;
- maintenance of adequate foreign exchange reserves as a precautionary measure; and

▣ changing the composition of foreign capital inflow in favour of stable items and reducing short-term loans.

THE BALANCE OF PAYMENTS

The balance of payments (BoP) is a systematic record of all transactions between the economic units of one country (households, firms, and the government) and the rest of the world. It consists of two parts: the current account and the capital account.

The current account covers transactions in goods and services and transfers during the current period.

$$Current\ account = value\ of\ exports - value\ of\ imports\ +\ net\ transfers\ from\ abroad$$

$$= net\ exports + net\ transfers\ from\ abroad$$

Net exports (NX) is the *trade balance.* If net transfer from abroad is positive, that means foreign residents are transferring less out of India (in the form of gifts or remittances, for example) than Indians are doing from abroad. Since India tops the list of remittance receivers in the world, this item has a large positive value in our current account. Net foreign aid received by India during a particular period is also part of transfers.

If the right-hand side is positive (negative), it is a case of current account surplus (deficit). Note that large transfers from abroad may put the current account in surplus even if net exports is negative. In subsequent analysis, the 'net transfer' term will be ignored for simplicity. So current account will consist of net exports or trade balance only.

Exports and imports include trade in services as well as in goods. When an American company pays for the maintenance of its factory in Karnataka, or for the services of an Indian employee in Texas, India receives payment for exporting a service. Tourism is another major service export. Trade in services is often called *invisible,* because they cannot be seen to cross national borders.

A current account deficit means that the revenue from exports is less than the expenditure on imports. This deficit can be financed only by borrowing from foreigners (selling bonds, usually to foreign banks) or drawing down foreign assets. *Net foreign assets* (NFA) of India is the excess of foreign assets owned by Indians over the assets owned by foreigners here. Deficit (surplus) in current account leads to a reduction in (addition to) NFA of a country.

The capital account records transactions in assets.

$$Capital\ account = receipt\ from\ sale\ of\ domestic\ assets$$

$$- spending\ on\ buying\ foreign\ assets$$

Taking the two accounts together

$$Balance\ of\ Payments = current\ account + capital\ account.$$

BoP is in surplus (deficit) if the combined current and capital accounts have surplus (deficit). Thus, a deficit in current account by itself does not create a BoP deficit. It may be outweighed by a sufficiently large surplus in capital account. The USA, for example, has been able to sustain a large and persistent deficit in the current account by its ability to attract foreign capital on an even larger scale. This option, unfortunately, is not available to a country like India, which faces borrowing constraints in the global capital market.

It will be very useful to keep the basic rule of BoP accounting in mind.

Basic Accounting Rule

Any transaction leading to a net receipt of foreign exchange creates a surplus (credit) in the corresponding account. Any transaction leading to net payment to foreigners creates a deficit (debit) in the corresponding account.

If India's exports exceed imports in value (NX > 0), our exporters receive foreign exchange, so this is a current account surplus for India. When sales of bonds to foreigners (borrowing abroad) exceeds purchase of foreign bonds (lending to foreigners) by Indians, we are acquiring foreign currency on balance. This is a surplus on capital account. A surplus (deficit) on capital account is called a *net capital inflow* (*outflow*) to the country. When India borrows abroad to fill the gap between its export and import, its current account deficit is being offset by a capital account surplus. Repayment of foreign loan is a deficit in capital account as it involves payment (outflow) of foreign exchange.

Box 7.1   Double-Entry Bookkeeping

BoP accounting follows the system of double-entry bookkeeping in which every transaction is recorded twice, once as a credit and once as a debit. Any transaction giving rise to a payment from (to) the rest of the world is a credit (debit). The payment itself is recorded as an offsetting entry to the transaction which is its cause.

Suppose that India exports cotton textiles to Japan. Since the Japanese importer will have to pay for the purchase in some way, this is a credit in the current account for India. The actual payment can take various forms: a bank draft in yen (or even possibly dollar), or the granting of credit by the Indian exporter to the Japanese importer. In both cases India's foreign assets go up and this must be recorded as an offsetting debit in India's capital account.

Since BoP accounting follows double-entry bookkeeping, the balance of payments *always* balances in principle, that is, the total value of credit entries must equal the total value of debit entries. In practice this never happens mainly due to problems with the availability or recording of data. Therefore, an item for *errors and omissions* is included to make the overall balance zero.

The corollary is that an increase in the country's foreign assets (or decrease in foreign liabilities) is a debit entry and that a decrease in foreign assets (or increase in foreign liabilities) is a credit entry in the capital account.

Table 7.2 presents India's balance of payments for some years.

Table 7.2   India's BoP

(Rs crore)

Item	1991−2	1999−2000	2000−01	2001−02
Current account				
Exports (f.o.b)	44,922	162,753	205,287	214,351
Imports (c.i.f.)	51,417	240,112	270,663	274,778
Trade balance	−6495	−77,359	−65,376	−60,427
Invisibles (net)	4258	57,028	53,954	67,146
Current Account Balance	−2237	−20,331	−11,431	6719
External assistance (net)	7394	3915	2079	5830

(Contd)

Table 7.2 (Contd)

Item	1991–2	1999–2000	2000–01	2001–02
Foreign investment (net)	340	22,501	23,267	28,275
Commercial borrowings (net)	3807	1360	18,832	−5432
NRI deposits (net)	1008	6709	10,567	13,127
Total Capital Account	10,005	45,328	41,599	45,724
Overall Balance	7768	27,770	27,620	56,592

Source: Statistical Outline of India, 2002–3.

The large increase in net invisible receipts has been caused chiefly by the large rise in remittance income and sustained growth in software service exports. Software service exports are included under the 'miscellaneous receipts' category in the account for invisibles. Remittances (earnings from the export of labour) are recorded as private transfers by convention.

The BoP and the Central Bank

All Central Banks, including the RBI, hold reserves of foreign currencies. This stock can be used to help finance a current account deficit. Suppose that India has a current account deficit of Rs 100, but capital account surplus of only Rs 80 (India cannot borrow more than Rs 80). Overall BoP deficit is Rs 20. It can be met if the RBI sells the equivalent foreign exchange to Indian importers who use it to pay the foreigners. Or, if the current account is in balance, the RBI sales of foreign currency can finance foreign lending or repayment of foreign loan (capital account deficit) by Indians. Similarly, if either the current or the capital account is in surplus, the RBI can buy foreign currency to add to its reserves. Purchases and sales of foreign exchange by the Central Bank are called *official reserve transactions*.

An overall BoP surplus implies net purchase of foreign exchange by the RBI, which adds to its stock of foreign assets (foreign exchange reserves). This raises money supply by boosting the monetary base. Conversely, a BoP deficit equals net foreign exchange sales by the RBI, which depletes its stock of foreign assets and, hence, reduces the monetary base

Let us consider an example to illustrate. Suppose that India has a current account surplus of Rs 60 crore and a capital account deficit of Rs 20 crore. Then we can infer: (i) the overall BoP shows a surplus of Rs 40 crore; (ii) if the RBI intervenes, its net foreign assets will be increasing; and (iii) the RBI is purchasing foreign currency (selling home currency).

If the Central Bank decides that in no case will it engage in buying or selling foreign currencies, the exchange rate(the value of the home currency relative to foreign currencies) will have to adjust, to eliminate surpluses or deficits in the BoP. A system where the Central Bank does not intervene at all in the foreign exchange market is called a *fully flexible system of exchange* or a *clean float* of the currency.

In the example given above, if the RBI does not intervene, the BoP surplus will be eliminated through an appreciation of the rupee.

The current account of India has showed a surplus for two years in a row—2001 and 2002. This is only the second time that this has happened, since the early 1950s. This is not necessarily a healthy development, as the major contributory factor has been the decline in private and public investment.

Box 7.2   Should a Current Account Deficit always be a Cause for Alarm?

Recall from the discussion of Chapter 3, that in an open economy

$$Y = C + I + G + X - M$$

or

$$CAD = M - X = (C + I + G) - Y.$$

Since $(C + I + G)$ is the aggregate demand or total planned expenditure in an economy in a particular period, deficit in the current account indicates that a country is spending more than its income and building up debt to the outside world. Whether CAD is a matter for concern or not depends on the nature of the excess spending involved. Long-term growth prospects are not harmed if the expenditure is on *productive I* or *G*. The debt plus interest can be repaid in future out of the growth dividend reaped. In this case, CAD is actually a sign of health of a vigorous economy, which is borrowing abroad to supplement domestic resources for development. If, however, the CAD is triggered by unproductive *I* or *G* or current consumption, then it is indeed a bad omen for the economy.

Financing Current Account Deficit

A deficit in the current account or the excess of spending over income in the current period must be financed by a net capital inflow into the country. This may take several forms.

Foreign direct investment (FDI): Foreign firms, typically multinational companies, may decide to expand operation in the country by setting up a subsidiary unit to run a production plant or by taking over a domestic firm. Foreign exchange brought in for this purpose is available for meeting the deficit

Foreign portfolio investment (FPI): Foreign investors, typically institutional investors like mutual funds, pension funds, and insurance companies purchase bonds or company shares or other financial assets. These constitute an important source of funds.

External borrowing: The country may borrow from international agencies like the IMF or the World Bank or from foreign governments and commercial banks.

Foreign asset reserves: The country may draw down its accumulated stock of foreign reserves to meet the gap between spending and income.

FDI, governed by long-term considerations, is the most stable type of finance, while short-term loans (maturity of less than a year) are the most volatile. Excessive reliance on short-term borrowing has been a major contributory factor behind BoP crisis in many countries in Latin America and Asia. (The Asian Crisis is discussed in Box 7.5.) Policy planners in India keep a close watch on the volume of outstanding short-term debt of the nation. They try to encourage non-debt creating flows like FDI or purchase of shares, rather than short-term loans.

EXCHANGE RATE CONCEPTS

The exchange rate is usually quoted as the number of units of the domestic currency required to purchase one unit of foreign currency. It is the price of foreign currency in terms of the home currency. Dollar–rupee exchange rate of 40 means that Rs 40 can be used to buy one dollar in the foreign exchange market. Similarly, there will be exchange rates between the rupee and the yen, the rupee and the euro, the rupee and the mark, and so on. Economists distinguish between:

Nominal Exchange Rate (NER): It is the exchange rate of a currency against any other. It is thus a bilateral concept.

Effective Exchange Rate (EER): It is the weighted average of nominal rates, the weights being the shares of the respective countries in the trade of the country (either export or import) for which the EER is being calculated. Suppose that India trades only with the USA (share 60 per cent) and Japan (share 40 per cent) and NERs of the rupee are 50 for the dollar and 10 for the yen. Then EER = 0.6 (50) + 0.4 (10) = 34. For Rs 34 one can buy a basket consisting of 0.6 dollar and 0.4 yen.

Real Exchange Rate (RER): It is designed to measure the rate at which home goods exchange for foreign goods rather than the rate at which currencies themselves are traded. India's NER with respect to the USA, is the amount of rupees to be given up to get one dollar, whereas our RER is the quantity of domestic goods which is to be given up to get one unit of USA goods. Denoting the home price level by P and the foreign price level by P^f:

$$RER = NER(P^f/P)$$

Real Effective Exchange Rate (REER): This is the overall RER for the economy. It is the weighted average of the RERs for all its trade partners, the weights being the shares of the respective countries in its foreign trade. It may be interpreted as the quantity of domestic goods which is to be given up to get one unit of a given basket of foreign goods. Usually, only the major trade partners are included. Thus a 5-country REER for India is the weighted average of our RERs with five of our most important partners in trade.

For simplicity we shall henceforth assume that India has a single trading partner—the USA. So, EER = NER, and REER = RER. Let us denote the (nominal) exchange rate by e and suppose $e = 40$, that is, Rs 40 are needed to buy one dollar. Let $P^f = \$4$ and $P = $ Rs 10, so that RER = 16. This means 16 units of the home good are needed to buy one unit of USA good. (Value of 16 units of home good = Rs 160 = \$4 at the exchange rate e = value of 1 unit of good in the USA, because $P^f = \$4$.)

Note that since P^f is in dollars and EER or e is rupees per dollar, the numerator of the expression for RER is the value of foreign price in rupees. The denominator is the domestic price in rupees. Thus, the RER stands for prices abroad, relative to those at home. It is often taken as a measure of the country's *international competitiveness*. A rise in RER implies that foreign goods have become more expensive relative to home goods. This is an improvement in the competitiveness of our products. A fall in RER stands for loss of competitiveness.

A rise in the nominal exchange rate is known as *depreciation* of the home currency. More units of the home currency are required to buy one unit of the foreign currency. The opposite change is

Table 7.3   India's NEER and REER

(base: 1985 = 100)

Year	NEER	REER
1990–1	67.20	75.58
1991–2	52.51	64.20
1992–3	43.46	57.08
1993–4	44.69	61.59
1994–5	43.37	66.04
1995–6	39.73	63.62
1996–7	38.97	63.81
1997–8	40.01	67.02
1998–9	36.34	63.44
1999–2000	35. 46	63. 31

Source: India Development Report, 2002.

appreciation. Depreciation makes home exports more attractive to foreigners and imports less attractive to domestic consumers. Let us take an example.

Suppose that initially $e = 40$ (Rs 40 exchanges for one dollar) and a refrigerator made in India costs Rs 40,000. This will sell for $1000 in the USA. Now there is a depreciation of the rupee so that $e = 50$. The refrigerator becomes cheaper in dollars ($800) and thus more competitive with refrigerators from other countries to the US market and its demand (our exports) will increase. At the same time, as a result of the rise in e, our imports from the USA (say, cars) will become more expensive in rupees and decline in volume.

Currency depreciation improves the trade balance by stimulating exports and reducing imports. Currency appreciation has the opposite effect.

However, if along with the depreciation of the rupee our price level P also rises to the same extent (with P^f staying constant), there may not be any change in RER and export will not rise. In terms of our numerical example, if along with the rise in e from 40 to 50, the domestic price of the refrigerator goes up to Rs 50,000, the dollar price stays the same as before ($1000) and there will be no effect on competitiveness and sales.

In this case, *nominal depreciation* (rise in e) has failed to gene *real depreciation* (rise in RER). Exports will not change. For real depreciation to take place, nominal depreciation must not be offset by domestic inflation (rise in P).

DETERMINATION OF THE EXCHANGE RATE

Being the price of one currency in terms of another, the value of the exchange rate will be determined by the forces of demand and supply in the market for foreign exchange. We assume that India trades only with the USA. The price levels P^f and P are assumed to be constant, so that nominal changes and real changes in e are the same.

Demand for dollars comes from the following sources. Indian consumers wishing to import American goods will sell rupees to buy dollars with which to pay the American suppliers, Indian tourists in the USA will exchange rupees for dollars, if an Indian company intends to buy a bond of the US government or share in an American company or to set up a branch office in New York, it will convert rupees into dollars.

Demand for dollars (foreign exchange) arises as a result of import of goods and services and outflow of capital. Conversely, supply of dollars is created by export of goods and services and inflow of capital.

When demand and supply are equal in the foreign exchange market, import and capital outflow are equal to export and capital inflow. Hence, the BoP must be in equilibrium. When demand exceeds supply, the BoP is in deficit and when supply exceeds demand, it is in surplus.

Flexible Exchange System

In Figure 7.1, the demand and supply curves of foreign exchange are plotted against the exchange rate e. We have seen that, a rise in e (depreciation of rupee or rise in the price of dollar relative to rupee) will reduce our imports and stimulate our exports. If the exchange rate is higher then (i) the rupee cost of imports is higher and therefore the demand for foreign exchange is lower and (ii) the dollar cost of exports is lower and therefore the supply of foreign exchange is higher. (More dollars will be sold to get the rupees needed to pay for higher imports from India.) This explains the upward slope of the supply curve and downward slope of the demand curve in Figure 7.1 The equilibrium(market clearing) value of e ($= e^*$) is given by the point E_1.

Since at point E_1 demand and supply of foreign exchange are equal, the BoP must also be in equilibrium with zero surplus or deficit.

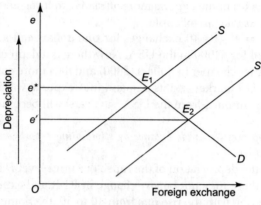

Fig. 7.1   Exchange Rate Determination

When the exchange rate is determined purely by demand and supply conditions without any intervention by central banks, the situation is known as a *flexible exchange system* or *floating exchange system*.

Let us consider the impact of some exogenous changes on the exchange rate. American investors want to buy more shares in Indian companies or to set up more production plants in India. This will increase the demand for rupees on their part, which is the same thing as an increase in the supply of dollars. In Figure 7.1, the supply curve shifts to the right and at the new equilibrium at E_2, the value of e is lower. The rupee has appreciated in value as a result of greater capital inflow.

An increase in the USA's demand for imports from India (due possibly to an improvement in the quality of our products) will produce the same outcome. If, on the other hand, our import demand increases, the demand curve for dollars will shift outwards and e will rise, causing a depreciation of the rupee.

Discovery of major oil deposits in the Arabian Sea reduces our dependence on imported oil. The fall in imports causes a decline in the demand for dollars. The demand curve shifts down causing an appreciation of the rupee.

Fixed Exchange System

In a flexible exchange system, the Central Bank does nothing to influence the rate. This is an extreme case. At the other extreme, we have the fixed (or pegged) exchange system in which the central bank of a country fixes (pegs) the value of e. An upward (downward) revision in the fixed value of e is called *devaluation* (*revaluation*) of the home currency.

Box 7.3   A Subtle Distinction

When the value of e increases (falls) in a flexible exchange system due to changes in market conditions, this is depreciation (appreciation). When the value of e is raised (lowered) as part of policy in a fixed exchange system, it is devaluation (revaluation). Devaluation or revaluation are, thus, resetting of fixed values of the exchange rate. Like depreciation, devaluation may be nominal or real.

Suppose that the equilibrium $e^* = 5$ in Figure 7.2, but the RBI wants to fix it at $e = 3$. At the fixed rate, the rupee will be *overvalued* or, equivalently, the dollar will be *undervalued*. The price of dollar in terms of rupee is being artificially kept at 3, rather than 5. These terms mean that if the market forces of demand and supply were free to operate, the value of e would rise to clear the market. At the fixed rate of $e = 3$, the demand for foreign exchange exceeds the supply (the gap AB in the figure) which implies that the BoP is in deficit. If the RBI does not intervene, this excess demand for dollars will drive its price up to the equilibrium level. To maintain any fixed rate different from the equilibrium rate, the Bank must stand ready to buy and sell rupees at that rate. In this particular case it must meet the excess demand, AB, by selling dollars from its own reserves in exchange for rupees. This neutralizes the upward pressure on the price of dollars.

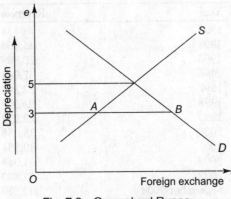

Fig. 7.2   Overvalued Rupee

India's Rising Foreign Currency Reserves

In recent years, India's dollar reserves have reached very high levels. This is the direct consequence of the RBI's exchange rate policy. Attracted by the prospect of higher return, foreign savers are buying shares in the Indian stock market on a large scale. This inflow of capital is adding to the supply of dollars (demand for rupees).

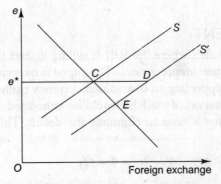

Fig. 7.3   Central Bank's Reserve Accumulation

Suppose that, initially, the exchange rate is at e^*—the equilibrium value. The RBI wants to keep it fixed at that level. Inflow of foreign funds in the domestic stock market pushes the dollar supply curve to the right and equilibrium is driven down to E. The rupee has an appreciation. The authorities do not want this to happen, because a stronger rupee will hurt our exports and make remittance to India less attractive.

To prevent the value of e from falling, the RBI will have to buy up CD amount of dollars from the market. This will raise the value of its dollar reserves. The trend of the RBI's foreign exchange assets are presented in Table 7.4.

Table 7.4   India's Foreign Reserves

(US$ million)

Year	Reserves
1993	6434
1994	15,068
1995	20,809
1996	17,044
1997	22,367
1998	25,975
1999	29,522
2000	35,058
2001	39,554
2002	51,049
2003	71,890
September 2004	112,919

Source: RBI Reports, various issues.

Accumulating a large stock of reserves is justified on precautionary grounds. It acts as a cushion against potential disruptions to foreign trade and flow of funds which may cause serious damage to the economy. A comfortable position, in respect of foreign assets, is also interpreted by foreign investors as a sign of the health of the economy. Improvement in the credit rating of a country enables it to access the international capital market on more favourable terms. Continuous accretion to foreign currency reserves has facilitated further liberalization of restrictions on international current and capital account transactions.

DOMESTIC ADJUSTMENT

Consider a situation of BoP deficit where the RBI is selling dollars (buying rupees) to prevent a rise in the exchange rate of the rupee (depreciation). The rupee is overvalued relative to the equilibrium. It is clear that the process of supporting an overvalued currency cannot continue indefinitely, because eventually the foreign asset reserves of the RBI would be exhausted. Before that point is reached, the Bank would have to take policy actions to eliminate the deficit. This calls for domestic adjustment. Recall from Chapter 3 that

$$NX = X - M = Y - AD = Y - (C + I + G).$$

To improve the trade balance NX, three options are available: (i) reduce AD with Y the same; (ii) raise Y, with AD the same; or (iii) allow devaluation, by raising the pegged value of e closer to e^*. The second option requires growth in the productivity of factors combined with harder work and longer working hours, which is neither palatable nor easily achieved in the short run. This leaves cutback in AD and devaluation as the only alternatives.

Cutback in AD is painful, as unemployment is likely to rise in the economy and there will be a decline in the general standard of living as consumption is reduced. Devaluation is likely to create inflationary pressures by making import of consumer goods and intermediate inputs more costly. (Devaluation is discussed in more depth, later in this chapter.) So governments are usually reluctant to initiate the process of adjustment in the face of falling foreign reserves. Too often this leads to a BoP crisis.

Box 7.4   Collapse of the Bretton Woods System

The best example of a long-term fixed exchange arrangement was the Bretton Woods System. In 1944, the Allies met in Bretton Woods, New Hampshire, USA, to develop an international monetary system to promote global trade after the War. Under the agreement, Central Banks bought and sold their own currencies to keep the exchange rates fixed. The USA, which pegged the dollar to gold, at the rate of US$ 35 per ounce, became the reserve currency country of the world. Most countries chose to hold their foreign reserves in US dollars. Two international institutions were created—the IMF and the World Bank.

To support fixed exchange rates when nations had BoP deficits and were losing foreign reserves, the IMF extended loans and exhorted the deficit countries to pursue contractionary policies to ease the problems in their external sectors. If the problem still persisted, devaluation was permitted, subject to approval by the IMF. Countries with persistent BoP surplus were required to revalue their currencies.

In practice, adjustments in exchange rates proved very difficult. Deficit countries were reluctant to devalue as it would trigger inflationary pressures by raising the price of imports. Moreover, the possibility of devaluation generated the possibility of speculative attacks on the currency. (See the following section for a discussion on speculation.) Surplus countries were under no pressure to revalue. As a result of these factors, some countries, like the UK, developed chronic deficits and others, like Germany, developed chronic surpluses.

Most damaging to the system was the fact that the USA itself became a chronic deficit country after the economic recovery of Japan and Western Europe. The dollar became overvalued. Severe inflationary pressures in the USA in the late 1960s, caused by the Vietnam war, worsened the crisis. The presumption that it would have to be devalued soon, led to loss of confidence in the dollar as a reserve asset. In 1972, the dollar was devalued and there was an attempt to establish a new set of fixed exchange rates. This, however, proved unsuccessful and the system finally collapsed in 1973. Since then, most currencies have been allowed to float under control (managed or dirty float).

BoP CRISIS AND SPECULATIVE ATTACK ON CURRENCY

As the RBI's holding of reserve assets dips low, foreign lenders lose confidence in the government and either reduce loans or begin demanding higher interest rates. This exacerbates the deficit in the BoP. Worse, a speculative attack on the rupee might begin.

Diminishing stock of foreign reserves undermines the ability of the Bank to defend the overvalued rupee. This triggers the expectation of devaluation of the rupee in the near future. So there will ensue a rush to sell off rupees and buy dollars. By selling those dollars, when the price of the dollar goes up after possible rupee devaluation, one can make profits. Suppose the current exchange rate is $e = 1$, but it is expected to go up to $e = 2$ soon. If a speculator sells Re 1 now to get \$1, he can sell it for Rs 2 after devaluation—a profit of 100 per cent! Imminent devaluation induces people to move out of the rupee and this makes it even harder for the Bank to defend the rupee because now it has to sell scarce dollars to Indians who want to shift their wealth (either to make profit or avoid loss) out of rupees and into dollars. Its low stock of dollars begins to run out faster and ultimately makes devaluation inevitable. Thus, expected devaluation brings about actual devaluation, an instance of *self-fulfilling expectations*.

In the event of speculative attack, some countries try to defend their currencies by raising the domestic interest rate—often to extraordinarily high levels—in the hope that it will stop the flight out of the currency. But historically, in most cases, this type of *interest defence* has failed to stem the tide of speculation and caused severe contractions in domestic output and employment. The RBI followed a tight money policy in response to the outbreak of the Asian Crisis (see Box 7.5) to discourage capital outflows and prevent contagion.

Box 7.5   The Asian Crisis

During the 1980s, and the first half of the 1990s, the economies of Hong Kong, South Korea, Thailand, Indonesia, Malaysia, and Singapore grew at spectacularly high rates and experienced steady improvement in the standard of living. Most of these newly industrializing countries (NICs) had removed all exchange controls and pegged their currencies to the dollar. Foreign credit expanded wildly as investors perceived little or no exchange risk and domestic interest rates were high. A growing percentage of this huge inflow of short-term credit (with maturity period of one year or less) was finding its way into speculation, particularly in real estate. Under implicit guarantee by corrupt government officials, banks and finance companies borrowed dollar and yen freely from foreign banks (most of the time without covering their exposure in the forward market) and granted loans to speculators.

The crisis struck in January 1997 with the bankruptcy of Hanbo Steel, a big Korean conglomerate. The following month, a major Thai corporation defaulted on its debt. A deep recession in Japan, accompanied by a falling yen, led to a sharp reduction in exports from the region. Under a flexible rate system, this would have caused a fall in the value of the local currencies, but the authorities tried to defend the pegged rates by intervening in the market. Soon it became clear that such intervention could not be sustained. Expectation of devaluation opened the floodgates to the sale of local currencies as hot money took flight. Devaluation of the Thai baht triggered a downward spiral in which competitive devaluation and speculative attacks on currencies became the norm. Steep currency depreciation had a shattering impact on banks and finance companies burdened with enormous foreign currency debts. Growth became zero or negative for most of the 'tigers'.

The lesson from the crisis, for countries like India, is simple and clear. There should be no hurry in dismantling controls on movement of short-term funds and the domestic financial system should be under strict supervision.

Financial capital flows, across national borders, in response to interest differential and expected changes in exchange rates of currencies. It flows out of countries where the interest rate is low and/or devaluation is expected. The part driven by expected devaluation or revaluation is mostly speculative in nature. It is called *hot money* in contrast to *cool money*, which is investment in durable capital governed by long-term considerations. To contain the disruptive influence of hot money, most governments favour imposition of capital controls on the movement of short term finance in and out of their countries.

INTERNAL AND EXTERNAL BALANCE UNDER FIXED RATE

In an open economy under fixed exchange regime, policymakers are faced with a potential conflict between achieving domestic targets and maintaining equilibrium in the BoP. Suppose that the economy is in a depressed state with high unemployment of resources. All prices including the exchange rate are assumed constant. The Keynesian approach outlined in Chapter 3 prescribes that expansionary fiscal and monetary action be taken to boost AD, that will raise income and employment. But as income Y rises, imports M will rise. If exports X are exogenously given, the result will be a decline in net exports,

NX, causing a worsening of the external trade balance. The nature of the dilemma can be brought out clearly in a simple diagram.

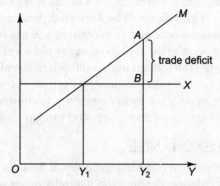

Fig. 7.4   Internal and External Balance

In Figure 7.4, the upward sloping line plots the import demand function $M = u + mY$, where $m > 0$ is the marginal propensity to import. Exogenous export X is shown by the horizontal line. Equilibrium in the current account ($X = M$, zero trade balance) occurs at Y_1. Ignoring the capital account for the moment, this is also a situation of BoP equilibrium. But there is no reason why Y_1 should also be the optimal level with regard to domestic goals. If the optimal level from the point of view of domestic employment is Y_2, then a conflict appears. If the internal target is attained through appropriate demand management, the trade balance will be in deficit ($= AB$); whereas if the economy is at Y_1, the level of employment will be too low.

If the exchange rate is made flexible, policymakers need not worry about the external balance problem.

FLEXIBLE EXCHANGE AND INSULATION FROM FOREIGN SHOCKS

A major advantage claimed for flexible exchange rate is that it affords full protection against shocks originating abroad. Consider an economy that is initially in full internal and external equilibrium, with output at the optimal level and the BoP in neither deficit or surplus. This corresponds to point E_1 in Figure 7.5. Suppose now that there is a recession abroad that reduces foreign income. Fall in income

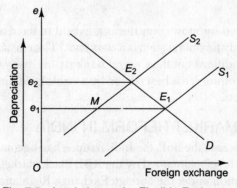

Fig. 7.5   Insulation under Flexible Exchange

induces a fall in foreign country's imports, which is the same as a decline in home exports. This decline leads to a fall in the supply of foreign exchange. The supply curve shifts to the left.

At the old equilibrium value of e, a deficit appears in the BoP, shown by the gap ME_1. Under flexible exchange e will rise to e_2. The deficit will be corrected through a fall in the price of the home currency (a depreciation). Domestic income and employment will not be affected.

If, instead, the exchange rate were to be kept fixed at the old level, the exogenous fall in exports would cause home Y to fall through the foreign trade multiplier. (Recall the discussion of Chapter 3.) Thus the recession abroad will have a contractionary effect on the domestic economy in a fixed exchange system. Under flexible system the home economy is completely insulated against a wide variety of external shocks. Closed economy multipliers and foreign trade multipliers are the same.

ADVANTAGES OF FIXED EXCHANGE

If flexible exchange can be so effective in resolving the internal balance–external balance dilemma by keeping the BoP continuously in balance, the question naturally arises why it is not the only system in operation. Does the fixed rate system have any points in its favour? The proponents of the fixed rate maintain that:

- Fluctuations in the exchange rate introduce a large element of uncertainty in the production and investment plans of firms. This is the *exchange rate risk* of foreign trade. The profits earned in pounds by an American company operating in England will suddenly shrink in dollar value if the dollar depreciates relative to the pound. Import plans of households will also be upset by unexpected changes in prices caused by unstable exchange rates. Exchange rate volatility adds to the uncertainty of producing for foreign markets or buying from foreign suppliers and makes it difficult to plan into the future. Such unpleasant contingencies can be mitigated by the use of forward exchange contracts, but *hedging* does not eliminate risk completely and adds to the transaction costs of trading. The cost of hedging is higher when exchange rate fluctuations are larger.
- Countries enjoying surplus in BoP do not usually like to see their currencies appreciate, because that makes their imports cheaper and exports dearer to foreigners. This threatens output and employment at home. So surplus countries often sell their currencies and acquire foreign currency reserves. Deficit countries are often reluctant to let their currencies depreciate as, by making imports more expensive, this would add fuel to inflation. So they may choose to defend overvalued currencies.

The current system followed by most countries is a hybrid of fixed and flexible rates. It is called *managed float* or *dirty float*. (A fully flexible system is a *clean float*.) The exchange rate is allowed to change daily in response to market conditions but the Central Bank stands ready to intervene to prevent large swings in value. International commerce is best served by a stable medium of exchange that minimizes uncertainty and transaction costs.

FOREIGN EXCHANGE MARKET REFORM IN INDIA

By 1991, due to serious imbalances in the BoP, the Indian rupee had become grossly overvalued relative to most major currencies at the level maintained by the RBI. Black marketing in foreign currencies was rampant in spite of strict regulation under the Foreign Exchange Regulation Act (FERA). A substantial devaluation was announced in July 1991 and a dual exchange rate was introduced the following year. The rates were subsequently unified and allowed to float. Between June 1991 and March 1993 there was a big depreciation, relative to the dollar. It was a real devaluation of no less than 25 per cent vis-à-vis our major trading rivals. This gave a welcome boost to exports. And the black market almost disappeared.

The draconian FERA was replaced by the much more lenient Foreign Exchange Management Act (FEMA). The RBI has delegated considerable power to authorized dealers to handle foreign exchange for a variety of purposes.

The rupee has been made convertible for current account transactions with acceptance of Article VIII of the Articles of Agreement of the IMF. Measures are being taken to lift controls on capital transactions and move the system gradually to full convertibility on the capital account in the near future.

The number of financial instruments available in the foreign currency market has increased dramatically. A rupee–foreign currency swap market has emerged and authorized dealers are permitted to use innovative products like cross-currency options, interest and currency swaps, and forward rate agreements in the international market.

Significant liberalization measures include the following. Authorized dealers are now able to borrow and lend in overseas markets subject to some restrictions, banks are permitted to fix interest rates on non-resident deposits, use derivative products for balance sheet management, and exercise other investment options subject to the RBI's approval, Indian investors have more freedom to invest abroad and FIIs (foreign institutional investments) and NRIs are permitted to trade in some important financial instruments.

The RBI intervenes on a daily basis to maintain orderly conditions in the market for the rupee. Although there is no explicit target, the 5-country REER has stabilized around a value of 52 to 53 per cent (with 1985 = 100) in recent years.

India's exchange rate policy has been very successful in insulating the economy against the turbulence in global financial markets that prevailed in the late 1990s, in the wake of the Asian Crisis. The reform process is going on and, compared to a decade ago, India is now in a much better position to participate fruitfully in the burgeoning international trade in financial assets. The ability of the banking system to handle foreign funds has improved considerably, but it is still far from the best international standards.

DEVALUATION AND PURCHASING POWER PARITY

When prices—domestic and foreign—are not changing, nominal devaluation (rise in e under fixed rate) and real devaluation (rise in RER) are synonymous. Here we shall allow P^f and P to be variable and consider the effects of *real* devaluation (rise in RER $= eP^f/P$). Devaluation, henceforth, will be taken to mean real devaluation.

Devaluation implies a rise in (P^f/P), that is, foreign goods become more expensive relative to home goods. This is expected to shift demand in favour of our goods both in India and in our trading partner, the USA. The resulting improvement in our $NX (= X - M)$ will be stronger, the larger the rise in our exports (USA's imports) and the fall in our imports, in response to the rise in (P^f/P). Thus, the impact of the rupee devaluation on India's net exports (and, hence, aggregate demand) is critically dependent on the responsiveness (elasticity) of import demand of the two countries to changes in relative price of commodities. Larger import elasticities raise the stimulating power of devaluation.

Even if import elasticities are high, the favourable impact of devaluation on BoP (rise in surplus or reduction in deficit) does not materialize overnight. There is a time lag between the announcement of devaluation and price revision by sellers and a further lag before consumers revise their purchase plans in response to the change in price. These lags vary from country to country, depending on the structure of markets and government regulations relating to price change and other institutional factors that influence the speed of reaction of buyers and sellers.

Suppose that at a particular point in time, in a situation of deficit, a devaluation is announced that raises the relative price of imports. The short-term impact is to increase import prices with little change in the volume of imports (and exports). Therefore, the trade balance initially worsens. Over time, as quantities begin to adjust to the price change, exports rise and imports begin to decline. The trade balance eventually improves if the elasticities are sufficiently large. This pattern of adjustment in trade balance following devaluation—first falling and then rising—is referred to as the *J-curve effect*.

DEVALUATION AND INFLATION

One major reason why most countries are not very keen to make use of (nominal) devaluation to improve BoP is that there is a close link between devaluation and inflation. The set of commodities that become more costly after devaluation includes not only imported consumer goods but also imported intermediate inputs used in industry and agriculture. Higher cost of production will pass through to higher product price, particularly in markets in which the market power of the seller is high. As the cost of living rises, workers will start demanding higher wages to protect their real income. To the extent they succeed, this leads to another round of price escalation. In the presence of domestic inflation nominal devaluation may fail to translate into a real devaluation and exports may fail to get the desired boost.

The final impact of a nominal devaluation on consumer prices will depend on

- the importance of imported inputs in production;
- the power of the sellers to pass on cost increases to buyers;
- the import content of consumption and;
- the power of workers to extract a rise in wages to counter the escalation in cost of living.

Another problem is that, although, a single country may improve its export prospects by devaluing its own currency, the effect may vanish if its rivals also follow suit. Under *competitive devaluation*, the relative position of the exporting countries stay unchanged, while the importing nations benefit from the reduction in price. The exporters suffer the adverse effects without any compensating gain. This dilemma was very much evident during the Asian Crisis.

The policy of import-substituting industrialization, now largely abandoned by the GOI, involved numerous restrictions on import of manufactures. Thus, the demand for foreign exchange (supply of rupee) was artificially restricted leading to an overvaluation of the rupee, relative to its market-clearing level. This reduced the competitiveness of our exports. In its determined effort to turn LDCs away from import substitution to export promotion, the IMF puts relentless pressure for devaluation. At the same time to make devaluation real and not merely nominal it urges cut in the fiscal deficit to contain inflationary pressures. Real devaluation in tandem with strict fiscal and monetary discipline forms the core of the IMF's stabilization package.

For a real devaluation to take place, nominal devaluation must not be offset by a rise in domestic inflation relative to inflation in the foreign country. A currency is said to maintain *purchasing power parity* if it depreciates by an amount equal to the excess of domestic inflation over foreign inflation. In this case RER will stay unchanged.

The Purchasing Power Parity (PPP) Principle

Movements in exchange rates reflect differences in relative inflation rates across countries. If prices rise (fall) in one country the exchange rate will depreciate (appreciate) by just the right amount to keep RER constant.

Empirical evidence does reveal positive correlation between movements in exchange rates and inflation rates, but the correlation, contrary to the prediction of the theory, is far from perfect.

When the inflation rate in a country exceeds that of its trade partner, holding the exchange rate fixed would imply steady loss in international competitiveness. To avoid this, many countries adopt a policy of *crawling peg exchange rate* in which the exchange rate is devalued at a rate roughly equal to the inflation differential between the home country and its trading partners. This maintains the RER at a constant level as e is raised at the same rate as (P/P^f). For example, if India is on a crawling peg and inflation rates in India and the USA are 8 per cent and 6 per cent, respectively, rupee will be devalued with respect to dollar at 2 per cent.

We end this chapter with an observation on macroeconomic policy in an open economy. The ability to run a trade deficit dampens domestic inflationary pressures, at least in the short run. When domestic demand rises, a trade deficit tends to appear, but the imports will absorb part of the pressure created by demand. In a closed economy, excess domestic demand is spent entirely on domestic output, resulting in higher pressure on P. The large and persistent deficit run by the USA, since the 1980s, has contributed to keep inflation in check in that country. Unfortunately, the policy of maintaining large deficits over significant periods is not a feasible option for countries for which financing the deficit through borrowing is a serious problem.

Summary

- Openness of an economy comprises openness of goods, capital, and factor markets.
- The BoP consists of the current and the capital accounts.
- BoP surplus adds to money supply by raising the foreign assets of the Central Bank.
- Important exchange rate concepts are: NER, EER, RER, REER.
- The exchange rate is determined by demand and supply of foreign exchange.
- Under fixed exchange, the Central Bank must stand ready to buy and sell foreign exchange at the fixed rate. It has to hold reserves of foreign currency for that purpose.
- There is a dilemma between maintaining internal and external balance and the currency may be vulnerable to speculative attack. Flexible exchange confers insulation from foreign shock.
- The Indian foreign exchange market has been substantially reformed in recent years.
- Devaluation may be inflationary.
- PPP does not command solid empirical support.

Exercise

1. For each of the following transactions, state to which account—current or capital—in India's BoP it belongs and whether it is a surplus (credit) or a deficit (debit) item:
   (i) purchase of a Japanese VCR by an Indian national;

    (ii) purchase of share in an Indian company by a French mutual fund;

   (iii) GOI borrowing from an American bank;

   (iv) export of bed linen by an Indian firm to Belgium;

    (v) an African tourist paying cash for a meal in a restaurant in Agra;

   (vi) an Indian national purchasing a house in Lima;

  (vii) an American investor making a deposit in the State Bank of India.

2. Suppose that the rupee is appreciating steadily against the dollar. How would this affect you if
   (i) you want to visit the USA as tourist;
  (ii) you are an exporter of handicrafts to the USA;
 (iii) your NRI uncle sends you a gift cheque for $100?

3. 'If the domestic currency is weak, the prime minister is unhappy but the exporters are happy.' Explain.

4. Suppose that a country has a current account deficit of $9 million and a capital account surplus of $11 million.
   (i) Is the BoP in deficit or surplus?
  (ii) If the Central Bank intervenes, does it buy or sell the home currency?
 (iii) If the Bank does not intervene, what will be the impact on the home exchange rate?

5. What is the real exchange rate? Carefully distinguish between nominal and real devaluation.

6. Comment on the effectiveness of devaluation as an instrument for correcting external imbalance.

7. Suppose that a country devalues its currency by 12 per cent, but at the same time domestic prices rise by 10 per cent. What real devaluation has been achieved? What if prices have risen by 15 per cent?

8. 'A current account surplus is equivalent to a decrease in the net foreign liabilities of a nation.' True or False?

9. If Central Banks never engaged in foreign exchange transactions, could there be a surplus or deficit in a country's BoP? What is the possible justification for Central Bank intervention in the currency market?

10. Discuss the domestic adjustments called for to support an overvalued currency under a fixed exchange system.

11. Explain the mechanism linking BoP and money supply when the exchange rate is fixed. What can be the justification for sterilization?

12. Suppose that the RBI embarks on a tight money policy. What is the likely impact on India's exports under
   (i) fixed exchange rate and;
  (ii) flexible exchange rate?

13. Decline in the price of oil in 1985–6 led to a sharp depreciation of the currency of Mexico, a major oil exporter. Explain this fact using a suitable diagram.

14. What is the relationship between trade balance and the level of economic activity when the exchange rate is fixed? How does this relationship create a potential conflict between internal and external balance?

15. Discuss the relative advantages and disadvantages of fixed vis-à-vis flexible exchange rates.

16. Unlike a closed economy, an open economy can raise its investment even if domestic saving remains unchanged. Explain. (Hint: rewrite the relation $S = I + NX$ as $I = S + \text{CAD}$, where $\text{CAD} = (-NX)$.)

17. Suppose that a large deposit of a rare metal is discovered by the Geological Survey of India and our country starts exporting it on a large scale. What will the impact on
   (i) the exchange rate of the rupee; and
   (ii) your welfare if you are an exporter of traditional handicrafts?

Appendix 7.1
The World Trade Organization

India is a member of the World Trade Organization (WTO) which was established in 1995 to act as a forum for international cooperation on trade-related policies and for the creation of codes of conduct for member governments. The major agreements administered by it are the General Agreement on Tariffs and Trade (GATT), General Agreement on Trade in Services (GATS), Trade-related Intellectual Property Rights Agreement (TRIPS), and Trade-related Investment Measures Agreement (TRIMS). The organization is headed by a ministerial conference of all members that meets at least once every two years.

There are now 142 members. After a long period of waiting China finally became a member in December 2001. The WTO replaces the earlier GATT, an informal agreement made in 1947 that tried with a large measure of success to promote multilateral free trade among nations in the decades following the Second World War.

Box A7.1   From GATT to WTO: Major Steps

1947: GATT is set up among 23 countries. The Agreement comes into force on 1 January 1948.

1948: In March 53 countries sign The Havana Charter proposing to set up an International Trade Organization (ITO).

1950: China withdraws from GATT. The US Congress fails to ratify the ITO.

1955: Japan accedes to GATT. The USA is granted a waiver from GATT discipline for certain agricultural policies.

1965: Part IV (on trade and development) is added to GATT to promote the interest of the developing countries.

1974: The Multifibre Arrangement (MFA) comes into force. It restricts export growth in clothing and textiles to 6 per cent per year. It is renegotiated in 1977, 1982, and extended in 1986, 1991, 1992.

1986: Uruguay Round is launched in Punta Del Este, Uruguay.

1994: In Marrakesh on 15 April the final act is signed establishing the WTO.

1995: On 1 January the WTO starts functioning.

1999: Ministerial meeting in Seattle fails to launch a new round.

2001: A new round of trade talks is agreed on in Doha. In December, China becomes a member.

2003: Ministerial meeting in Cancun collapses.

The WTO differs in a number of important respects from GATT–1947. They may be summarized as:

- The WTO agreement is a 'single undertaking'—all its provisions apply to all members without exception. There is no opportunity for any country to opt out of specific disciplines. The earlier GATT allowed much more latitude in this respect.
- The WTO's coverage is much wider than that of GATT–1947. Its rules and guidelines extend far beyond import tariffs and non-tariff barriers to cover investment flows undertaken by multinational corporations across national boundaries, services trade, and intellectual property (patent) rights. The old Indian Patent Act of 1970 was replaced by the new patent regime from January 2005. The system now is essentially that of uniform product patent for all goods including food and pharmaceuticals for a period of twenty years.

  The potentially harmful effects of the new regime on the welfare of the developing countries are sought to be limited through The Doha Declaration on TRIPS Agreement and Public Health. It clearly states that TRIPS should not prevent members from taking measures to protect public health and, in particular, to promote access to medicine by all.
- Dispute settlement procedures are much stricter and less time-consuming under the WTO. The principal instrument is the 'negative consensus rule' which states that all members must oppose the findings of the Dispute Settlement Body in a case of dispute to block adoption of reports.

Unlike the World Bank and the IMF where voting rights are determined by the financial stakes of governments, the WTO is governed by the principle of 'one nation one vote' and it tries to operate by consultation and consensus. In order to hammer out outlines of acceptable proposals and negotiating agendas, informal discussions are periodically held among the major members of the Organization for Economic Cooperation and Development (OECD) and the major developing countries such as China, Brazil, India, and South Africa. This is the so-called 'Green Room Process'.

Transparency is a basic pillar of the WTO, without which enforcement of commitments will be impossible. The function of the Trade Policy Review Mechanism (TPRM) is to conduct regular and systematic review of the trade policies of the members. The European Union, the USA, Japan, and Canada are subject to review by the General Council every two years, the next 16 largest traders are to be reviewed every four years and the remaining members, every six years.

Although the overwhelming thrust of the WTO is towards unhampered international movement of goods, services, and investible funds, under specific circumstances, governments are given power to restrict trade. The provisions in this connection include: (i) articles allowing for policies to protect public health, national security, and industries seriously injured by imports; (ii) the right to fight 'unfair competition' by imposing countervailing duties on subsidized exports and anti-dumping duties; and (iii) the power to intervene in cases of serious BoP difficulties or to nurture infant industries of national importance. These provisions act as safety valves for developing countries like India.

Appendix 7.2
Economic Policy in an Open Economy

We shall now consider monetary, fiscal, and exchange rate-related policies in an open economy that participates in foreign trade and international flow of financial capital. Not surprisingly, the effects of policy actions will be different, in important aspects, relative to our previous results (Chapter 5) for the closed economy. The nature of the exchange regime—fixed or flexible, and the assumptions regarding the degree of capital mobility will play vital roles in the analysis.

In the first section, for the sake of manageability, only trade in goods and services will be considered and the capital account will be taken as completely closed. Capital movements will be allowed in the next section.

IS–LM WITH FOREIGN TRADE

We have seen that depreciation (rise in e) raises exports X and decreases imports M and thus raises NX ($= X - M$). Also, since M depends positively on Y, NX varies inversely with Y. Export X ($=$ import of the foreign country) will depend positively on foreign income Y^f. Therefore, NX depends positively on e, Y^f and negatively on Y. The equation of the IS curve is

$$Y = C(Y - T) + I(r) + G + NX(Y, Y^f, e).$$

This differs from the IS curve of a closed economy (Chapter 5) only in the last NX term. As before, any autonomous rise in C, I, G or cut in T will shift the curve to the right. The new element, that can cause a rightward shift, is a rise in NX brought about by a rise in Y^f or rise in e (depreciation). The exchange rate e is a given parameter in a fixed exchange system. Raising the fixed value of e to a higher level constitutes a policy of devaluation.

Since neither the demand nor supply of real balances is affected by foreign trade or the exchange rate , LM is represented as before by

$$M^s/P = kY - hr.$$

The determination of Y and r in an open economy (under fixed exchange and with a closed capital account), for given values of G, T, X (included in NX), Y^f and e is shown in Figure 7.6.

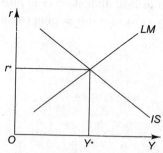

Fig. 7.6   Determination of Y, r in Open Economy under Fixed Exchange

FISCAL AND MONETARY POLICY AND DEVALUATION UNDER FIXED EXCHANGE (NO CAPITAL FLOWS)

If G is increased or T is cut, IS shifts outwards. At the new equilibrium Y and r are higher. The rise in Y reduces NX by raising M. Easy money (rise in M^s) raises Y and reduces r (LM shifts to right). NX declines once again. An increase in foreign income Y^f shifts IS outwards by boosting NX. The impact on Y and r is the same as under fiscal expansion, but the ultimate effect on NX is positive now. (Recall the discussion in Chapter 3.)

If e is raised (devaluation), NX is boosted and IS is pushed outwards. Both Y and r increase. Table A7.2.1 summarizes the results.

Table A7.2.1   Policy Analysis under Fixed Exchange (No Capital Flows)

	Fiscal expansion	Rise in money supply	Rise in foreign income	Devaluation
Y	Rises	Rises	Rises	Rises
r	Rises	Falls	Rises	Rises
NX	Falls	Falls	Rises	Rises

OPEN ECONOMY WITH CAPITAL FLOWS (THE MUNDELL–FLEMING MODEL)

Now we allow mobility of capital (lending and borrowing or trade in financial assets) between trading countries. Analysis of open economy macroproblems under capital mobility is called the Mundell–Fleming Model in honour of its original developers, Robert Mundell and Marcus Fleming.

Box A7.2.1   Capital Mobility in India

After decades of very strict controls, Indian capital market was opened up to foreign investors in 1992. Since then, India's corporate sector has been allowed to tap international capital market through American Depository Receipts (ADR), Global Depository Receipts (GDR), Foreign Currency Convertible Bonds (FCCB), External Commercial Borrowings (ECB), Overseas Corporate Bonds (OCB), and non-resident Indians have been allowed to invest in Indian companies. FIIs such as pension funds, mutual funds, and insurance companies are allowed to hold all types of domestic securities including government securities and they have full freedom to convert rupee earnings into foreign currency (full capital convertibility). FIIs are the second largest, after the promoters, in terms of shareholding in the Sensex companies. They also hold the largest chunk of free-float or tradable shares of these companies. This implies a substantial influence on prices.

FDI, in which foreign investors acquire control over the management of assets they invest in, has also been on the rise in recent years, but at a much slower pace compared with the portfolio investment by FIIs.

India does not yet have full capital account convertibility for all types of investors or all types of investment. She is moving towards that goal in a phased manner. Full capital convertibility is a major pillar of international financial integration. Indian rupee is already fully convertible for current account transactions.

Capital mobility can be of two types. When domestic and foreign assets (bonds) are perfect substitutes and investors, who are perfectly informed, can costlessly and without any hindrance move their funds from one to the other (zero transaction costs), we have a situation of *perfect capital mobility*.

Clearly, in this case, domestic and foreign interest rates (return on bonds) cannot be different. If one rate was even slightly higher, investors would immediately switch to that asset and keep on putting money into it until the rate was driven back down to equality. For the case of imperfect mobility, domestic and foreign bonds are not perfect substitutes, or there may be restrictions on movement of funds across national boundaries, and as a result, rates of interest may not be equalized.

In order to keep the analysis simple, we shall consider the case of perfect capital mobility only. This is not a bad assumption because, driven by the forces of globalization, capital markets all over the world are moving towards greater openness at a fairly fast pace.

POLICY UNDER PERFECT CAPITAL MOBILITY

Absence of transaction costs will lead to international equalization of the rates of return on bonds. Thus, we have $r = r^*$. In addition, the foreign rate of interest is taken to be given, uninfluenced by domestic policy.

(i) *Fixed exchange, fiscal policy* In Figure 7.7, the economy is initially at E_1. The IS, and LM Curves intersect on the horizontal BB line which shows that due to perfect capital mobility, domestic rate of interest cannot get out of line with the fixed foreign interest rate. Expansionary fiscal action (rise in G or a cut in T) shifts IS_1 to IS_2. As the rate of interest goes up to r_1 above r^*, there is massive capital inflow (investors buy domestic bonds on a massive scale). The exchange rate can be kept fixed in the face of the inflow (spurt in demand for rupee), only if RBI buys up dollars from the market in exchange for rupees. This action will cause domestic money supply to expand and LM will shift to the right. Final equilibrium will be achieved at E_2 when LM has shifted all the way to LM_2 to restore $r = r^*$ once again. The shift in LM adds to the initial fiscal thrust and the positive impact on Y is maximum.

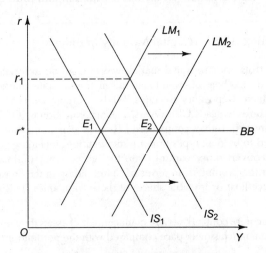

Fig. 7.7   Fixed Exchange, Fiscal Policy

(ii) *Fixed exchange, monetary policy* The relevant diagram is given by Figure 7.8.

An increase in domestic money supply shifts LM to the right, pushing the domestic r temporarily to r_1 below r^*. This will induce a massive outflow of capital (investors will be selling off Indian bonds on a massive scale and demanding dollars). To keep the exchange rate fixed, the RBI will have to sell

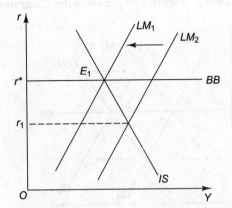

Fig. 7.8   Fixed Exchange, Monetary Policy

dollars from its stock. This will cause domestic money supply to fall and the process will continue until LM shifts back to its original position. Only then the capital outflow and the drop in money supply will stop. But then income will also be back at its initial level.

Under perfect capital mobility and fixed exchange, monetary policy loses its effectiveness completely.

(iii) *Flexible exchange, fiscal policy* The impact of fiscal expansion under flexible exchange and full capital mobility is illustrated in Figure 7.9. Now the RBI does not intervene in the foreign exchange market.

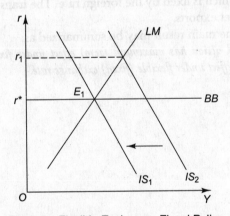

Fig. 7.9   Flexible Exchange, Fiscal Policy

The IS curve moves to the right from IS_1 to IS_2, driving the domestic interest rate to r_1 above r^*. The emergence of this interest differential triggers a massive capital inflow and the rupee appreciates as a result. This causes a decline in NX and the IS shifts back to the left. Equilibrium will be restored only when it has shifted back to its original position. With $r = r^*$, capital inflow and exchange appreciation will stop. Output is back to its initial level. Fiscal action is completely ineffective. This is in sharp contrast to the case of fixed exchange. In this case, *crowding out* occurs not through a rise in r (as in the case of a closed economy), but through a fall in NX induced by currency appreciation.

(iv) *Flexible exchange, monetary policy* Figure 7.10 provides the illustration.

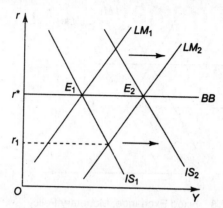

Fig. 7.10   Flexible Exchange, Monetary Policy

Increase in money supply pushes LM outwards, causing r to drop temporarily to r_1 below r^*. Massive capital outflow is triggered. Since the RBI does not intervene, the rupee depreciates in consequence. Net exports get a boost as export rises and import falls. Rise in NX causes IS to shift to the right. Final equilibrium is at E_2, with $r = r^*$ once again. Monetary policy has maximum impact on Y in this case.

A contrast with the closed economy model should be noted. Here, monetary policy does not operate through the interest rate, which is fixed by the foreign rate. The transmission channel, instead, is through the exchange rate and net exports.

Taking all the cases together, the main result may be summarized as:

Given full capital mobility, fiscal action has maximum (zero) effect under fixed (flexible) exchange rate. Monetary action has maximum (zero) effect under flexible (fixed) exchange rate.

8. Determination of the Aggregate Price Level

So far, except briefly in the discussion of real devaluation, we have retained the assumption of a constant price level P. It will be relaxed now to show the determination of the aggregate price level through the forces of aggregate demand (AD) and aggregate supply (AS). The difference with the treatment of aggregate demand of Chapter 3 is that P is not a constant any more. Bearing this important distinction in mind, we shall continue to use the term AD in the present chapter and in the chapters that follow.

AGGREGATE DEMAND (UNDER PRICE FLEXIBILITY)

The aggregate demand (AD) relation shows the link between P and aggregate output. It is derived from equilibrium in the commodities market and the money (asset) market. Note that in earlier chapters when P was held fixed, AD was taken as $(C + I + G + NX)$, total spending in real terms in the economy. Now P is an endogenous variable and AD captures the relation between varying P and equilibrium output.

The price level P did not figure in the IS relation, but it did in the LM relation. Given the supply of nominal money M, changes in P altered the supply of money in real terms and the equilibrium values of Y and r changed accordingly. Figure 8.1a shows the impact of a rise in P from P_0 to P_1. As (M/P) falls, the LM Curve shifts to the left, while IS stays unchanged. In the new equilibrium, Y is lower. Figure 8.1b plots the AD Curve showing the dependence of equilibrium Y on P. It is negatively sloped.

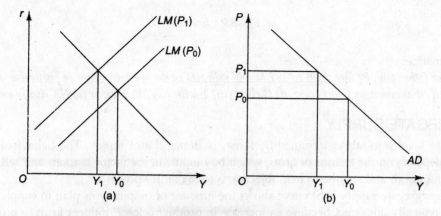

Fig. 8.1 Derivation of the AD Curve

The AD curve is negatively sloped because:

■ Increase in P reduces the real supply of money (supply of real balances);

- Fall in real balances pushes up r, the rate of interest, to preserve equilibrium in the money market;
- Rise in r leads to a decrease of planned investment I; and
- Fall in I causes Y to fall.

Shift of AD

Note that in deriving AD we are changing P, holding M^s constant. Thus, the nominal money stock is an exogenous variable for AD. The exogenous variables of the IS curve will also play a role as AD is obtained through joint interaction of IS and LM.

For any given level of P, anything that shifts the IS curve rightwards (LM staying unchanged) or the LM curve rightwards (IS remaining unchanged), will bring about an increase in the equilibrium level of Y. This is equivalent to a rightward shift of the AD curve (since Y is higher at each level of P).

Let us illustrate by considering a rise in government expenditure G. In Figure 8.2a, at $P = P_1$ the equilibrium $Y = Y_1$. This is shown as point A in the second panel. Now let G go up with P constant at P_1. This causes IS to shift to the right. In Figure 8.2a as IS_1 shifts to IS_2, Y rises to Y_2. This is shown as a new point B in Figure 8.2b. Since Y rises for each given value of P, the new AD Curve after the rise in G must lie entirely to the right of the old one.

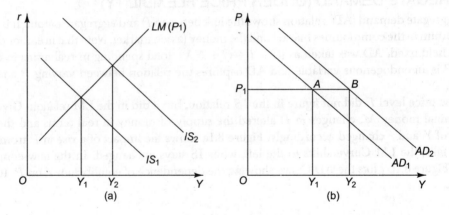

Fig. 8.2   Shift of AD

To summarize:
Any factor (other than P) that shifts IS or LM will shift AD in the same direction. In particular, AD will shift to the right if (i) autonomous C or I rises; (ii) G rises; (iii) T falls; (iv) M^s rises; or (v) NX rises in an open economy.

AGGREGATE SUPPLY

The price level is jointly determined by forces of demand and supply. The behaviour of aggregate supply depends on the actions of firms, which buy inputs in the factor markets and sell output in the market for goods and services. Their objective is to maximize profits.

The aggregate supply (AS) curve shows the amount of output firms plan to supply at each level of P. It typically slopes up, because an increase in product price P induces firms to produce and sell more. Let us examine the link more closely.

For simplicity we take labour, denoted by L, to be the only variable factor of production. Other factors like physical capital stock and land are held fixed. Let the money (or nominal) wage rate be w.

For example, $w = 50$ implies that a worker gets Rs 50 per hour of work done. *Real wage* $(= w/P)$ is obtained by dividing (deflating) w by the product price P. Unlike money wage w which is in units of rupees, real wage is in units of the commodity. Thus if $P = $ Rs 2 and $w = $ Rs 50, real wage $w/P = 25$ units of output per hour. That is, by working one hour, a person gets 25 units of the product. (He gets Rs 50 as money wage, with which 25 units of the good can be purchased at $P = $ Rs 2.)

The amount of L that a profit-maximizing firm will wish to hire depends negatively on *real* wage. A cut in money wage w will not lead to more employment if it goes with a fall in the product price P that keeps w/P unchanged. Suppose initially $w = 50$, $P = 2$, so that $w/P = 25$ and the firm is hiring 200 units of L. (Labour hour to be precise, but we shall use labour to stand for labour hour as well.) Now if w falls to 25 but at the same time P falls to 1, the firm has no incentive to change its use of labour. Labour is cheaper, but so is the product that the firm sells. The *real* cost of labour has not decreased. Real wage is unchanged at 25. To induce business to hire more L, real wage (w/P) must decline. In our example, when w falls to 25 (from 50) real wage will fall and labour demand will rise if P stays constant at 2 or rises or falls to 1.25. And more employment implies more production and supply of output.

The relationship can be derived more formally using the notion of marginal product of labour, which is defined as the addition to output as one extra unit of L is employed. For example, if production equals 200 units for 15 workers, 230 for 16 workers, and 248 for 17 workers, the marginal product (MP) of the sixteenth worker is 30 $(= 230 - 200)$ units of output and MP of the seventeenth worker is 18 $(= 248 - 230)$ units.

One very important assumption about technology is that MP diminishes as more L is hired. This occurs because, as more workers are added to the same fixed quantity of capital and land, the extra output added by the last worker decreases. This is the *law of diminishing returns*. In our example, MP of the seventeenth worker is less than that of the sixteenth.

The firm hires L up to the level where MP equals the real wage.

$$\text{MP}(L) = w/P \tag{8.1}$$

(MP depends on the value of L. That is why we use the function notation $\text{MP}(L)$.)

The logic is simple. Suppose that $w/P = 25$ and MP$= 35$ at $L = 100$. Then an additional unit of L adds 35 units to output but costs only 25 units of output. So it will be profitable to hire that extra unit. As long as $w/P > $ MP, employment should increase and it should decrease if $w/P < $ MP. (Use numerical values to show that in the latter case profit can be raised by reducing employment.) The optimum profit-maximizing value of L is reached when equation (8.1) holds.

The labour demand curve shows the quantity of L hired at each value of w/P. Since (8.1) holds at the point of maximum profit, the labour demand curve is nothing but the $\text{MP}(L)$ curve. By assumption $\text{MP}(L)$ decrease as L increases. So the labour demand curve slopes down. It is shown in Figure 8.3.

To go from labour demand to the AS schedule, we first proceed on the assumption that money wage is constant. This is known as the Keynesian case of money wage rigidity. Later we shall treat what is called the classical view of the labour market. The distinction is crucial because the two opposing views lead to radically different policy conclusions.

If w is constant, a rise in P implies a fall in w/P and demand for L will be stimulated. With more employment, output Y will rise. Thus, we have a positive relation between P and Y. Equivalently, the AS curve is upward sloping.

Shift of AS

If labour productivity improves due to technological progress, cost of production will come down even without any change in real wage and this should give a boost to employment. $\text{MP}(L)$ is higher than

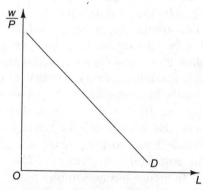

Fig. 8.3   Labour Demand

before at each value of L, so that the MP(L) curve shifts up. This is equivalent to an outward shift of the labour demand curve. More L will be hired at any given w/P. Since w is assumed to be constant, this implies that more L will be employed (and more Y produced) at each P. The AS curve shifts to the right.

Suppose that, in addition to L, production requires another important material input, Z (petroleum, for example). In deriving the relation between P and Y, the prices of labour (money wage) and of Z are held constant. If now the price of Z goes down with w and P staying unchanged, average cost of production will decline, giving a boost to planned supply. Since output increases even at the same P, the AS curve shifts to the right.

AS shifts to the right if (i) labour productivity improves; (ii) prices of material inputs fall.

Figure 8.4 shows the simultaneous determination of P and Y through the interaction of AD and AS.

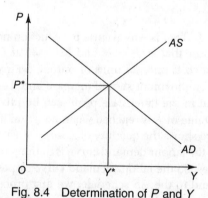

Fig. 8.4   Determination of P and Y

FISCAL AND MONETARY POLICY, DEMAND AND SUPPLY SHOCKS

An increase in budget deficit (rise in G and/or a cut in T) shifts AD to the right and the result is a rise in both Y and P. A rise in M^s also has exactly the same impact. Figure 8.5 illustrates.

Let us trace the economic process set in motion by a rise in nominal money stock. At the initial price level, M/P rises, which depresses r and I increases as a result. Planned total expenditure $(C + I + G)$ exceeds the level of current output Y. This excess of demand over supply puts upward pressure on P. As P rises, with money wage w remaining unchanged, real wage declines. Firms hire more labour and output expands. The process continues until the new equilibrium values P and Y are reached. Real

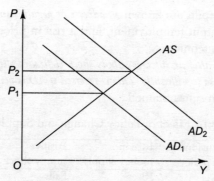

Fig. 8.5   Rise in Money Supply

wage is lower and real money balance is higher but the increase is less than the rise in M as P is also higher. The rate of interest is lower because M/P is higher.

Rightward (leftward) shift of AD is sometimes called a favourable or positive (adverse or negative) *demand shock*. Apart from changes in fiscal or monetary action, such shocks may be generated by changes in the autonomous components of AD (autonomous C or I or NX). A sudden fall in exports is an example of a negative demand shock.

Although there is no difference between fiscal and monetary expansion as far as the effects on P and Y are concerned, the *composition* of aggregate output is likely to differ, as in the IS-LM model. Fiscal expansion increases Y and, thereby, causes money demand to rise. With M/P falling (M unchanged, P rising) r will increase and investment will be depressed as a result. This fall in I partially crowds out the rise in G. When M^s rises, the impact on r is to make it lower. So there is no cause for crowding out. In fact I is higher. But in either case, the upward adjustment in P dampens the expansionary impact compared to the $IS-LM$ context where P was held constant.

The extent of rise in Y and P following fiscal or monetary expansion (or a positive demand shock in general) depends on the slope of the AS curve. If it is very steep, P does most of the adjusting and Y moves very little. This is reversed if AS is very flat.

Now suppose that there has been an increase in the price of an intermediate input. Imported petroleum becomes costlier, for instance. The AS curve shifts to the left. The result is a fall in Y combined with a rise in P. Figure 8.6 illustrates. Effect of a decline in labour productivity or a rise in money wage (it stays constant but moves to a higher level) is the same. Fall in productivity of factors

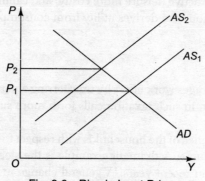

Fig. 8.6   Rise in Input Price

and increases in the prices of inputs are known as *adverse or negative supply shocks* to the economy. Such shocks lead to reduction in output (employment) and a rise in price. Favourable or positive supply shocks produce the opposite outcome.

If the AD curve is very steep, after an adverse supply shock (leftward shift of AS), adjustment will be mostly borne by P and Y will not decrease significantly. This is reversed if AD is very flat.

Table 8.1 summarizes the results obtained.

Table 8.1   Effect of Policy Change and Supply Shocks

	Expansionary fiscal policy	Rise in money supply	Positive supply shock	Adverse supply shock
P	Rises	Rises	Falls	Rises
Y	Rises	Rises	Rises	Falls
r	Rises	Falls	Falls	Rises

The interest rate declines, following a positive supply shock, because the fall in P raises M/P.

FULL WAGE PRICE FLEXIBILITY (CLASSICAL CASE)

Under this view, called the *classical approach*, money wage is not constant. Rather, balance between demand and supply of labour simultaneously determines the real wage and the level of employment in the economy.

Because of diminishing marginal returns, demand for labour is inversely related to real wage. The supply of labour, on the other hand, depends positively on real wage. Labour creates disutility because it involves sacrifice of leisure, which is a source of utility. But work has a positive side too. Through it, one earns income that can be used to purchase goods and services for consumption. *The optimum supply of labour (hours of work) is determined by balancing the disutility of work with the real return from work* (see Appendix 8.1 for a formal derivation of labour supply). Once again, it is the real wage that matters, not the nominal wage. Suppose that, initially, $w = $ Rs 50 per hour and $P = $ Rs 2, implying real wage of 25 units of the product. By working one hour, a person gets Rs 50 with which he can purchase 25 units of the commodity. If now w increases to Rs 100 per hour and at the same time P rises to Rs 4, real wage does not change and the person can obtain only the same amount of consumption goods (25 units) as before for an hour's work in spite of the rise in w. So he will not change his labour supply. If, instead, P had remained unchanged following the rise in w, real wage would have increased to 50 units of the product, making work more attractive (leisure more costly) and calling forth more hours of work. Thus labour supply of a rational person who derives utility from consumption and leisure will be positively related to real wage.

Shift in Labour Supply

A tax on labour income discourages work effort by transferring a part of the real wage from workers to the government. So a reduction in such taxation calls forth more supply of labour. The supply curve shifts to the right.

Change in taste and preference of the households with respect to participation in the labour market will cause labour supply to change. A dramatic example is the steep rise in the rate of participation of women in the labour force in recent years. A general change in attitude towards working for pay has played a major role. Figure 8.7 brings labour demand and supply together to depict balance in the market for labour.

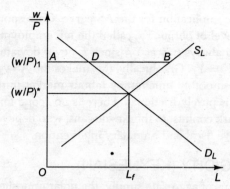

Fig. 8.7   Labour Market Equilibrium

The equilibrium levels of real wage and employment are $(w/P)^*$ and L_f, respectively. Since demand and supply of L are equal at this value, L is called the *full employment* level. Everybody looking for work can find work at $(w/P)^*$. Employment will be continuously maintained at this level through flexibility in w and P.

Suppose for some reason, the prevailing real wage is at $(w/P) > (w/P)^*$. The result is unemployment. (Supply of labour = AB exceeds demand = AD.) But this disequilibrium will be eliminated by a fall in w/P brought about by the pressure of unemployment. As the real wage falls, demand will improve and supply shrink and the gap will be closed and full employment restored at point E. According to this view of a frictionless labour market adjustment, persistent unemployment is an impossibility unless some factors (such as minimum wage laws or trade union resistance) hold up the required downward adjustment in w/P.

Box 8.1   Types of Unemployment

Full employment does not imply that there is absolutely no unemployment of any sort. At any point in time, there will be new entrants to the labour force looking for their first job, workers who have left an old job to find a better one, and there will be employers looking for the right type of employee. Because searching takes time and proceeds by trial and error, there will always be some unemployment even in the best organized labour market. This is called *frictional* unemployment.

Structural unemployment: This is caused by a mismatch between skill requirements of jobs and current skill availability. When an economy is undergoing structural transformation in response to technological upgradation or radical reorientations in policy (such as the decision to liberalize and globalize on a significant scale), workers losing jobs in the shrinking activities may not have the required skills to be absorbed in the expanding sectors. Structural unemployment will be quite high in such cases, particularly during the period of transition.

Even when no large-scale relocation of labour is taking place, unskilled or low-skilled workers are often unable to find long-term jobs. Typically, they hold jobs for short periods at low remuneration. Such chronically unemployed persons are part of structural unemployment.

Natural rate of unemployment: This is the unemployment created by normal labour market frictions that persists even when the labour market is in equilibrium. It reflects unemployment due to frictional and structural causes.

Cyclical unemployment: This is caused by deviations from full employment in the course of business cycles, going down in booms and shooting up in downswings.

This view has a dramatic implication for the AS curve. Corresponding to L_f, given the stocks of capital and land, there is a level of output Y_f, called the full employment output. Perfect flexibility in real wage ensures that Y will always stay at Y_f (since L never deviates from L_f). Thus, whatever the value of P, we always have $Y = Y_f$. Graphically, this makes the AS vertical at Y_f.

The classical view of a smoothly functioning labour market implies that output Y is always at Y_f and any unemployment is purely frictional. There is no scope for government action to combat unemployment. This is in stark contrast to the Keynesians, who believe that cyclical unemployment is serious enough to justify active fiscal and monetary intervention.

WAGE AND PRICE RIGIDITY (KEYNESIAN)

Coming back to the conditions of aggregate supply, the polar opposite to the classical approach is the supposition by Keynes that, at low levels of output and employment, P (as well as w) can be taken to be constant. This produces a horizontal AS curve. Here, although unemployment is high, the real wage does not fall to clear the labour market. Conversely, when labour demand goes up, more supply is forthcoming to meet demand with no increase in wages. The modern-day followers of Keynes, called *new Keynesians*, have advanced sophisticated arguments to defend the assumption of non-flexible wages and prices. The two most important ones—efficiency wages and menu costs—are discussed below.

Efficiency Wage Hypothesis

Keynes believed that money wage would not adjust quickly enough in the short run to preserve full employment all the time. Wage contracts between employers and workers are usually made in terms of money wage and, once made, stay in effect for a number of years. They are not subject to continuous revision in response to changing prices or pressures of labour demand or supply.

New Keynesians claim that there are additional reasons why the firms, who are assumed to have the power to fix wages, may set the real wage at a level higher than the market clearing value $(w/P)^*$ of Figure 8.7. High real wage and unemployment will be simultaneously present in equilibrium.

The chief explanation is in terms of the *efficiency wage theory* which implies that it may be in the best interest of firms to offer a high real wage. There are several reasons why firms may decide to do so. Labour turnover is costly to a firm. Every time an existing worker quits, it has to incur expenditure to recruit a new one and retrain him for the job. If a high wage is paid, fewer workers quit and firms minimize turnover costs. Moreover, a labour force that is well paid is motivated to work more productively in return for the 'fair treatment' offered by the employer and this adds to the firm's profits. Also, by offering high remuneration a company raises the cost of losing the job and this is expected to deter shirking on the job. Fear of unemployment acts as a disciplining device.

To summarize, a real wage that is higher than the market clearing level enables a firm to build up a more experienced and more efficient labour force. Being the outcome of deliberate choice by firms, it ceases to be a variable that moves up and down to keep the economy always at full employment.

New Keynesians claim that P may be rigid if costs are associated with changing nominal prices, and the market is monopolistically competitive. This explanation is known as the *menu cost hypothesis*.

Menu Cost Hypothesis

When a restaurant wants to change the prices of its offerings, it has to incur the expenditure of printing a new menu card. This is the origin of the term *menu cost* of price change. These costs are usually small, but a firm may choose not to change the price if the lost profit from doing so is smaller than the (small) cost of changing price. Whether this will be the case, depends crucially on the nature of market competition.

In a perfectly competitive market, the elasticity of demand facing an individual seller (who constitutes a tiny part of the total market) is very high. Even a very small deviation from the going market price, which is beyond its control, will cause large swings in sales and, hence, in profits. The cost of not hitting the right price is very high and it will certainly outweigh any small menu cost. So, a competitive firm will always adjust its price in response to changing conditions of cost or demand.

However, the situation is different for a seller who has monopoly power in the market. The demand for his product responds much less sharply to changes in price and, the loss in profit, from mispricing, is correspondingly small. If this loss is less than the menu cost of changing prices, the seller will not adjust the price.

There are also indirect costs of price change. Frequent changes entail a loss of customer goodwill. To minimize this loss, firms typically revise price only when it is made 'necessary' by significant change in costs. Price cutting, when demand falls, may trigger a price war and oligopolists are fully aware of the disruptive consequences of such warfare. Therefore, a tacit collusion often emerges among big sellers not to change the going price in response to every little flutter in demand or costs.

All these factors go a long way towards explaining why prices may be sticky and the AS curve tends to become horizontal or very flat at the going price.

KEYNESIAN AGGREGATE SUPPLY

In this case, firms are willing to produce any amount of output demanded at the given P. The AS Curve is horizontal. Shifts in AD produce change in Y of equal amount in the same direction. There is no dampening through the rise in P, following a fiscal or monetary expansion. Conversely, the full impact of any fall in demand falls on output and employment.

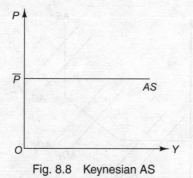

Fig. 8.8   Keynesian AS

Evidently, the assumption of absolutely fixed wages (nominal or real) and prices is extremely unrealistic. But it serves to highlight what would happen if wages and prices are slow to adjust to changing conditions in labour or commodity markets.

CLASSICAL AGGREGATE SUPPLY

Here wages and prices are fully flexible (there are no menu costs or any other barriers to price adjustment) and real wage adjusts instantly (rising if demand for labour exceeds supply and falling if there is unemployment) to ensure full employment all the time. Supply of output is always at the full employment level, implying a vertical AS Curve.

Now any change in AD is totally powerless to affect output and employment. The entire burden of adjustment falls on P. Let us trace the impact of a rise in the stock of money.

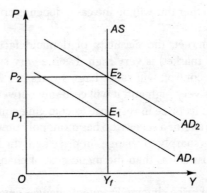

Fig. 8.9   Classical AS and Rise in Money Supply

As the money supply expands, AD shifts to the right and equilibrium moves from E_1 to E_2 in Figure 8.9. Output is unchanged at Y_f, P is higher. The money wage w moves up in the same proportion as P to keep (w/P) at its equilibrium level. Money is *neutral* in the sense that changes in its supply cannot influence output and real wage.

The Keynesian case of absolutely fixed w and P (horizontal AS) and the classical case of perfectly flexible w and P (vertical AS) represent two extreme assumptions about labour market adjustment. Reality is likely to be in the middle. The Keynesian hypothesis is reasonably accurate for low values of Y in the short run, while the classical analysis comes into force as the economy approaches full capacity production and, wages and prices have more time to adjust in the long run. In the intermediate range AS is likely to have an upward slope. Figure 8.10 shows an AS Curve that combines the features of the Keynesian and the classical cases and has an intermediate range.

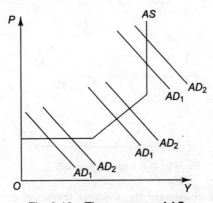

Fig. 8.10   Three ranges of AS

In the Keynesian zone, a rise in AD causes Y to rise with P unchanged, in the intermediate zone, it raises both Y and P, and in the classical zone only P rises leaving Y unchanged. Money is neutral only in the classical zone.

Summary

■ The AD Curve shows combinations of P and Y that maintain equilibrium in the commodity and asset markets. It is negatively sloped.

■ The AS Curve shows the profit-maximizing level of Y at each level of P. Under the Keynesian assumption of constant money wage, AS is positively sloped due to diminishing marginal product of labour. In the classical case of complete wage–price flexibility, the curve is vertical at full employment level of Y.

■ The extent of rise in P, Y following AD changes depends on the slope of AS. The steeper the curve, the greater the change in P.

■ New Keynesians use efficiency wage hypothesis and the menu cost hypothesis to justify rigidity of real wage and product price, respectively.

Exercise

1. 'As the price level falls, the equilibrium output determined in the IS–LM model also falls.' True or False? Give reasons.

2. What will happen to the position of the AD Curve if a cutback in government spending G is accompanied by
   (i) a fall
   (ii) a rise in money supply?

3. If money demand is independent of the rate of interest, what effect will a rise in G have on the AD Curve?

4. 'Demand for labour varies inversely with the real wage because of diminishing marginal productivity.' True or False? Explain.

5. If business cycles are caused by demand factors, P should move procyclically (in the same direction as output), if caused by supply shocks P moves countercyclically (in the opposite direction of output). Use the AD–AS graph to illustrate.

6. Suppose that an economy suffers an adverse supply shock in the form of a rise in the price of imported oil. Show the consequences in an AD–AS diagram. How should the Central Bank respond if it wants to stabilize output?

7. How would you use the AD–AS graph to differentiate between (i) negative supply shock and demand contraction, (ii) positive supply shock and demand expansion?

8. Show that
   (i) if the AS Curve is relatively flat, adjustment will be done mostly by Y, rather than P, following a contraction in demand;
   (ii) if the AD is relatively steep, adjustment will be done mostly by P, rather than Y, following an expansion of supply.

9. Explain why the classical AS Curve is vertical. What is the mechanism that ensures continuous full employment in the classical analysis?

10. Discuss how the idea of efficiency wages may be used to defend the Keynesian AS Curve.

11. Why does r rise after an adverse supply shock to the economy?

12. In an economy, the labour demand and supply curves are given by

$$L_d = 2000 - 8(w/P), L_s = 1000 + 12(w/P).$$

Find the real wage and employment in equilibrium.

Appendix 8.1
The Microeconomics of Labour Supply

In deciding how much labour to supply (how many hours to work), Mr Sen weighs the cost of work against its benefit. Suppose the hourly nominal wage rate is w and the general price level is P. Then by working one hour in the market Mr Sen obtains w/P units of goods and services. Consumption of goods gives him utility. But work involves sacrifice of leisure which is also a source of utility. The optimum hours of work involves a balancing of the utility of the consumption gain and the disutility of work (sacrifice of leisure). Figure 8.11 explains the choice.

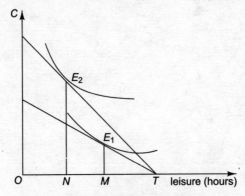

Fig. 8.11   Labour Supply Decision

The vertical axis plots the consumption level of Mr Sen and the horizontal axis, his consumption of leisure. The total (fixed) number of hours to be allocated between work and leisure is OT. The slope of the budget line is the real wage w/P because, by giving up one hour of leisure (moving one unit to the left from T), he gets w/P of goods to consume. For a given real wage, the initial equilibrium is E_1, where OM hours of leisure are consumed (or, TM hours are devoted to work). If the real wage goes up, the budget line shifts up and in the new equilibrium E_2, hours of work have gone up to TN. In this way we get a positive relation between real wage and labour supply of Mr Sen. The aggregate labour supply of the economy at any particular real wage is obtained by summing the labour supplies of all individual agents for that real wage.

A possible objection to the analysis outlined above is that, in reality, individuals are not free to choose their hours of work. Most jobs in the formal sector specify the number of hours that must be worked (say, per week). Once accepted, hours on the job cannot be altered. Nevertheless, the situation is different in the informal sector (unregistered small-scale manufacturing units, for example). Moreover, through choice of overtime or part-time work or variation in the number of family members who are working, control over labour supply may be exercised.

Shift of Labour Supply

Any factor that alters the willingness to work at a given real wage will *shift* the labour supply curve. Some of the more important factors are:

- If Mr Sen suddenly wins a large prize in a lottery or comes into an inheritance, his lifetime wealth rises and he may choose to work less and enjoy more leisure at the current wage rate. The labour supply curve will shift to the left.

- If the real wage is expected to rise in future, Mr Sen feels wealthier and may decide to work less now. The curve shifts to the left.

- If the working age population expands, aggregate labour supply will rise. The curve will shift rightwards.

- If more persons (Mrs Sen, for example) choose to join the labour force due to economic necessity or change in attitude to work, labour supply will rise in the economy.

- If there is a tax on labour income, a reduction in its rate will bring forth greater labour supply by improving the take-home real wage.

9. The Problem of Inflation

DEFINITION AND COSTS

Inflation is defined to be a condition of *persistent* rise in the *general* level of prices. Of course, it does not mean that all prices are rising without exception. Since there are thousands and thousands of goods and services of extremely diverse types, some prices may actually be falling at any particular point in time. However, in an inflationary situation, the general trend of prices is upwards. This is statistically captured by the persistent upward movement of some aggregate price index, usually the WPI or the CPI.

Inflation in India

Judged by the standards of the developing countries, inflation in India has been rather mild. Low inflation has contributed to social welfare by protecting the real income of the poorer sections of the population. Table 9.1 presents figures for the years 1991–2002.

Table 9.1   Inflation in India

(per cent)

Year	WPI	CPI
1991–2	13.7	13.5
1992–3	10.1	9.6
1993–4	8.4	7.3
1995–6	8.0	10.0
1996–7	4.6	9.4
1997–8	4.4	6.8
1998–9	5.9	13.1
1999–2000	3.3	3.4
2000–1	7.2	3.7
2001–2	3.6	4.3

Source: Statistical Outline of India, Tata Services Limited 2002–3.

The sudden jump in CPI (IW) in 1998–9 was due to the exceptional spurt in food prices, especially potatoes and onions, during that year. The steep rise in WPI was caused by higher oil prices. In general, inflation in India is very closely correlated with the performance of the agricultural sector. Shortfalls in food production are directly transmitted to CPI via the rise in the prices of essential items of mass consumption. Agriculture also supplies raw materials of different types to many industries (agro-based industries). Bad harvest pushes up the cost of these inputs. This exerts an upward pressure on prices by causing the supply curve to shift up (adverse supply shock, recall the discussion of Chapter 8).

The second half of 1993–4 witnessed a surge in foreign capital inflow and the monetary base or reserve money shot up almost by 25 per cent. As money supply expanded in response, inflation also got a boost in 1994–5. By the following year, the RBI had taken contractionary measures to curb the expansion in money supply and at the same time there was growth in industrial production as well as imports. This had a moderating influence on the rise in P. Currently, the rate of inflation (measured by the WPI) hovers around 6 per cent per annum. When measured by the CPI, a more appropriate measure, the rate is higher, but not very much. This relatively low value is the result of two factors—moderate increase in money stock and stagnation in aggregate demand due mostly to a deceleration in investment.

Government investment in India has declined by approximately 1.5 per cent of GDP after the reforms. Since 1995-6, private investment has fallen by about 3 per cent of GDP. Growth of exports, another component of AD, has suffered a sharp setback in the last five years (1998–2003). Future prospects are clouded by a slowing world economy and the inability to improve our international competitiveness.

Although price controls and subsidies have been reduced or removed on many items in recent years, the remaining ones continue to provide an anti-inflationary cushion.

Costs of Inflation

Inflation entails a loss in the purchasing power of money. With the same amount of money, smaller amounts of goods and services can be obtained in the market. This has a deleterious effect on the general standard of living. But the loss of purchasing power is not uniformly distributed over the entire population. Some groups are better able to protect their real income in the face of rising prices than other groups. If money income stays constant or fails to rise at the same rate as P (the general price level), real income and, hence, the standard of living declines. This is the fate of workers whose wages are not fully indexed to P and of bond holders and retired persons receiving income flows fixed in nominal terms. In general, the economically weaker sections of the population are less able to shield themselves against rising prices than the rich. Inflation has socially harmful consequences for the distribution of income and wealth in a community.

Borrowers are happier than lenders in a regime of rising prices, because the burden of debt and its repayment gets lighter in real terms. The real rate of interest (= the nominal rate – the rate of inflation) is adversely affected by inflation and lenders suffer in consequence. The real return is protected only if the nominal rate of interest can be raised to exactly match the rise in P. Although there is some evidence that this may be true in the long run, over shorter periods, inflation reduces the real return on saving and lending.

Inflation increases the cost of holding money balances. As a result, people try to economize on holding cash by making more frequent trips to banks. The disutility of this and other efforts for managing with less cash in daily affairs is known as the *shoe leather costs* of inflation. These efforts reduce the time available for leisure or productive work.

A very significant cost of inflation is created by the interaction between inflation and the tax system. This problem, known as *bracket creep,* arises because the income levels corresponding to different income tax rates are not revised systematically with inflation. A person moves into a higher tax bracket and pays more tax just because his money income—but not necessarily real income—is higher due to inflation.

Due to the existence of lags in collection, tax revenue fails to keep pace with inflation and the real value of tax revenue declines. This adds to the fiscal burden of the government. On the other hand, by reducing the load of the national debt and interest payments in real terms, rising prices work to the government's advantage. To calculate the real burden of government borrowing, fiscal deficit is adjusted for inflation according to the following relation:

Adjusted Fiscal Deficit $(AFD) = FD - \pi B$

Here π is the rate of inflation and B, the stock of outstanding public debt.

AFD as proportion of India's GDP has declined from 2.96 per cent over 1980–90 to 1.56 per cent over 1990–2000.

When inflation is high, there is more uncertainty about future price levels and inflation rates than when prices are either stable or not rising too fast. Uncertainty is welfare reducing because it makes planning more difficult.

Inflation Tax

Inflation confers one positive benefit on the government. It supplies a handy instrument for financing its spending. This is known as *inflation tax* or *seignorage*. Through its monopoly power of printing money, the government can create command over real resources for itself simply through deficit financing (debt monetization). Addition to money supply raises the level of P and this reduces the purchasing power of households. In effect, the government is able to raise its own purchasing power without having recourse to higher taxation. Let us illustrate. Suppose currently 100 units of output are being produced and $P = 2$. The household's income is Rs 200, just sufficient to purchase 100 units. Now the government wants to take for its own use 10 units of output. It can do so in two ways (i) raise Rs 20 through taxation and buy 10 units at $P = 2$ which will reduce the household's disposable income to Rs 180 or (ii) indulge in deficit finance (borrow from the Central Bank, which is equivalent to printing money), so that the money supply expands and as a result P rises enough to ensure that with its income of Rs 200 (there is no explicit tax now) the private sector can buy only 180 units. The government is able to purchase 10 units without raising taxes, simply by debasing the currency through inflation.

This way of raising revenue through money creation is called seignorage or inflation tax. Understandably, it is very popular in countries that do not have well-developed machinery for imposing or collecting direct and indirect taxes.

The purchasing power of extra money creation (at current prices) is:

$$\text{Seignorage} = \Delta M/P = (\Delta M/M) \cdot (M/P)$$
$$= g_M(M/P) \tag{9.1}$$

It is thus the product of the growth rate of money supply times the stock of real balances held by the public. The larger the real balances held, the larger is the inflation tax or seignorage corresponding to a given money supply growth.

In India the seignorage ratio (= seignorage/GDP) over 1980–2000 has remained between 2–3 per cent on average. This is fairly low by developing country standards. For Latin American countries, the figure has often touched the level of 5–6 per cent.

CAUSES OF INFLATION

The major explanations of inflation are broadly classified into (i) demand pull factors and (ii) cost push factors. Both can be explained using shifts in the AD–AS Curves. Recall the discussion in Chapter 8.

Demand Pull Consider any factor that shifts AD to the right. It may be increase in autonomous C, I or G or M. If AS slopes up, P (and Y) will go up as a result (see Figure 9.1). Now, a one-time rise in P is not inflationary. To be inflationary, the rise in P must be sustained. This can happen only if AD keeps shifting as when, for example, the government continues to raise G period after period and finance it continuously through money creation (borrowing from the Central Bank). This is the link between budget deficit (BD) and inflation.

It is important to note that the inflationary impact of deficit financing (BD financed by monetized debt) depends on the slope of the AS curve. If AS is flat—as it is likely to be in the short-run with

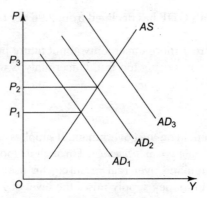

Fig. 9.1 Demand-pull Inflation

underutilization of labour and other resources—the impact will be zero on P. Only Y is stimulated. As the AS becomes steeper, the inflationary impact becomes more and more pronounced. When in the long-run (as a result of perfectly flexible w and P) AS is vertical, BD is 100 per cent inflationary.

Cost Push Consider a rise in money wage w from a fixed level to a higher one. This will shift AS to the left. With AD unchanged, the effect is to raise P (see Figure 9.2). Once again, for the change to be inflationary, w must keep rising to higher and higher levels.

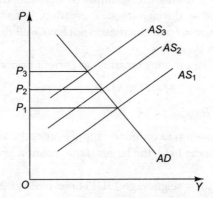

Fig. 9.2 Cost-push Inflation

There is good reasons for w to keep rising. Suppose the initial rise in w was aimed at obtaining a gain in real wage w/P. As P rises, however, the gain is eroded and real wage tends to fall back to its initial value. To counter this, workers demand another hike in w. This causes P to rise further, which provokes the demand for another pay revision and so on. This *wage–price spiral* can ignite and sustain a process of inflation.

The same effect on P would have been obtained if, instead of a cumulative rise in w, there had been a sustained increase in the price of any complementary material input (imported petroleum or some industrial chemical, for instance) or adverse supply shocks sustained over time.

One interesting point emerges. In demand pull inflation (shifting AD curves in Figure 9.1), output Y rises along with P. In cost push, by contrast, the rise in P is accompanied by a fall in Y (shifting AS curves in Figure 9.2). The behaviour of output may, thus, help one to identify the source of inflation.

Cost Push Inflation through Mark-up Pricing

Surveys of the methods of pricing used by business reveal that for almost all manufactured products, the most commonly used rule is that of mark-up pricing. According to this rule, price includes a mark up on estimated average cost (or unit cost) of production. For simplicity, we take labour to be the most important factor of production. Firms set P to cover unit labour cost and add a mark up on it to take care of non-labour costs (of capital and other complementary inputs).

The labour cost, per unit of output, is the number of labour hours it takes to produce one unit of output, denoted by d, times the wage per hour. Thus if $d = 7$ and $w = $ Rs 40, unit labour cost = Rs 280. The labour requirement coefficient d is the inverse of average labour productivity (= output per unit of L). Improvement in labour productivity implies a fall in d. Mark-up pricing states that price equals average or unit cost plus a mark-up on that cost.

$$P = (1 + m)dw, \quad m > 0 \tag{9.2}$$

where (dw) is the unit labour cost and m the constant mark-up chosen by the firm. The (mdw) part ensures that non-labour costs are accounted for. With $m = 0.1$, $d = 7$, $w = $ Rs 40, P will be Rs 308.

Price equation (9.2) says that: P is higher if (i) w is higher, (ii) non-labour costs are higher, calling for a higher m and (iii) d is higher, that is, labour productivity is lower.

Mark-up pricing provides a cost push explanation of inflation by establishing a direct link between increases in costs of production and the resulting increase in P. Sustained upward movement in the prices of inputs or decline in productivity of labour (rise in d) will trigger off a process of inflation. This will occur even if the mark-up factor m remains constant.

Denoting average labour productivity by z $(= 1/d)$, equation (9.2) can be rewritten as

$$P = (1 + m)(w/z).$$

Assuming m to be constant, this gives the rate of inflation as (see Result B in Appendix 1.1):

$$g_P = g_w - g_z. \tag{9.3}$$

That is, the proportionate change in P equals the rate of wage inflation minus the rate of growth of labour productivity. Prices rise when money wages rise in excess of the rise in productivity. For example, if w rises at 5 per cent while productivity of L grows at 3 per cent, inflation will equal 2 per cent.

INFLATION AND UNEMPLOYMENT: THE PHILLIPS CURVE

The original Phillips Curve was a relationship between the rate of unemployment and the rate of change of money wages. The relationship is a negative one—as unemployment (u) falls, wage inflation increases.

The reason for the negative slope is as follows. As u declines (due, possibly, to an increase in demand for L), the bargaining power of workers increases and they are able to extract wage increase at a higher rate. On the other hand, when u is high (there is lot of slack in the labour market), the rate of wage increase will be dampened.

The original Phillips Curve provided a link between g_w and u. But it was modified to set up a link between the rate of unemployment and the rate of inflation. This is how the Phillips Curve is interpreted in modern macroeconomics. The simplest way to understand it is to use equation (9.3). If labour productivity is not changing, $g_z = 0$ and $g_P = g_w$. In this case a relation between g_w and u leads to an identical relation between g_P and u. This is plotted in Figure 9.3.

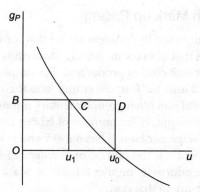

Fig. 9.3   Phillips Curve

The point of intersection with the horizontal axis shows the rate of unemployment consistent with price stability. Unemployment less than (in excess of) u_0 is inflationary (deflationary). This level of unemployment is called the *Non-accelerating Inflation Rate of Unemployment (NAIRU)*.

The negative slope of the Phillips Curve can be explained from another angle. Starting from a position of zero inflation (point u_0 in Figure 9.3), suppose the government increases AD by raising G or cutting T or by boosting the money supply. At the initial level of output, this extra demand causes inflation to rise from zero to OB per cent. This reduces the real wage, which induces firms to expand production. Unemployment falls to u_1, the economy moves to C. Thus, a fall in unemployment can be 'purchased' at the price of higher inflation.

However, the conclusion will be upset if money wage adjusts very quickly to price rise. As soon as workers realize that inflation has risen to OB per cent and their real wage has fallen in consequence, they increase their nominal wage demand. If they succeed in pushing w up to the full extent of the hike in prices, real wage and unemployment return to their original levels and only inflation is higher. The economy moves from C to D. The Phillips trade-off between inflation and unemployment is likely to be a short-run phenomenon, because it depends on the time lag between the rise in inflation and the resulting money wage revision. If, however, the wage revision is partial (less than the extent of inflation), real wage stays below the original level and some reduction in unemployment can be maintained at the cost of higher inflation.

Friedman strongly criticized the original Phillips Curve approach for ignoring the role of expectations in setting wages and other nominal prices. Workers' expectation about inflation is a major factor that determines wage changes. Since workers try to protect their real earnings, they are concerned with the wage adjusted for any expected change in the price level. When expected inflation is higher, they bargain for higher wages and, employers are also willing to grant a raise because the prices of the products they sell are expected to rise. This actually raises costs and prices. The *expectation-augmented Phillips Curve* takes this into account. It is written as

$$g_P = f(u) + P^e.$$

In this equation, expected inflation appears as a shift parameter. A rise in P^e will cause the curve to shift up by pushing up actual inflation even if unemployment stays the same.

THE LONG-RUN PHILLIPS CURVE

In the long-run, expected price fully adjusts to the actual price. The implication is quite dramatic for stabilization policy. It is illustrated in Figure 9.4. Each Phillips Curve (PC) is drawn for a particular expectation of the inflation rate P^e. The lowest curve passing through A is based on an expectation of stable prices ($P^e = 0$). Suppose that in Figure 9.4, the system is at A with unemployment u_0 (NAIRU) to begin with. Inflation is zero.

The government stimulates AD to reduce unemployment. In the short-run, employment increases because the rise in P following the rise in AD is not immediately perceived by the workers and their expected price remains the same, and real wage falls as a result. Suppose, for the sake of illustration, the inflation rate is 2 per cent. In Figure 9.4 we move from A to B.

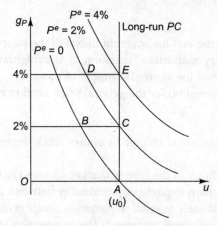

Fig. 9.4   Long-run Phillips Curve

As suppliers of labour come to realize that prices have risen by 2 per cent, they press for a rise of 2 per cent in nominal wage. Once this is achieved, real wage (and, hence, unemployment) is back to its original level and the economy moves to C on a higher PC ($P^e = 2\%$). If policymakers persist in stimulating AD further, inflation will rise to, say, 4 per cent. Until workers come to anticipate this, unemployment falls below u_0 (at point D). But, eventually, they will adjust fully and the system will move to E, where u is back to NAIRU. Thus the long-run Phillips Curve is the vertical line, and the trade-off between inflation and unemployment has vanished. The result is summarized as:

The long-run Phillips Curve is the relation between inflation and unemployment when expectation of inflation has time to adjust fully to actual inflation. It is vertical, implying that attempt to force inflation below NAIRU will cause inflation to accelerate without any change in employment or output.

From this analysis it is easy to see why *anticipated* inflation may fail to generate any reduction in unemployment. In this case, wage claims will be automatically (or very quickly) adjusted upwards to match the rise in inflation, real wage will not fall, and labour demand will not be stimulated.

THE QUANTITY THEORY OF MONEY

According to this theory, which has a very long history in economics, the value of P, the general price level, and its movement over time is determined by the demand for and supply of money balances in the economy. This is in sharp contrast to the analysis of Keynes, in which supply and demand for money fixes the equilibrium value of r, the rate of interest. The group of economists who use the quantity theoretic approach to the determination of P and changes in P are known as *Monetarists*. According to the members of this group, inflation is always and everywhere a monetary phenomenon, because an upward spurt in general prices, caused by demand-related or cost-related factors, cannot be sustained over a long period, if not backed by continuous monetary expansion.

So far as the supply of money is concerned, the monetarists, just like the Keynesians, take M^s to be an exogenous policy parameter controlled by the Central Bank. But, on the demand side, they deny the influence of r and consider only the transactions demand.

$$M^d = kPY.$$

Thus, people hold a constant fraction k of their money income in the form of money balances. (Equivalently, demand for real balances, M^d/P, is a fraction k of real income Y.) In equilibrium,

$$M^s = kPY. \tag{9.4}$$

The value of k is taken to depend on payment habits of the people and other institutional factors. If M^s is fixed by the monetary authorities, equation (9.4) straightaway gives money income of the economy, as a unique multiple of the aggregate supply of money.

Equation (9.4) gives an expression for the general price level in equilibrium

$$P = M^s/kY. \tag{9.5}$$

The behaviour of P in response to change in money stock depends crucially on the behaviour of real national income Y.

If perfect wage-price flexibility in the labour market ensures continuous full employment, we can set $Y = Y_f$ and equation (9.5) then implies proportionality between M and P.

A change in money supply will cause an equal proportionate change in the general level of prices. Values of real income and other real variables will remain unchanged. This is 'neutrality of money' once again.

Inflation is a purely monetary phenomenon and the blame for it can be squarely laid on the Central Bank for its inability to control the growth of money supply. The quantity theory in its strong form states:

Quantity Theory

Price level is proportional to money supply, so that the rate of inflation equals the rate of growth of money supply $(g_P = g_M)$.

Let us illustrate with an example. Suppose that $k = 1/10$ and, initially, $M^s = 100$ and $Y = 50$, so that $P = 20$. Now M^s is raised to 180. At the initial value of P, demand for money remains equal to the old supply (= 100). The excess supply of 80 units of money is spent on buying goods and services. With output staying unchanged at 50, P has to rise to 36, so that once again money demand (= $1/10 \times 36 \times 50$) equals the new supply (= 180).

The assumption is that when people have more money on their hands than what they want to hold, they spend it directly on purchasing goods. With supply fixed, 'too much money chases too few goods' and prices are driven up. In Keynesian analysis, in contrast, when people have a larger stock of money than they want to hold, they buy bonds so that bond prices rise or the interest rate falls. This causes aggregate demand to rise by stimulating investment. The impact of a rise in money supply on the commodity market, thus, works indirectly through a fall in the interest rate. The final impact on P depends on the slope of the aggregate supply (AS) curve. Thus, generally, money is not neutral in the Keynesian system.

It should be noted that we do not need full employment for the validity of the quantity theory in its strong form. The proportional relation between M^s and P will hold if Y is fixed for some reason (not necessarily at Y_f) and does not respond to a change in M^s. The quantity theorists take the short-run to be a period over which resources are in fixed supply. Production technology and the structure of the economy also do not change significantly. As a result Y may be treated as fixed in the short-run.

Historical evidence supports, in a particular sense, the monetarist claim that inflation is basically a monetary phenomenon. Almost every country that has experienced high inflation over long periods has also experienced sustained, high growth of money stock. In the short-run and during mild inflation, the link, however, is much weaker.

Over longer periods, the value of Y rises with the growth of the labour force, capital accumulation, and technological innovations that raise the productivity of factors. If Y is changing, equation (9.5) predicts:

$$g_P = g_M - g_Y. \tag{9.6}$$

The rate of growth of real output is subtracted from the growth of money supply to arrive at the rate of inflation. Thus, if the economy is growing at 6 per cent per annum, for maintaining price stability $(g_P = 0)$, the increment in money supply planned by the Central Bank must also be 6 per cent. Otherwise there will be inflation or deflation, neither of which is deemed desirable.

In the modern version of quantity theory, money is treated as a luxury good in the sense that an increase in income leads to a more than proportionate increase in the demand for money, that is, the income elasticity of money demand is greater than one. (When demand is proportional to income, this elasticity equals one.) In this case

$$g_P = g_M - \beta g_Y \tag{9.7}$$

where $\beta (> 1)$ is the income elasticity of money demand. Now, for maintaining price stability $(g_P = 0)$, the Central Bank has to fix the rate of growth of M higher than the rate of growth of real income. This approach was the basis for the Chakravarty Committee's (1985) rule for monetary targeting in India. On the basis of an estimated value of $\beta = 2$ and an expected growth rate of (real) national income of 5 per cent, the Committee recommended that the annual growth rate of M be limited to 14 per cent $(= 2 \times 5 + 4)$ to ensure that inflation did not exceed 4 per cent per annum. The RBI continues to follow essentially the same rule in setting the limit to the growth of broad money, $M3$.

Equation (9.7) implies that when both money supply and real income are growing, the two forces exert opposing pressures on the price level. Money supply expansion by itself $(g_M > 0)$ makes for rising P $(g_P > 0)$, while rising real income $(g_Y > 0)$ tends to curtail inflation. The net impact depends on the relative strengths of the two effects. Rising real income causes demand for real balances to rise and this reduces the inflationary potential of rising money supply. Equation (9.7) can be recast in a more general form, which may be called the modern quantity theory.

Modern Quantity Theory

Inflation rate equals the growth rate of nominal money stock minus the growth rate of real money demand.

The major factors influencing real money demand (or demand for real balances) are (i) real income Y; (ii) the interest rate, r, which is the cost of holding money; (iii) financial innovations and institutional change; and (iv) expectations of future inflation.

If r rises, real money demand declines and any given nominal money growth leads to less inflation. Introduction of new financial instruments, like credit cards, reduces the need for holding cash for transactions and puts upward pressure on P. Also, if people expect the rate of inflation to pick up in future, they economize on the holding of cash (whose value will be eroded at a faster rate) and this adds fuel to inflation. Thus, *inflationary expectations* are self-fulfilling. Such expectations induce workers in the organized sectors to press for wage hikes and this is likely to set the wage-price spiral in motion.

In India inflation has consistently remained below the growth of money stock, as shown in Table 9.2. The quantity theory in its strong form does not hold, but the weaker version represented by equation

(9.7) is not a bad approximation. Price controls and production subsidies in combination with restrictive monetary policy have played a major role in keeping inflation low. The experience of most other LDCs, those in Latin America in particular, has been much worse in this respect.

Table 9.2   Money Growth, Inflation, and Seignorage in India

Year	Money growth	Inflation (%)	Seignorage (%)
1990–1	13.13	10.95	2.15
1991–2	13.35	14.71	2.15
1992–3	11.33	8.56	1.77
1993–4	25.17	9.40	4.30
1994–5	22.07	9.91	3.87
1995–6	14.87	8.17	2.58
1996–7	2.84	4.6	0.41
1997–8	13.20	4.4	1.96
1998–9	14.55	6.9	2.14
1999–2000	8.08	3.3	1.15

Source: India Development Report, 2002.

VELOCITY OF CIRCULATION OF MONEY

There is an old tradition in economics that analyses the link between inflation and the quantity of money in terms of the velocity of circulation of money.

The income velocity of circulation of money (or velocity, in short) is the ratio of nominal GNP to the nominal money supply($= GNP/M^s$). It is the number of times per year that the money stock turns over to finance national income. Thus, for example, if GNP is Rs 20,000 and $M =$ Rs 2000, velocity, $V = 10$. The definition of $V (= PY/M)$ can be rewritten as:

$$P = MV/Y.$$

If V and Y are constant, P is proportional to M. This is a restatement of the quantity theory in its strong form. $(1/V)$ takes the place of k in equation (9.5). If prices are rising very fast (hyperinflation), there is flight from money in the sense that money changes hand very quickly. Nobody wants to hold cash which is losing purchasing power at a fast pace. This means that V rises continuously during hyperinflation. If Y is constant, the rate of inflation will exceed the growth of money stock. (Why?)

BUDGET DEFICIT AND INFLATION

Deficit financing, it may be recalled, is the part of budget deficit that is covered by borrowing from the Central Bank. We have seen that the effect is to increase the base money or reserve money by the same magnitude. The aggregate money supply expands by a multiple of the rise in reserve money, through the operation of the money multiplier, provided certain conditions are met (explained in Chapter 6). This increment in M will cause P to rise by shifting the AD curve. (This has already been explained in Chapter 8.)

A temporary budget deficit financed by money creation leads to a one-time shift in AD, which results in a one-time rise in P. Once the deficit disappears, AD does not shift any more and there is no inflation. Thus, temporary budget deficit cannot be a source of inflation. But persistent deficit may well be. According to the monetarists, who believe in the quantity theory, the rise in P in the short-run will be proportional to the jump in M. If deficit financing persists at a constant rate leading to a steady growth in the stock of money, the economy will be suffering a constant rate of inflation. Over a longer span of time, when real income also is growing, the rate of inflation will be given by equations (9.6) or (9.7).

Financing budget deficit persistently through money creation (borrowing from the Central Bank) will lead to sustained inflation. If the deficit is financed by issuing bonds to the public (non-monetized debt), there is no impact on money supply and the general price level. (In the latter case the burden of public debt will grow over time.)

Reliance on deficit financing may land a government in a trap, as inflation tends to worsen the deficit. Expenditures keep pace with rising prices, but revenues do not. Tax revenue falls in real terms and so does seignorage revenue, as higher inflation causes a flight from money (reduction in real balances held). Still more money creation becomes necessary, adding further fuel to inflation.

It is worth remembering that the magnitude of the impact of deficit financing on the money stock depends crucially on the ability of the commercial banks to find borrowers for their loanable funds. If there is no dearth of borrowers (banks are fully loaned up), the change in M equals deficit financing times the money multiplier. No secondary expansion of money supply takes place if banks cannot find suitable borrowers. The increment in M then equals the amount of deficit financing.

Table 9.3   Deficit Finance in India

(Rs crore)

Year	Deficit Finance or Monetized Deficit	DF as % of GDP (current prices)
1988–9	6503	1.64
1989–90	13,813	3.02
1990–1	14,754	2.75
1991–2	5508	0.89
1992–3	4257	0.60
1993–4	260	0.03
1994–5	2130	0.22
1995–6	19,855	1.77
1996–7	1934	0.15
1997–8	12,914	0.91

Source: India Development Report, 1999–2000.

There is no automatic link between BD and inflation. Actually, in the early stages of inflation, programmes to reduce deficits are often inflationary. Fiscal consolidation starts by raising the controlled prices of public sector units and subsidized goods and services. This exerts upward pressure on the price level.

Although the correlation between BD and inflation is not always high, high deficits invariably tend to create high inflation sooner or later. There has been massive BD in all the episodes of hyperinflation, such as that in Bolivia in 1984–5, when prices soared by over 11,000 per cent in one year. (The most celebrated hyperinflation is that of inter-War Germany. The price index rose from 262 in January 1919 to 126,160,000,000,000 in December 1923—an incredible factor of 481.5 billion!)

Friedman, the leader of the monetarists, made a famous statement that inflation is always and everywhere a monetary phenomenon. This is essentially correct. However, governments generally print money to cover their budget deficit. Rapid money growth without fiscal imbalance is possible but very unlikely. In this sense inflation is almost always a fiscal phenomenon.

IMPOSING DISCIPLINE ON THE CENTRAL BANK: CURRENCY BOARDS AND INFLATION

The system of currency boards is a novel attempt to control the ability of Central Banks to create money. Under it, the domestic money supply has to be totally backed by foreign reserves and the authorities must stand ready to exchange domestic currency for foreign currency at a fixed rate. The Central Bank can no longer conduct an independent monetary policy, nor can it print money at the government's behest to finance budget deficits. This is because it cannot hold claims on the government.

In a desperate attempt to control inflation that had been running at 800 per cent per annum in 1990, Argentina adopted the currency board system. The peso–dollar rate was fixed at one to one and the money supply had to have a 100-per cent dollar backing. An Argentine citizen could go to the central bank and exchange a peso for a dollar any time he chose. Money supply could expand only when people wanted to change dollars into pesos. Inflation dropped dramatically to 5 per cent by the end of 1995 and the growth rate of the economy picked up.

Unfortunately, in the aftermath of the Mexican currency crisis, people became very nervous and started converting pesos into dollars on a big scale. The sharp contraction in money supply led to a severe recession in which the unemployment rate shot up almost to 20 per cent. Hong Kong, which also had a currency board, faced a severe banking crisis in 1998. In January 2002, Argentina abolished the currency board and let the peso float relative to the dollar. A sharp devaluation followed, which led to some recovery in the current account balance, but at the same time many holders of dollar-denominated debt were forced to default on loans.

Policymakers have become much more sceptical about the magical properties of currency boards.

THE BURDEN OF PUBLIC DEBT

Now that the GOI has drastically reduced powers to finance deficit by borrowing from the RBI, it will be forced to rely more on borrowing from the public. This type of non-monetized debt does not add to reserve money and, hence, is not inflationary. But does it mean that this mode of finance is costless? In fact, there is a view that government debt is costless if it is held solely by domestic citizens. (External debt owed to foreigners is always a burden for the economy.) But this view is not correct.

Box 9.1   The Money–Inflation Link in India

Manohar Rao attempted to test the predictions of monetarists using annual data on the Indian economy over the 40-year period 1950–1 to 1990–1. The results suggested that for a constant level of real output (long-run full employment equilibrium), the inflation rate is nearly equal to the growth rate of nominal money supply. This bears out the basic monetarist contention that, in the long run, when all adjustments have taken place, sustained money growth leads to an equal increase in the rate of inflation.

However, the same exercise implied that in the short-run, inflation was significantly affected by the growth of output, particularly in the agricultural sector.

An important study by Balakrishnan, Surekha, and Vani (1994) found that for the period 1952–80, change in the prices of foodgrains was more important than money supply in explaining inflation in India. Empirical work has consistently failed to lend robust support to any particular theory of inflation in the Indian situation. But the performance of the agricultural sector has been found to be significant, almost without exception.

Source: Balakrishnan, Surekha, and Vani (1994); Rao (1997).

First, if government borrowing pushes up the rate of interest, private investment may be adversely affected. This is the crowding-out effect. Setback in investment will result in a smaller capital stock for future generations. Their consumption possibilities will be lowered.

Second, if the internally held debt grows over time, the interest burden of servicing the debt will grow with it (even with r remaining unchanged) and this will add to the deficit, calling for higher borrowing unless taxation can be raised sufficiently to meet the gap. (If inflation is present, the relevant cost is the real rate of interest, which equals the nominal rate minus the rate of inflation.) The rise in the volume of debt by itself may not be a serious problem if GDP is also rising at the same time. What matters is the evolution of the debt–GDP ratio. This ratio will stabilize at a constant level if there is zero primary deficit (PD = non-interest expenditure minus tax revenue) and the interest rate, r, to be paid on the debt equals g, the growth rate of GDP (see Box 9.2 for the general formula for the evolution of this ratio).

If for some reason, r rises above g, the ratio can be kept stable only with a decline in PD. But reducing PD calls for lower government expenditure and/or higher taxes. For a number of reasons, governments may be reluctant to do this. If the PD is cut, the result may be contractionary, implying a fall in g. This, by widening the gap between r and g, will make debt stabilization harder to achieve.

Box 9.2   Algebra of Public Debt

Denoting public debt in any period by D, we have

$$\Delta D = G - T + rD.$$

The right-hand side is the budget deficit, the difference between total expenditure including interest payment on existing debt (rD) and tax revenue. $(G - T)$ is the primary deficit. Budget deficit leads to an equal addition to D (the left-hand side). Writing $d = D/Y$ (the debt–GDP ratio) and using the formula for the growth rate of a ratio, we obtain

$$\Delta d/d = \Delta D/D - \Delta Y/Y = \Delta D/D - g, \text{ where}$$

g is the growth rate of GDP.

$$\Delta d = \Delta D/Y - gd = (G-T)/Y + rd - gd = PD/Y + (r-g)d.$$

Once the debt reaches a very high level relative to GDP, investors might lose confidence in the ability of the government to service it through higher taxation in future and this is likely to destabilize the financial market and cause r to rise steeply. The growth of national debt may turn out to be unsustainable over time and the system may lurch towards bankruptcy.

Whether a rising public debt should be a cause for alarm depends crucially on the use to which the proceeds are put. If the government spending (which is generating the deficit that is being financed through borrowing) is for productive purposes, growth of output (g) will be stimulated and debt may be sustainable. If, however, the budgetary deficit is driven mostly by unproductive revenue expenditure of the government—the case in India—a rising public debt is a bad omen for the health of the economy. More than 70 per cent of the borrowing by the GOI goes to meet current (revenue) expenditure.

To reduce the burden of debt servicing, the GOI in recent years has been taking steps to reduce the interest rate down to a very low level, barely ahead of the rate of inflation. This is the soft option, given the inability to rein in the primary deficit. Pensioners, in particular, have been hit hard by the move.

Table 9.4   Outstanding Liabilities of the GOI

(per cent of GDP)

	1997–8	1998–9	1999–2000	2000–01	2001–02
Internal debt	47.5	47.9	49.7	52.4	55.1
External debt	10.6	10.2	9.6	9.0	8.7
Total debt	58.1	58.1	59.3	61.4	63.8

Source: Economic Survey, GOI, 2002–3.

MONEY GROWTH, INFLATION, AND INTEREST RATE

The real interest rate is obtained by subtracting the rate of inflation from the nominal rate of interest. What is the likely impact of monetary growth on interest rates? Here economists talk of two effects, which are explained below.

Let us consider the case where demand for real balances (real money demand) depends positively on Y and negatively on the nominal rate of interest r. Initially, at the original value of P, an increase in M translates into an increase in real money supply, M/P, and with real demand unchanged this causes r to fall. This is called the *liquidity effect* (increase in money supply = increase in liquidity). As Y begins to rise (due to the boost in I resulting from the fall in r) combined with rising P, demand for money begins to rise relative to supply and r is gradually pushed up. This is called the *income effect*. Ultimately, after full adjustment, an increase in inflation is fully reflected in an equal increase in the nominal interest rate. Thus, in the long-run, the *real* interest rate is unaffected by monetary factors. However, before the process has fully worked itself out, r lags behind inflation and this reduction in real interest causes hardship to lenders (savers) and makes life easier for borrowers.

A simpler way of viewing the link is as follows. In the presence of inflation, lenders try to protect the real value of their interest income. So nominal interest charged by them tends to incorporate a premium equal to the expected rate of inflation. As inflation persists over long periods, the actual value is anticipated more or less correctly (expected inflation = actual inflation) and we have:

$$Nominal\ r = real\ r + rate\ of\ inflation.$$

Thus, in the long-run, a change in inflation (actual or expected) will translate into an equal change in the nominal rate of interest leaving real interest unchanged. This is known as the Fisher effect.

Summary

- Inflation is a sustained rise in the general price level. It reduces the purchasing power of money, the return on lending, and acts as a tax on the holding of money.
- Through inflation, the government can collect an inflation tax and seignorage revenue. Its real fiscal deficit is reduced. Adjusted Fiscal Deficit captures this effect.

- Causes of inflation are classified into demand pull and cost push. Cost push inflation often operates through mark-up pricing.
- The Phillips Curve is an inverse relation between unemployment and inflation that holds in the short-run. Adjustment of workers' expectation to inflation gives a vertical Phillips Curve in the long-run.
- The Quantity Theory, in its traditional form, equates the rate of inflation with the growth rate of money supply. In the modern version, the rate of growth of real money demand due to growth in output is subtracted from the growth in money supply to arrive at the rate of inflation. Velocity of circulation is taken to be constant in both versions.
- Though persistent budget deficit financed by borrowing from the Central Bank leads to inflation, there is no automatic link between inflation and budget deficit.
- Currency boards impose discipline on Central Banks by tying money supply rigidly to foreign exchange reserves.
- In India, empirical evidence supports the Quantity Theory in the long-run but in the short-run, the output level, particularly in the agricultural sector, is an important determinant of inflation.
- The debt–GDP ratio stabilizes if primary deficit is zero and the rate of interest equals the growth rate of GDP.
- In the long-run, increases in inflation are transmitted one for one to the nominal rate of interest.

Exercise

1. The old and the poor are hurt more by inflation than the young and the rich. Can you explain why?

2. Suppose the inflation rate is 2 per cent, while r, the nominal interest rate, is 6 per cent. If inflation rises to 10 per cent, by how much should r rise to keep real r the same?

3. Rapid inflation induces people to economize on real balances (flight from money). What is the implication for the behaviour of V? Argue that inflation in this case may exceed the growth of money stock.

4. Use the idea of mark-up pricing to explain why a year of bad monsoon may cause inflation in a country like India.

5. Higher growth of money stock (and the attendant inflation) often leads to a decline in real balances held by the public. Use equation (9.1) to show that there may be a particular rate of money growth that maximizes seignorage revenue.

6. Inflation has both costs and benefits for government finances. Explain.

7. Discuss how the behaviour of output may help to identify the type of inflation—demand pull or cost push.

8. Explain why the Phillips trade-off depends crucially on the speed of wage adjustment.

9. Are budget deficits always inflationary? Comment on the Indian experience in this context.

10. Recent years in India have witnessed a rapid growth in the use of credit cards and ATMs in urban areas. Use the modern quantity theory approach to examine the likely impact on prices.

11. If the income elasticity of money demand is expected to go down along with a fall in expected growth of real income, what is the implication for monetary targeting?

12. RBI had forecast a GDP growth of 5.5 per cent for 1995–6 and targeted an increase of 15.5 per cent of money supply for price stability. What is the implied elasticity of money demand?

13. Currently, in an economy, the primary budget surplus is 4 per cent of GDP, the rate of interest is 8 per cent, and the growth rate of GDP is 5 per cent. Inflation is absent. Will the debt–GDP ratio rise or fall?

14. Fiscal consolidation (reduction in budget deficit) and/or tight money policy are universal prescriptions for fighting inflation. Can you give any reason why such policies may actually worsen the situation?

10. Economic Growth

As indicated in Chapter 3, the time series plot of the GDP of most economies display cyclical fluctuations (business cycles) around a long-run trend. While the annual growth rate varies over the cycle (rising in booms and falling in recessions), the trend gives the average rate of progress over a relatively long span of time (say, fifty years). The theory of economic growth is an important branch of macroeconomics that tries to highlight the factors that influence the *long-run trend growth* of an economy. Growth is important for a nation because, without it, the general standard of living of its citizens cannot improve over time. This is supported, without exception, by the historical experience of all the industrialized countries of the world.

Growth of real GDP, sustained at a high level enabled, Japan to catch up with the advanced industrialized countries of Europe and North America within a quarter century after the Second World War. A comparable catching up was subsequently accomplished by four other Asian economies—Hong Kong, Singapore, Taiwan, and South Korea. In each case, carefully designed and implemented growth-enhancing policies played a vital role in the process.

Since the focus of growth theory is entirely on the supply side or the productive capacity, the problem of deficiency in aggregate demand is assumed to be absent. Moreover, the economy is taken to be a closed one, so that there is no foreign trade. Thus, planned saving (S) equals planned investment (I) at each point of time.

Table 10.1 Growth of the Indian Economy

(per cent)

Period	National Income (factor cost, constant prices)	Per Capita Income (constant prices)
First Plan (1951–6)	3.7	1.8
Second Plan (1956–1)	4.1	2.1
Third Plan (1961–6)	2.4	0.2
3 Annual Plans (1966–9)	3.7	1.5
Fourth Plan (1969–74)	3.3	1.0
Fifth Plan (1974–9)	5.0	2.7
Annual Plan (1979–80)	–6.0	–8.2
Sixth Plan (1980–5)	5.4	3.2
Seventh Plan (1985–90)	5.7	3.6
2 Annual Plans (1990–2)	2.6	0.6
Eighth Plan (1992–7)	5.2	4.7
2001–2	5.7	3.9

Source: Statistical Outline of India, Tata Services Limited 2002–3.

Growth theory had its beginning in the years following the Second World War when the war-ravaged economies embarked on the programme of reconstruction. With the stock of productive capital lying in ruins, the most urgent task confronting the nations was to build it up as quickly as possible. This called for high saving (curtailment of current consumption), so that resources could be devoted to investment (the production of capital, goods). The role of saving and productivity of capital, in the process of economic expansion, can be brought out in very simple terms.

The Data Series on National Accounts Statistics for 1950-1 to 2001-2 (1993-4 prices) published by the Economic and Political Weekly Research Foundation (EPWRF) reveals that India's per capita GDP at factor cost was $124.7 in 1950-1 and $386.7 in 2001-2. This threefold rise over fifty years gives a long-term trend growth of 2.1 per cent. Trend growth of some other countries are: 1.8 per cent (USA 1870-2000), 2.95 per cent (Japan 1890-1990), 5 to 6.5 per cent on average (South Korea, Singapore, Taiwan 1960-90).

THEORY OF GROWTH

Let us denote the saving ratio $(= S/Y)$ by s. That is, s is the fraction of GDP withheld from consumption and invested. For simplicity, let us assume there is no depreciation of capital, so addition to capital stock equals I (gross investment). Let v denote the incremental capital output ratio (ICOR), the inverse of the marginal productivity of K. For example, $v = 4$ means that it takes 4 additional units of K to raise Y by 1 unit. The higher is v, the less productive is capital. Thus, v or the ICOR is a measure of the overall efficiency of the economy—how well it utilizes its physical capital (and complementary resources) in the process of production. We assume v to be constant.

(i) $S = sY$

(ii) $I = \Delta K$

(iii) $\Delta K / \Delta Y = v$

(iv) $S = I$

The first equation is the proportional relation between S and Y. The second says that in the absence of depreciation, investment leads to an equal increase in the capital stock. Absence of depreciation is just a simplifying assumption. The third equation is the assumption of constant ICOR. The final equation shows the equality of saving and investment as condition of macro balance. The four equations can be combined to yield the expression for the equilibrium rate of growth of an economy.

$$g^* = \Delta Y/Y = s/v \tag{10.1}$$

To take an example, if $s = 20$ per cent and $v = 5$, $g^* = 4$ per cent. The higher the rate of saving (s), and lower the ICOR (v), the faster is the growth of the economy. Equation (10.1) provided the theoretical foundation for the economic plans undertaken by numerous developing economies throughout the world in the post-War years. India belonged to this group.

The Indian Planning Commission uses equation (10.1) to estimate the investment (= saving) requirement of meeting a specified growth target. For example, it calculates investment to be 32.6 per cent of GDP (at current prices) corresponding to a growth target of 8 per cent per annum for the Tenth Plan period. This figure is based on the Commission's projected value of 4.08 for the ICOR over 2002-7. There seems to be an upward bias in the estimate for ICOR, because the value appears to have settled around 3.7 in recent years.

Although equation (10.1) captures in a useful form the interrelationship between the growth rate, the saving rate, and the productivity of capital, it ignores the role of labour altogether. We now proceed

Table 10.2   India's Incremental Capital Output Ratio

Period	ICOR
1988–92	4.13
1989–93	4.88
1990–4	4.84
1991–5	4.54
1992–6	3.71
1993–7	3.79
1994–8	3.71
1995–9	3.73

Source: India Development Report, 2002.

to rectify this omission and develop a more general approach which is called the Solow model after its originator, Robert Solow.

THE SOLOW MODEL OF GROWTH

The basic building block is the concept of an aggregate production function for the entire economy.

$$Y = AF(K, L)$$

This says that aggregate output (Y) in any period is determined by the inputs of capital (K) and labour (L). The multiplicative term A captures the current state of technical knowledge and the overall efficiency in the use of the factors of production, K and L. If there is technological improvement (rise in overall efficiency) over time—introduction of new and better methods of production—A will increase and Y will be higher for *given* levels of the factor inputs, K and L. This is equivalent to a general improvement in the productivity of factors.

It may strike one as odd that the production function does not include land or intermediate inputs. This, of course, does not mean that they are unimportant for production. Land does not appear because, for the economy, its supply is essentially fixed, even in the long run. Only variable factors have been included in the production function. K changes through saving and investment and L changes due to population growth that adds to the labour force. For simplicity, the labour force is taken to be a constant fraction of the population. Value of intermediate inputs has been subtracted from gross output to arrive at net value added in the economy, so that Y stands for GDP.

Constant returns to scale (CRS) is taken to prevail in production, which means that if the factor inputs are increased by a certain proportion, output rises by exactly the same proportion. For example, if $Y = 100$ when $K = 20$ and $L = 15$, then $Y = 200$ for $K = 40$, $L = 30$. CRS tells us the impact on Y of a *balanced* change in K and L. Diminishing returns is assumed to hold for *unbalanced* change in factors. If capital per unit of labour (K/L) increases, output per head (Y/L) is assumed to increase at a decreasing rate. CRS is not incompatible with diminishing returns in this sense, as the following production function illustrates.

Let the production function be $Y = 5K^{1/2}L^{1/2}$. This obeys CRS. For $K = 3$, $L = 12$, $Y = 30$ and for $K = 9$, $L = 36$, $Y = 90$. A threefold rise in factor input has led to a threefold rise in Y. Dividing through by L we get per capita output as a function of capital per head.

$Y/L = 5(K/L)^{1/2}$ or $y = 5k^{1/2}$, denoting Y/L by y, K/L by k.

This displays diminishing returns in the sense that a doubling of k will lead to a less than doubling of y. (Check with suitable numbers.) Diminishing returns to factors (not to be confused with returns to scale, which is constant) gives a relationship between y and k of the type shown in Figure 10.1. We call this relation the *per capita production function*.

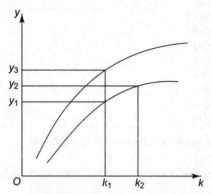

Fig. 10.1   Per Capita Production Function
(before and after Technical Progress)

The curve gets flatter and flatter as k increases. This is due to the operation of diminishing returns as the input of K rises relative to L. Technical progress is captured by a rise in A, which shifts the curve up, because y becomes higher at each level of k.

Two Sources of Growth

Per capita output (or income) of an economy can grow for two reasons:

- Growth of capital stock per worker k. In Figure 10.1, if k rises from k_1 to k_2, y rises from y_1 to y_2. An increase in k is known as an increase in *capital intensity* of production.
- Technical progress or improvement in factor productivity (rise in A). The curve shifts up, so that y rises to y_3 from y_1 even if k stays at k_1.

Steady State (Balanced Growth)

Initially, we assume no change in A, the productivity factor. Change in productivity will be treated later. For simplicity of exposition we also assume (i) the labour force is growing over time at an exogenously given rate n, that is, $\Delta L/L = n$; (ii) $I = sY$; and (iii) a constant fraction d of the existing capital stock depreciates each period, so that the amount of total depreciation in any period is dK. Thus we have

(i) $Y = AF(K, L)$ or $y = Af(k)$

(ii) $\Delta K = I - dK$

(iii) $I = S = sY$

(iv) $\Delta L/L = n$

Equation (ii) states that addition to capital stock equals net investment, which is gross investment minus depreciation.

A *steady state* or *balanced growth* is defined to be a situation where Y, K, and L are growing at the same rate over time. Since L, by assumption, is growing at n, in steady state:

$$\Delta Y/Y = \Delta K/K = \Delta L/L = n \qquad (10.2)$$

Since Y and L are changing at the same rate, Y/L or y is constant. Similarly, k is also constant, as the growth rate of K equals that of L.

Since the growth rate of a ratio is equal to the difference between the growth of the numerator and the denominator, we have:

$$\Delta k/k = \Delta K/K - \Delta L/L = \Delta K/K - n$$
$$= (I - dK)/K - n = I/K - (n+d)$$
$$= sY/K - (n+d)$$

or $\qquad \Delta k = sY/L - (n+d)k = sy - (n+d)k \qquad (10.3)$

The first term on the right-hand side (sy) is the investment per worker and the second term $(n+d)k$ is the gross investment per worker, needed to keep k unchanged, for a labour force growing at n. The excess contributes to the growth of k.

In steady state, k does not change.

$$\Delta k = 0 \text{ or, using equation (10.3), } sy = (n+d)\,k \qquad (10.4)$$

The steady state values of k and y are depicted as k^* and y^* in Figure 10.2.

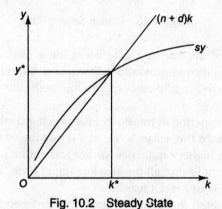

Fig. 10.2   Steady State

Since s is a fraction (say 10 per cent), the sy curve is obtained by scaling down the value of y by 10 per cent for each value of k. To the left of k^*, $sy > (n+d)k$ and, hence, $\Delta k > 0$ by (10.3). So k will increase towards k^*. To the right of k^*, $sy < (n+d)k$ and k will fall in obedience to equation (10.3). Thus k converges to k^* from either direction.

Starting from a value less than k^*, the capital per worker will gradually increase towards k. Output per head will rise towards y^*.

In long-run steady state (balanced growth) without productivity change, Y, K, and L are growing at the same rate n. Capital stock K is growing at n although gross investment is growing at $(n+d)$ because dK is eaten up by depreciation. Since K and L grow at n, Y also grows at n owing to CRS. Capital–labour ratio k and output per worker y are constant.

In steady state, the positive impact of investment on k just balances the negative effects of depreciation and growth of labour force.

Impact of Change in Saving Ratio

Consider a rise in s. This causes the sy curve to shift upwards. The result is an increase in the steady state values of k and y. In Figure 10.3 the equilibrium moves from E_1 to E_2. However, there is no effect on the steady state rate of growth, which remains equal to n (= the growth rate of L). So a higher s improves social welfare by raising output per worker, but has no influence on the long-run rate of growth.

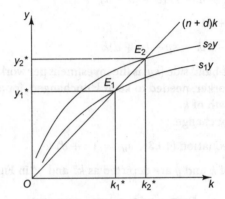

Fig. 10.3   Rise in Saving Rate

The immediate impact of the rise in s is to boost the growth of k (from the relation $\Delta k/k = s(Y/K) - (n + d)$) and this in turn improves the growth of y, but this gradually dies down due to the operation of diminishing returns to additional capital. Ultimately, the growth rate returns to the original value of n.

It should be noted that the period of transition over which growth of y remains higher than n may be quite substantial in length. In this sense, a rise in s is conducive to growth. Also, as noted above, higher s results in *permanently* higher capital per worker and output per worker. However, s cannot be raised indefinitely (100 per cent is after all the absolute upper limit) and, therefore, raising output per head continuously through rise in s is not feasible.

The prediction of the model that long-run growth is independent of saving and investment is considered unsatisfactory by most economists. The theory of endogenous growth, a new approach to the problem of growth developed in the 1980s, restores the positive role of saving. This is discussed below.

Technical Progress and Growth

We have seen that, with A remaining unchanged, the system has a tendency to converge to steady state where per capita income y becomes constant and growth *in per capita terms* comes to a halt. However, if factor productivity or efficiency in input use improves, A will go up and, even with s unchanged, the economy will move to a new steady state with higher k and y. This is shown in Figure 10.4 as a movement from E_1 to E_2.

In the new equilibrium, growth rate is the same as before (equal to n, the rate at which K, L and Y are growing), but k and y are higher due to the rise in A. This can be stated as:

A sustained rise in living standards supported by a sustained rise in output per head needs a sustained improvement in productivity (continuous technical progress).

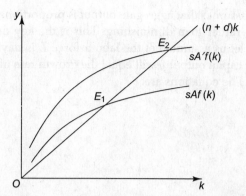

Fig. 10.4 Technical Progress in the Solow Model

Technical progress, captured by the rise in A, has been taken to be *exogenously* given. In reality, technical improvements do not just happen, they require conscious, well-planned effort. The major factors responsible for productivity growth in a modern economy are investment in research and development (R&D) and accumulation of skill through formal education and on-the-job training.

So far, by capital, we have meant *physical* capital—factories, buildings, and machinery. But *human capital* is equally important. Human capital consists of the economically valuable skill and knowledge embodied in the workforce. This is determined basically by levels of formal education and on-the-job experience. Labour's contribution to output depends both on its quantity and quality. The greater the human capital embodied in labour, the better is the quality. The spectacular growth of per capita income of the Asian economies of South Korea, Taiwan, Hong Kong, and Singapore was rendered possible through rapid accumulation of both physical and human capital.

On-the-job experience of workers and managers is an important source of improvement in technical knowledge. Practice sharpens skills and suggests new ideas for innovation. This phenomenon of *learning by doing* is encapsulated in the learning curve, which shows an inverse relation between average cost of production and cumulative output since the beginning of production. Cumulative output is a good index of the stock of accumulated experience. Major industries in which the learning curve is important include shipbuilding, aircrafts, and semiconductors. The empirically observed 80 per cent learning phenomenon suggests that average cost will fall by 20 per cent (due to rise in labour productivity) if total cumulative production doubles.

The modern approach to economic growth that does not take productivity growth as exogenously given, but instead tries to account for it within the model is known as *endogenous growth theory*.

Endogenous Growth

The analysis of growth, discussed in the previous section, yielded the result that, without exogenous productivity growth, the long-run (steady state) growth rate cannot be affected by changes in saving or investment. Endogenous growth theory makes one crucial departure from the standard assumptions and arrives at a different result.

This *new growth theory* emphasizes the role of investment in physical capital in stimulating the growth of human capital. As new factories are built and new machines put into use, more resources are devoted to schooling, health care, on-the-job training, and R&D. Workers learn new techniques and their knowledge becomes embodied in human capital. As the society's stock of human capital improves, this tends to offset the fall in the marginal product of physical capital. The simplest version of endogenous growth theory assumes that aggregate output is proportional to K, so that the marginal product of capital is constant, rather than diminishing. This is the key departure from the standard growth model. For simplicity, let us assume that the labour force L is staying constant. In this case of fixed L, the growth rate of per capita output y will equal the growth rate of output $\dot{Y}$ (= growth rate of K as Y is proportional to K). The equations are:

(i) $Y = AK$

(ii) $S = sY$

(iii) $\Delta K = I - dK$

(iv) $S = I$

Simple manipulation yields

$$\Delta K/K = \Delta Y/Y = sA - d. \tag{10.5}$$

Equation 10.5 says that, under endogenous growth, the economy's growth rate depends positively on the saving rate. This is in contrast to the earlier model where the long-run growth was independent of s. Higher saving helps growth by stimulating investment in physical capital which promotes human capital formation in the society. Improvement in human capital boosts the productivity of physical capital. Growth of productivity is not something accidental or purely exogenous, it is brought about by greater investment in human capital and R&D. National governments can play a critical role in the process of development if, by choosing the right mix of policies, they can promote saving, investment and human capital formation.

TOTAL FACTOR PRODUCTIVITY

Total Factor Productivity (TFP) refers to the part of growth in total output that is not accounted for by growth in the use of inputs. It is thus a measure of the overall efficiency of input use in the economy. The standard formula used is:

$$\text{Growth of TFP} = g_Y - (\theta g_L + (1 - \theta)g_K) \tag{10.6}$$

where θ and $(1 - \theta)$ are the estimated shares of L and K in national income. The increase in output that can be attributed to growth of the labour force is θg_L and the increase attributable to capital accumulation is $(1 - \theta) g_K$. The excess of actual growth in output over the combined contributions of labour and capital is the measure of technological progress or improvement in overall productivity of factors. For example, if the shares are 75 per cent and 25 per cent, L and K grow at 20 per cent and 8 per cent, respectively, while GDP grows at 20 per cent, then TFP grows at 3 per cent.

Growth in TFP is different from growth in labour productivity or capital productivity, which equal $(g_Y - g_L)$ and $(g_Y - g_K)$, respectively. Attempts to measure TFP in Indian industry in the post-reform years do not reveal any significant improvement.

Consumption in Steady State and the Golden Rule

Since capital per worker is constant in steady state, total capital stock grows at the same rate as the labour force, that is at rate n. To achieve this, gross investment must be $(n + d)K$, so that, when depreciation dK is subtracted, net addition to K is nK. Since consumption is output less gross investment (= saving), we have in steady state

$$C = Y - (n + d)K \text{ or } c = y - (n + d)k = f(k) - (n + d)k \tag{10.7}$$

Equation (10.7) shows that a change in steady state k has two opposing pulls on consumption per worker. An increase in k raises output per worker in steady sate $f(k)$. On the negative side, it also raises the amount of output per worker that must be used for gross investment, $(n+d)k$. This lowers the amount available for consumption.

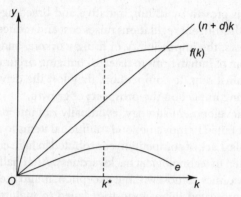

Fig. 10.5   Golden Rule Equilibrium

Figure 10.5 explicitly shows the relation between per capita consumption c and capital labour ratio k in steady state. The curve is obtained by plotting the vertical difference between $f(k)$ and $(n+d)k$. The value of k that maximizes c in steady state is called the *Golden Rule—capital–labour ratio*. It is given by the point where the slope of the $f(k)$ curve equals $(n+d)$. The Golden Rule steady state attains maximum long-run social welfare by maximizing per capita consumption of the citizens.

ECONOMIC REFORM AND GROWTH

Right-wing social scientists and policymakers never tire of insisting that government intervention in economic activities is harmful for growth. According to the supply-side economists, the sharp downturn of the US economy during the 1980s was due in large part to the proliferation of government regulations of business. The blame for the lacklustre performance of the European economies over the last decade (i.e., 1990s) has likewise been laid at the door of excessive government interference.

In the years following the Second World War, most LDCs, that had recently won independence from foreign rule were bent on achieving rapid economic growth through a process of careful economic planning. They were inspired by the success story of the USSR. It was believed that direct control of important sectors would facilitate macroeconomic management of the economy. State intervention was also deemed necessary to ensure an equitable distribution of income and wealth in a growing society.

In the sphere of foreign commerce in the pre-independence era, all the colonies were suppliers of raw materials to the industrialized countries. After independence, they naturally wanted to change this status by turning themselves into industrial powers as quickly as possible. In order to reduce the dependence on 'unequal trade', a policy of import substituting industrialization was universally adopted. To nurture the development of indigenous industry, numerous restrictions were imposed on manufacturing imports from foreign sources. This was an application of the traditional infant industry argument for trade protection. Doors were shut on private foreign capital as it had colonial overtones. In India, before the reforms, both the domestic and the foreign trade sectors were under pervasive government control.

Economic planning in India has produced many positive results. It has contributed to the building up of technological capabilities from a very narrow base and self-sufficiency has been achieved on many fronts. The record is far better than that of many countries of Africa and Latin America. But it also cannot be denied that the associated controls have been responsible for very serious negative results.

Excessive regulation harms growth by stifling initiative and breeding inefficiency and corruption on a wide scale. Complying with stringent regulations raises cost and reduces profitability. The licensing system, the minimum wage laws, the impossibility of firing workers, and myriad other rigidities had drastically restricted the freedom of Indian firms to react to changing circumstances. Assured of a captive domestic market sheltered against outside competition, they lost the drive to improve efficiency and quality. All this had a devastating impact on the prospects of growth.

Import substitution, as a development strategy, eventually ran into problems as opportunities for substitution were exhausted. It failed to move beyond traditional items to more sophisticated products like computers or precision tools. Lack of competition contributed to high costs and low quality. Absence of contact with foreign capital led to technological backwardness. After half a century of comprehensive planning, the Third World economies, almost without exception, found themselves mired in stagnation, sloth, and slack. Most of the protected infant industries failed to mature and contribute to national development.

After the collapse of the USSR and its eastern satellites, a wave of restructuring and reform began sweeping the world. The process is still continuing. In country after country, regulatory regimes were dismantled, restrictions on foreign capital inflow were lifted, and inward orientation was replaced by export promotion. The four Asian economies—Hong Kong, Singapore, South Korea, and Taiwan—became the role models of the new era. Their spectacular growth performance is generally attributed to the strategy of export orientation.

The Asian Tigers had successfully exploited existing export opportunities and created quite a few on their own initiative. Relying on the availability of cheap (but educated) local labour, they had started by specializing in the export of labour-intensive goods like textiles, apparel, shoes, and light electronics, but rapidly moved on to more sophisticated products. They were very successful in catching up with their more affluent trading partners within a relatively short time.

That trade liberalization and export orientation played a crucial role in the success story of the Asian Tigers is undeniable. The verdict, however, is ambiguous in respect of the role of the government. No clear lesson emerges. Hong Kong essentially relied on the operation of unfettered market forces, but South Korea and Singapore carefully regulated international trade and intervened extensively to foster the growth of particular industries through subsidies and directed credit programmes. There can be little doubt that what matters for growth is the *effectiveness* of regulations, rather than the existence of regulations as such. The champions of free markets would like to abolish all regulations lock, stock, and barrel. This, like all extreme positions, is wrong. What the developing world needs is less, but more effective, government intervention. The aim should be to get rid of clumsy and wasteful regulation and to make necessary regulation more efficient and flexible.

The *quality of governance* is now recognized as the key factor in explaining the economic, performance of nations. An important study by the economist, Robert Barro, of around 100 countries during 1960–90 has concluded that growth is stimulated by better schooling and life expectancy, lower fertility, lower government consumption, and better maintenance of the rule of law. Good institutions are the best capital that a society can have and the state should concentrate on the difficult task of creating and sustaining them.

India's growth record improved after the initiation of wide ranging reforms in 1991. For three years during 1994–7 there was a boom, with average annual growth of 7.5 per cent in real terms. But, it has decelerated since then and has remained between 5 and 6 per cent. This demonstrates that although a reduction in cumbersome government intervention and greater openness to foreign trade can temporarily help matters, sustained prosperity is impossible without a sustained upward trend in overall efficiency. That calls for continuous upgradation of infrastructure, both physical and social, higher rate of human capital formation, lower incidence of corruption, and fiscal consolidation at the central and state levels. All the high growth Asian economies not only had mostly outward-oriented trade policies, but had good scores on each of these counts. Despite some improvement in recent years, India's performance continues to be poor in respect of almost all the critical ingredients identified by Barro. The so-called second generation reforms should concentrate on these.

GROWTH, GLOBALIZATION, AND THE ENVIRONMENT

In the early stages of economic growth, increase in GDP involves a shift of activities from agriculture to manufacturing, which causes the pollution level to rise. At the same time environmental regulation is lax because the primary concern of the government at this stage is to bring about a rise in per capita output. Environmental quality deteriorates, as a result. Gradually, with further growth in income, composition of output shifts in favour of services which do not contribute much to pollution. At the same time, environmental consciousness grows and the government begins to attach much more importance to the preservation of natural resources and natural beauty. Affluence enables consumers to pay higher prices for products that meet higher environmental standards, and this, in turn, makes the adoption of more expensive, environment-friendly technology by producers possible. All these factors create a U-shaped relation between GDP growth and the quality of the environment.

However, even in the developed countries, there is a growing realization that a high level of GDP may not be sustainable in the long-run unless drastic measures are taken to bring down the current rate of consumption of exhaustible resources and the attendant destruction of natural capital.

Proponents of globalization have great faith in the power of export-led growth to pull the developing countries out of poverty and stagnation. But this may add seriously to environmental degradation in countries specializing in natural resource-intensive activities like mining, forestry, fishing, and wood products. The lowering of barriers to foreign investment and trade has enabled MNCs to expand their operations all around the world. Since profit is the primary objective and host-country regulatory standards are rather lax, there is a real danger that export production controlled by MNCs may have very serious environmental side effects.

Higher growth of GDP should enable governments to raise resources through taxation and other means for the abatement of pollution and the control of other harmful effects. But this will take time and governments in the poor countries may have other, more pressing, priorities for the use of their tax revenue.

Summary

- The theory of growth tries to isolate the factors that determine the long-run trend growth of an economy. Short-run fluctuations around the trend are ignored.
- For constant saving ratio (s) and ICOR (v) the growth rate is s/v.

- In the Solow model two sources of growth of per capita income are identified: (i) increase in capital–labour ratio and (ii) technological improvement. Increase in saving ratio raises the capital–labour ratio and output per head in steady state but has no effect on the long-run growth of output. Continuous technical progress is necessary for sustained rise in output per head.

- In endogenous growth theory, technological progress, driven by investment in human capital formation and R&D, offsets diminishing returns to physical capital. A rise in the saving ratio has a positive impact on long-run growth.

- Total factor productivity is a measure of technical progress. It is obtained by subtracting the sum of weighted growth in factor inputs from growth in output. The weights are the respective factor shares in total income.

- At the Golden Rule steady state, per capita consumption is maximum.

- Economic reform contributes to growth by improving the quality of governance and opening up the economy to foreign competition.

- Growth and globalization may have a harmful impact on the environment.

Exercise

1. What is a production function? State some of its major properties. How does it differ from the per capita production function?

2. Use numerical values to illustrate why s/v gives the growth rate of an economy.

3. What is meant by steady state? Explain the condition that must hold in a steady state in the Solow model.

4. What will be the impact of changes in n and d (consider the cases separately) on per capita output and the growth rate in long-run equilibrium in the Solow model? Draw graphs to illustrate.

5. Suppose that the level of technology jumps to a higher level and stays constant thereafter. What will be the effect on (i) output per head with capital–labour ratio constant and (ii) output per head and capital–labour ratio in new long-run equilibrium?

6. According to Solow's growth model, what should be the correlation between a nation's saving/investment ratio and its steady state growth in per capita terms? Is this consistent with the real world? Explain your answer.

7. An economy has the per capita production function $y = k^{1/2}$. Find the balanced growth value of k, given that the saving rate is 16 per cent, depreciation rate is 10 per cent, and population growth is zero.

8. 'Only steady technical progress can explain persistently rising living standards.' Explain, using the analytical apparatus developed in the chapter.

9. 'There is one saving rate that is best in the sense of maximizing per capita consumption in steady state.' Explain and use a graph to illustrate. How will this rate change if there is an increase in the rate of growth of the labour force?

10. Outline the basic differences between the theories of exogenous and endogenous growth. What type of government policy is recommended for development in the latter approach?

11. Comment on India's growth performance after economic reforms.

11. Special Topics

The monetarists were the first to put up a serious challenge to the Keynesian demand-side approach to macroeconomics. They had faith in the inherently self-correcting attributes of a free market economy and were against any discretionary intervention by the state. They were in favour of rules rather than discretion in economic policy. *New classical economics,* which emerged in the 1970s under the leadership of Robert Lucas, pushed the monetarist critique to its limit and emphatically declared the demise of the 'fundamentally flawed' Keynesian economics. They based their criticism on a rigorous theoretical model in which the hypothesis of rational expectations played a central role. The major charge levelled against the Keynesian approach was that it lacks micro foundations, in the sense that some of the crucial assumptions were not consistent with the behaviour of optimizing agents. Why, for example, should wages be inflexible when there is unemployment? In microeconomics, price falls in a situation of excess supply (supply exceeding demand). Why should the labour market be an exception?

In this chapter, we present a broadbrush survey of the major developments in modern macroeconomics. This is a very hotly contested terrain and our discussion highlights only the major points without doing justice to the nuances of the views of the different schools.

RATIONAL EXPECTATIONS AND POLICY INEFFECTIVENESS

As we have seen in Chapter 9, 'The problem of Inflation', the monetarists claimed that, once expectational factors are brought into the analysis, the Phillips Curve tends to become vertical in the long run. Policymakers can exploit the trade-off between inflation and unemployment only in the short-run when expectations have not yet fully adjusted to the new equilibrium values. A negatively sloped Phillips Curve exists only because misperception about the real wage can arise, making temporary deviation from full equilibrium possible.

For the new classicals, rational agents never make *systematic* mistakes and, therefore, the long-run equilibrium position is always achieved and sustained, except for random (non-systematic) errors. Government intervention in the form of fiscal or monetary action is powerless to affect the economy even in the short-run. This very strong conclusion is the result of two assumptions:

- All prices, including wages, are fully flexible. Full employment of labour is maintained all the time.
- Economic agents are rational, in the sense that they intelligently pursue their self-interest. They have *rational expectations* and seek to use all available information, including both past economic behaviour and expected future economic policy, when forming expectations of economic variables. In particular, they are aware of the basic relationships that determine the values of the relevant variables and expect the values that are generated by the model. For example, if the variable in question is the price level, the agents use their information about *AD* and *AS* factors to figure out the value at which the two will be equal and their expected value coincides with this particular value. Expectations of rational (intelligent and well-informed) agents are not exogenously determined, they are consistent with the predictions of the very model which is being

used to analyse the macrobehaviour of the system in which the agents are the actors. As John Muth, the originator of the idea of rational expectations, put it in his important article of 1961, 'Expectations, since they are informed predictions of future events, are essentially the same as the predictions of the relevant economic theory.'

To explore the policy implications of new classical economics, let us consider a one-time increase in the money stock. Under rational expectations, it is of crucial importance whether the policy change was *anticipated* (expected) or *unanticipated* (unexpected). Anticipated and unanticipated policy changes have radically different effects.

Rational agents know that a rise in money supply leads to an increase in AD and the price level. So, if the rise in money stock is fully anticipated, labour suppliers will adjust their money wage in equal proportion and, as a result, there will be an offsetting shift in the AS curve and real output, Y, will stay unchanged. This is illustrated in Figure 11.1.

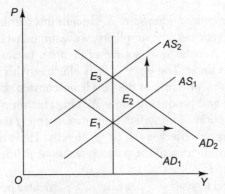

Fig. 11.1   Policy Neutrality under Rational Expectations

The AD curve shifts to AD_2 after the rise in money stock. Without any reaction on the supply side, the equilibrium will be at E_2 with a higher P and Y. But under rational expectations, the revision in wage claims would shift the AS up to AS_2 and the equilibrium will shift to E_3. When dealing with expectations, monetarists and Keynesians tend to assume that expectations are revised gradually with time lag, and until full adjustment is achieved, the economy can stay at E_2 where Y is higher (unemployment lower) compared to E_1. Under rational expectations, there is no perception or adjustment lag and the system jumps immediately from E_1 to E_2. There is no distinction between the short-run when expectations are unchanged and the long-run when they have fully adjusted. Money is neutral (cannot affect Y) even in the short-run. Likewise, any other anticipated demand-side policy would have left Y unchanged. This view was enshrined in the celebrated *policy ineffectiveness proposition.*

The Policy Ineffectiveness Proposition

If expectations are rational, anticipated changes in aggregate demand policy will be powerless to influence real output even in the short-run.

Results would have been different if the rise in money stock was *not anticipated.* In this case, workers do not expect the aggregate price level to change, and labour supply decision is not revised. With the AS curve staying unchanged, the shift of AD caused by monetary expansion will boost Y. Thus, the effect of unanticipated change in AD does not differ from that in the Keynesian framework.

The policy effectiveness, however, will vanish in the long-run, as workers learn about the policy change and revise their price forecast upwards. Output and employment will be back to their initial levels as in the monetarist analysis of the Phillips Curve.

SELLERS' MISPERCEPTION AND NON-NEUTRALITY OF MONEY

The strong conclusion of the new classicals that money is neutral in the short-run has not found empirical support. It has been observed that in many countries announced (and, hence, fully anticipated) monetary policy changes have been followed by changes in real output and employment.

For money to be non-neutral, the AS must not be vertical. If the assumption of perfect information is relaxed, it is possible to have an upward sloping supply curve in the new classical framework. The key assumption is that producers may misperceive changes in the aggregate price level and thus may be temporarily fooled into supplying more. According to the *misperceptions hypothesis*—rigorously formulated by Robert Lucas—when P rises above its expected value P^e, aggregate output is higher than its full employment level.

Consider the seller of a particular commodity X. He sells this particular commodity, but consumes a much larger set of goods and services. For simplicity, we assume that his own labour is the only input of production and that selling X is his only source of income. Let us denote the price of X by P_1. The general price level is P, as usual. The price of X is effectively his nominal wage and (P_1/P), the relative price of X, his real wage in terms of the goods he consumes. When the relative price rises, he responds by working more and producing more X. Thus, his supply decision hinges crucially on P_1/P. At this point the assumption of imperfect information enters the picture. The seller knows P_1 perfectly because, as the seller, he observes the price directly. He is not so well-informed about the general price level P. He has some idea of the possible value of P (the expected value P^e) and takes supply decisions on the basis of P_1/P^e.

Suppose that P_1 is observed to rise by 5 per cent in a particular period. The seller's response will depend on his expectation about the behaviour of the general price level. If he expected P also to rise by 5 per cent, that is, the rise in P^e also was 5 per cent, he will argue that the observed rise in P_1 is due to general inflation and relative price of X has not changed. So his output will not change. On the other hand, if his expected inflation (rise in P^e) was less than 5 per cent, say, 3 per cent, then the observed rise in P_1 of 5 per cent will signal a rise in the relative price of X to him and output will be raised. Here, the source of extra supply is the miscalculation or misperception on the part of the seller. His expected inflation fell short of the actual rise in the price of X.

The same logic applies to all sellers in the economy. An actual rise in the general price level, greater than the expected rise, will lead each seller to infer a rise in the relative price of his product and he will supply more. Total supply will, therefore, increase.

We can summarize the misperceptions theory as:

Aggregate supply depends on the actual price level compared to the expected price level. If the actual P exceeds (falls short of) the expected P^e, producers mistakenly think that the relative prices of their own products have increased (decreased) and this induces them to supply more (less).

This type of behaviour is represented by the equation:

$$Y = Y^* + a(P - P^e), a > 0 \tag{11.1}$$

Equation (11.1), gives the AS curve, often called the Lucas supply curve. It says that output Y will temporarily exceed full employment output when P exceeds P^e. Graphically, it gives an upward sloping short-run AS curve. Money is non-neutral because of the upward slope.

In the long run rational agents do not suffer from misperception ($P = P^e$), and the AS is vertical at the full employment level. Money is neutral once again.

KEYNESIAN COUNTER CRITIQUE

While admitting the validity of the point that the role of expectations and the response of rational agents to economic policy should be treated more carefully and that more attention should be devoted to making macro more consistent with micro, the Keynesians do not believe that new classicals have succeeded in destroying the case for activist stabilization policy. Their criticism is built around three main points:

- The hypothesis of rational expectations is too demanding. It fails the realism test by assuming that economic agents have perfect ability to process all available information to make sophisticated forecasts. It also ignores the costs of gathering and processing information. If such costs are high, rational agents may find it worthwhile to use limited information for forming expectations and forecast errors may be large in consequence.

- The economic system is too complicated for individual agents to know accurately the relationships that determine the values of the major macro variables. The hypothesis that agents do not make systematic errors in estimation or prediction may be broadly true in the long-run, but is not realistic in the short-run.

- Prices in reality are not fully flexible and, as a result, markets do not clear continuously. The new Keynesians offer several economic explanations (micro foundations) for the rigidity of prices of commodities or of labour. Rigidity of product prices may be due to menu costs of adjustment in a monopolistic market and real wages may not fall even in the presence of unemployment due to efficiency wage considerations (see the discussion in Chapter 8). Besides, if nominal wages are contractually fixed, as they usually are in a modern industrial economy, they will stay fixed for the duration of the contract and will not respond to changing labour market conditions. Wages are not constantly changing to find their market-clearing levels in competitive labour markets. Wage contracts are deliberately designed to incorporate long-term factors that influence the relationship between the employer and employees of a business organization.

Absence of rational expectations and rigidity of prices prevent the AS curve from being vertical in the short-medium run and aggregate demand management retains its usefulness as an instrument for influencing the economy.

REAL BUSINESS CYCLE THEORY

In Keynesian policy analysis, business cycles (periodic fluctuations in output and employment) are primarily caused by AD shocks, or shifting IS or LM curves. Cycles are undesirable because they cause human suffering by creating unemployment or inflation. Real business cycle theory emphasizes, instead, the role of workers' incentive to work in causing fluctuations in output. The main driving force is the *intertemporal substitution of labour*. Being the outcome of voluntary choice by workers, business cycles have no negative welfare implications and there is no justification for stabilization policy.

Workers are rational optimizers, in the sense that they choose the most desirable hours of work (labour supply) and hours of leisure by solving an intertemporal maximization problem. For simplicity, let us assume that there are only two periods in the working life of Mr Sen. The current wage rate is w_1 and the expected future wage is w_2. The (real) rate of interest is r. Since income earned in the first period can be saved to earn interest, one rupee in the second period is worth only $(1/1 + r)$ in the first. The intertemporal relative wage is given by the ratio of w_1 to $(w_2/1 + r)$ or $(1 + r)w_1/w_2$.

Mr Sen's decision about when to work and when to enjoy leisure depends crucially on his preference between consumption and leisure and this relative wage. Working in the first period becomes more attractive if this ratio becomes higher, which may happen if (i) w_1 goes up and/or (ii) r goes up. This provides the clue to business cycles. Aggregate economic shocks that cause the interest rate to rise or the wage to be temporarily high, stimulate more work effort, and output and employment go up, as a result. Low employment during recessions is not involuntary unemployment, it merely reflects the equilibrium response of Mr Sen to changing economic conditions. His cost–benefit calculation is telling him (and others like him) to enjoy leisure now and work harder in future. The labour market is in equilibrium all the time, fluctuations in output are being caused by workers' reallocation of work effort in response to changing relative wages.

Monetary policy can influence the behaviour of the real economy by changing the real interest rate. Fiscal policy can be effective not by means of an impact on aggregate demand but via *supply-side effects*. Changes in tax rates on labour income or interest income will produce changes in the labour supply decisions of optimizing agents.

Keynesians do not accept this view of business cycles. They point out that to explain real world output fluctuations solely in terms of work incentives requires implausibly high responsiveness of labour supply to changes in real wages. Most empirical studies reveal a relatively low value of elasticity of labour supply. Moreover, owing to sluggish adjustment in wages, the labour market is not in equilibrium all the time.

The view of the real business cycle theorists, that fiscal action can be effective only via supply-side effects, is in perfect accord with the view of a school of economists who champion what is known as supply-side economics.

SUPPLY-SIDE ECONOMICS

This body of thought won widespread *political* support during the late 1980s and 1990s. We have already pointed out (see Chapter 3) that a limitation of the Keynesian approach is its exclusive emphasis on demand management to the exclusion of supply-side considerations. Supply-side economics goes to the other extreme of denying any role to demand management whatsoever. It shares this bias with the new classical approach.

Supply-siders maintain that through a proliferation of bureaucracy, red tapism, and political patronage, governments have a tendency to become deeply entrenched sources of inefficiency and corruption and a burden on the backs of the people. Private-sector initiative is the motor force of economic growth. The full potential of this force cannot be realized unless the distortionary effects of taxes and subsidies and other types of state intervention are removed or minimized. After the collapse of the USSR, this view gained formidable force and provided ideological foundation to the sweeping programmes of deregulation and economic reform that were initiated in a large number of countries across the globe.

On the fiscal front, the Laffer Curve is used to advocate reduction in taxation. Tax cuts stimulate the economy by improving the incentive to work and to invest. Their role in stimulating AD, emphasized by Keynes, is downplayed. The Laffer Curve represents a hill-shaped relation between total tax revenue and the tax rate.

Total tax revenue is the product of the tax rate and the tax base (value of income). Revenue is obviously low when the rate is low. Not so obviously, it is also low when the tax rate is very high. The

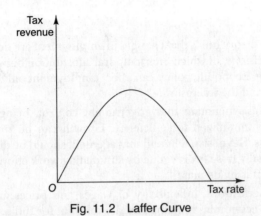

Fig. 11.2   Laffer Curve

reason is that a very high tax rate kills off the incentive to work or to invest and the level of income falls to a low value. The interesting policy conclusion is that when the tax rate is high, moving to a lower one would actually raise national income and tax revenue and the budget deficit will decline.

While the argument sounds logical, the chief difficulty is that the empirical evidence of labour supply response to tax cuts is not strong enough. And it is by no means easy to verify whether a country has really crossed the optimum. In the USA, the Reagan administration's (1981–8) policy experiments with tax cut ended up adding to the budget deficit as predicted by the followers of Keynes.

Supply-side economics, strongly promoted by the IMF and the World Bank, did play a major role in the reformulation of economic policy in India after the introduction of reforms in 1991. But the presence of excess capacity, particularly in the manufacturing sector, chiefly due to lack of adequate demand, is also a prominent feature of the Indian economy. Besides, capital markets are imperfect (implying the existence of borrowing constraints for a significant section of the population) and prices of many commodities and wages of different types of labour show a high degree of inflexibility. This means that Keynesian economics still retains its relevance for India. But it has to be liberally supplemented by relevant ideas borrowed from the other schools as and when the context demands.

Summary

- New classicals criticized Keynesian macroeconomics for lack of micro foundations.
- On the basis of rational expectations, new classicals enunciated the policy ineffectiveness proposition: Anticipated policy change cannot affect output or employment. Money is neutral even in the short-run.
- Seller's misperception of relative price may produce an upward-sloping AS curve and in that case money will be non-neutral in the short-run. In the long-run, there is no misperception and AS is vertical.
- Keynesian counter argument emphasizes the unrealism of rational expectations and offers efficiency wage hypothesis and menu costs of adjustment to justify the assumption of less than complete flexibility in wages and prices.

- Real Business Cycle theory holds that changes in employment are due to voluntary changes in labour supply decisions, in which intertemporal substitution between labour and leisure plays the crucial role. Economic policy can affect employment only through labour supply by changing wages and the interest rate.

- Supply-side economists maintain that government control, being a burden on private initiative, should be minimized for efficiency. Growth can be stimulated only through supply-side measures. Keynesian demand management should be discontinued. Reduction in taxation may actually raise tax revenue by stimulating work effort sufficiently. Empirical support for this claim is inadequate.

- Due to market imperfections, inflexibility of wages and prices and presence of excess capacity, Keynesian economics remains broadly relevant for India.

Glossary

Accelerator theory
Theory of business investment that relates planned investment to the rate of change of output. The flexible accelerator takes into account cost of adjusting the capital stock.

Aggregate demand
In the Keynesian model with fixed prices it is the sum of planned demand for an economy's output coming from four sources: households, firms, government, and foreign buyers. In the variable price model, it represents the relation between values of P and Y that maintain equilibrium in the goods and asset markets.

Aggregate demand shock
Shocks to an economy that shift the AD curve by shifting the IS or LM curves. Examples: change in government expenditure, increase or decrease in money supply.

Aggregate production function
The technological relation between aggregate output and the inputs (usually labour and capital) used in production.

Aggregate price level
The average price of goods and services in an economy, usually captured by some index.

Aggregate supply
The relation between P and the planned output Y derived from equilibrium in the labour market.

Aggregate supply shock
Shocks to an economy that shift the AS curve by affecting the production function or by changing the prices of inputs. Examples: increase in petroleum price, a drought, improvement in factor productivity due to better managerial practice.

Automatic stabilizer
The change in taxes and transfer payments that follow any change in national income Y without any deliberate policy change. When Y falls, under given tax and spending rules, budget deficit increases and this in turn tends to stabilize output by stimulating demand.

Autonomous spending
The part of planned demand for goods that does not depend on current income.

Average propensity to consume
The ratio of consumption to income (C/Y).

Balance of payments
A set of accounts summarizing an economy's transactions with the rest of the world. It consists of the current account which records transactions in currently produced goods and services and the capital account that records transactions in physical and financial assets. Purchase of Indian assets by foreigners is a capital inflow into India and purchase of foreign assets by Indians is a capital outflow from India.

Balance of payments crisis	Foreign exchange crisis stemming from problems in a country's balance of payments.
Bank reserves	Reserves that commercial banks have to maintain at the central bank at zero interest. It is usually set at a certain percentage of total deposits.
Barter	Direct exchange of goods for other goods without the use of money.
Bond	A financial asset promising a stream of payments over a specified period.
Bond rating	Assessment of a bond based on its default risk.
Bracket creep	In a situation of general inflation a person moves into a higher tax bracket and pays more tax just because his money income, and not necessarily real income, is higher.
Budget deficit	Excess of government expenditure over government revenue. Revenue deficit is the excess of revenue expenditure over revenue receipts. Primary deficit is the excess of expenditure excluding interest payment (non-interest expenditure) over receipts. Fiscal deficit is the excess of expenditure over receipts excluding government borrowing.
Business cycles	Short-term fluctuations in national income around its long-term trend.
Call money rate	The call money market is an interbank market for overnight loans. Once every fortnight, on a 'reporting Friday' banks have to satisfy reserve requirements which necessitates borrowing by deficit banks from surplus banks with excess reserves at the call money rate of interest. This rate is very volatile.
Capital account	See balance of payments.
Capital account convertibility	Absence of restrictions on the use and availability of a currency for buying and selling international assets. Unlike the current account, the rupee is not fully convertible on the capital account yet. The Tarapore Committee set up by the GOI specified three crucial preconditions for capital convertibility: (i) reduction in fiscal deficit relative to GDP; (ii) control of inflation; and (iii) strengthening of the financial sector. Of these, fiscal consolidation is way off the mark, actual inflation is close to the target and financial reform is still in progress and far from being comprehensive. So irrespective of the current stock of foreign exchange reserves, controls on capital transactions should not be hastily removed.
Capital accumulation	Growth in the stock of plants and productive equipment.
Capital controls	Restrictions on the holding of foreign assets by domestic residents and on the holding of domestic assets by foreigners. Capital controls have been substantially abolished in India in recent years.
Capital gain	Rise in the market value of an asset over its original price. The gain is realized at the time of sale.
Capital inflow, capital outflow	Borrowing from foreigners (foreigners acquiring domestic assets-surplus in capital account) is capital inflow. Lending abroad (residents acquiring foreign assets-deficit in capital account) is capital outflow.
Capital mobility	A situation in which foreigners can purchase Indian assets without difficulty and Indians can easily purchase foreign assets.
Cash reserve ratio	The fraction of total deposits of commercial banks that must be kept as reserves with the central bank.

Constant returns to scale	A proportional change in the level of all inputs leads to the same proportional change in output.
Consumer price index	It measures the retail prices of a fixed basket of goods and services purchased by households. In India three different indices are calculated for three different groups: industrial workers (IW), agricultural labourers (AL), and urban non-manual employees (UNME).
Consumption	Spending by households on goods and services.
Consumption function	A relationship between consumption and its determinants. In Keynesian analysis the chief determinant is disposable income. In permanent income theory it is permanent or lifetime income.
Constant money growth rule	Policy rule advocated by monetarists under which the central bank keeps the money supply growing at a pre-announced constant rate.
Convertible currency	A currency that can be freely traded for other currencies. Indian rupee is almost convertible now.
Cost push inflation	Rise in prices caused by increase in prices of labour and other inputs.
Crawling peg	Exchange rate system in which the exchange rate is allowed to move in line with the excess of domestic over foreign inflation. The purpose is to keep the real exchange rate stable.
Credibility	The degree to which market participants believe that an announced policy will indeed be carried through.
Credit rationing	A situation where a lender restricts the amount of loans granted to less than the amount sought even when the borrower is willing to pay the interest charged. Such rationing is a feature of an imperfect capital market.
Crowding out	The situation in which an increase in government spending fails to boost output because of an offsetting change in private spending. The effect usually operates through a rise in the rate of interest which depresses private investment spending. Crowding out may be partial or total.
Current account	See balance of payments.
Cyclically adjusted deficit (structural deficit)	What the budget deficit would be if output were at the full employment level. It represents the fiscal stance of the government.
Cyclical unemployment	Unemployment caused by business cycles, going down in booms and going up in recessions.
Default risk	Risk that the borrower (issuer of a bond) will not pay interest or the full amount promised when the bond matures.
Deficit finance	Budget deficit met by borrowing from the central bank. This adds to the money supply by raising the monetary base. As an important component of policy reform in India, GOI can no longer borrow from the RBI to meet its budget deficit. Also known as debt monetization or monetized debt.
Deflation	Falling prices, opposite of inflation.
Demand for money (real balance)	The volume of money in real terms that people want to hold in their portfolio.
Demand pull inflation	Rise in prices caused by increase in demand.
Depreciation	(a) Portion of the capital stock that wears out each year and (b) fall in the value of a currency in terms of another currency.

Devaluation	A policy induced increase in the exchange rate in a fixed exchange system.
Disposable income	The income the consumers have after paying taxes and receiving transfers.
Effective demand	Same as aggregate demand.
Effective exchange rate	The exchange rate between a country and its trade partners, computed as a trade share weighted average of bilateral exchange rates.
Efficiency wage	Profit maximizing firms pay a real wage higher than the level that would clear the labour market because workers exert more effort when they get a higher real wage. New Keynesians use the concept to explain real wage rigidity.
Endogenous growth theory	A branch of growth theory that explains productivity growth through investment in human capital. Also known as new growth theory.
Equation of exchange	$MV = PY$, where M is the quantity of money, V is velocity of circulation; P is the price level and Y the level of income. Under the assumption of constant V, this forms the basis of the tight link between M and PY emphasized by the Monetarists. Also known as the quantity equation.
Exchange rate	The price of one national currency in terms of another. Also known as the nominal exchange rate. It is usually expressed as the number of units of home currency per unit of a foreign currency. Rise (fall) in the exchange rate is depreciation (appreciation) of the home currency. In the fixed exchange system exchange rates are set at officially determined levels and changed infrequently only as part of exchange rate policy. In the flexible (floating) exchange system the exchange rate is determined in the market for foreign exchange without government intervention.
Expansionary policy	Monetary or fiscal policy that stimulates aggregate demand.
Expectations augmented Phillips curve	A modification of the standard Phillips Curve that recognizes the role of expected inflation as a determinant of actual inflation.
Fiscal consolidation	Move towards balanced budget through reduction in budget deficit.
Fiscal policy	Policy consisting of changes in the level and composition of government expenditure and taxation.
Fisher effect	The proposition that in the long run an increase in expected inflation causes an equal increase in the nominal rate of interest, leaving the real interest rate unchanged.
Flexible accelerator	See accelerator theory.
Flight from money	A situation in which money changes hand very quickly because nobody wants to hold an asset that is losing purchasing power very fast due to rapidly rising prices. Velocity of money increases continuously.
Flow variable	A variable that is measured per unit of time. Examples: GNP, consumption, saving, investment.
Foreign direct investment	Creation or extension of operating control over productive capacities in foreign countries.
Frictional unemployment	Unemployment resulting from workers 'search for suitable jobs and firms' search for suitable workers.
Foreign exchange reserves	Foreign assets held by the central bank.
Full employment output	The volume of output the firms supply after wages and prices have fully adjusted to their equilibrium values.

GDP	The value of final goods and services produced within a nation's geographical boundary in a year.
GDP deflator	The ratio of nominal GDP to real GDP, a measure of the overall price level.
GNP	The value of final goods and services produced by domestically owned factors of production in a year.
Golden rule capital labour ratio	The level of capital labour ratio that maximizes per capita consumption in steady state.
Government debt	The total value of outstanding government bonds at any point in time. Also known as public debt.
Government saving	The government's receipts minus its expenditure or the budget surplus.
High powered money	The liabilities of the central bank consisting of currency in circulation and bank reserves. This equals, on the asset side, the domestic credit extended by the central bank plus its foreign assets. Also known as the monetary base, base money or reserve money. Sometimes denoted by M0.
Human capital	The productive knowledge, skill, and training of the labour force.
Hyperinflation	Inflation at an extremely high rate.
Inflation	A sustained rise in the general price level.
Inflation tax	The product of the inflation rate and real money balances. Also known as seignirage, it is an instrument used by governments to raise resources by issuing money and raising prices.
Interest parity condition	When an Indian investor puts his money in Indian bonds he gets return at the domestic interest rate r. If instead he invests in American bonds he gets r^*, the American interest. If however the rupee is expected to depreciate, there is an additional source of return on foreign investment because the dollars earned will be worth more in rupee terms. Absent restrictions on flow of funds across countries, the two returns must be equal in equilibrium. Interest parity (or uncovered interest parity) is said to hold when domestic interest rate equals foreign interest rate plus the expected depreciation of the domestic currency.
Intermediate targets of monetary policy	These are mainly the growth of money supply or the various interest rates that a central bank tries to control in order to achieve the ultimate targets of price stability and growth of output and employment.
International reserves	The central bank's holding of foreign assets.
Inventories	Stocks of finished goods, goods in process and intermediate inputs held by firms. Addition to inventories is counted as part of investment.
Investment	Addition to plants and equipment (fixed investment) and inventories (inventory investment).
Invisible hand	The idea set out by Adam Smith, that if individuals conduct their economic affairs in their own best interests free from government intervention, the economy will operate at maximum efficiency. Also known as laissez-faire.
Keynesian approach	Macroeconomic analysis based on the assumption that wages and prices do not adjust quickly enough to maintain demand-supply balance in all markets. In contrast to the classical and neoclassical view, Keynesians argue that government intervention in the form of active fiscal and

	monetary policy is necessary to reduce unemployment and maintain stability in capitalist economies.
Labour force	The total number of people willing to work, including the employed workers as well as unemployed people actively looking for work.
Liquidity	Easy convertibility into cash.
Liquidity preference	Keynesian term for demand for money.
Liquidity preference theory of interest	Determination of the interest rate by the demand and supply of money as a portfolio asset.
Liquidity trap	A situation in which the rate of interest is very low and demand for money infinitely elastic, making it impossible for the monetary authorities to stimulate the economy through further reductions in interest rate.
Labour market rigidities	Restrictions on the ability of producers to adjust wages or employment.
Labour productivity	Average productivity of labour is total output divided by the number of workers. Marginal productivity of labour is the addition to total output caused by employment of an additional unit of labour, holding the level of other inputs constant.
Laffer curve	Curve showing the relation between tax revenue and the tax rate.
Loanable funds theory of interest	Determination of the interest rate through the interaction of saving (supply of loans) and investment (demand for loans).
Long run Phillips curve	A vertical line (with unemployment on the horizontal axis and inflation on the vertical), indicating that in the long run unemployment stays at the natural rate independent of inflation.
M1	The sum of currency and demand deposits in banks, assets that can be directly used in transactions. Also called narrow money. M2 = M1 + post office savings deposits M3 = M1 + net time deposits of banks. Also known as broad money or aggregate monetary resources.
Managed float	A system in which a central bank tries to influence the value of its currency by buying and selling currencies. Also known as dirty float.
Marginal propensity to consume (mpc)	The change in consumption spending induced by an additional unit of disposable income. Graphically, it is the slope of the consumption function.
Marginal propensity to import	The effect on imports of an increase in national income of one unit.
Marginal propensity to save	The change in saving induced by an additional unit of disposable income. (Equal to one minus the mpc).
Menu cost	The cost of changing price.
Misperceptions theory	Due to their inability to observe directly changes in the general price level, producers are fooled into supplying more output when the price level is higher than expected. The short run aggregate supply curve is upward sloping as a result.
Modern quantity theory	The rate of inflation equals the growth rate of money supply minus the growth rate of real money demand.
Monetarists	A group of economists who maintain that money supply is the primary determinant of the price level and aggregate output.
Monetary aggregates	The various measures of money supply used by central banks (M1, M2, M3)

Monetary base	Same as reserve money, base money, high powered money.
Monetary policy	The management of money supply, interest rates and credit by the central bank.
Monetary transmission mechanism	The process by which changes in money supply influence the economy.
Monetized debt	Same as deficit finance.
Money multiplier	The addition to money supply generated by an additional rupee in the monetary base.
Multiple deposit expansion	When the central bank supplies the banking system with additional reserves total deposits increase by a multiple of this amount.
Multiplier	The change in national income generated by an increase in autonomous demand (consumption or investment or net exports) by one unit.
National income	Same as GNP.
NAIRU (nonaccelerating inflation rate of unemployed)	Rate of unemployment consistent with zero inflation. The point where the Phillips Curve intersects the horizontal (unemployment) axis.
Natural rate of unemployment	Rate of unemployment consistent with full employment where demand for labour equals supply of labour. It reflects unemployment due to frictional or structural causes. Usually this is taken to be the same as NAIRU.
Neutrality of money	The proposition that an increase in money supply leads to a proportional increase in the price level leaving employment and output unchanged.
New classicals	A group of economists who believe that (i) the agents in an economy are fully rational; (ii) full employment is continuously maintained through wage-price flexibility in competitive markets; and (iii) anticipated policy has no macroeconomic effect.
New Keynesians	A group of economists who try to explain wage-price rigidity using basic economic theory of imperfect competition and imperfect information.
Nominal appreciation	A decrease in the nominal exchange rate in flexible exchange system.
Nominal exchange rate	The number of units of domestic currency per unit of foreign currency. Also known as the exchange rate.
Nominal GDP, GNP	GDP, GNP at current market prices.
Nominal interest rate	Interest rate that does not take inflation into account.
Okun's law	Relation between GDP growth and change in the unemployment rate.
Open market operation	Purchase and sale of securities by the central bank in the open market for the purpose of changing the money supply.
Overvalued exchange rate	In a fixed exchange system an exchange rate that is above the equilibrium (market clearing) level.
Paradox of thrift	People's attempt to save more may lead to fall in output with saving unchanged.
Phillips curve	An inverse relationship between inflation and unemployment.
Policy ineffectiveness proposition	The conclusion of the neoclassicals that anticipated policy has no effect on the economy.
Permanent income	The present value of the income stream an economic agent expects to earn over his entire working life.
Permanent income theory of consumption	The hypothesis that consumption spending is determined not by current income, but by permanent or life time income.

Present value	The value today of a payment to be received in the future. It equals the amount of money that must be invested today at a given interest rate to be worth the future receipt.
Price index	A statistical measure of the average level of prices for a given bundle of goods and services.
Price stickiness	The tendency of prices to respond slowly to changes in the conditions of demand and supply. Due to this, imbalance between demand and supply may persist. Another name for price rigidity.
Primary (budget) deficit	A measure of the budget deficit that excludes interest payments from government outlays.
Procyclical	Tendency to move in the same direction as GDP over the business cycle. Opposite is countercyclical.
Production function	See aggregate production function.
Productivity shock	A change in an economy's production function.
Purchasing power parity	The hypothesis that similar domestic and foreign goods should have the same price in terms of the same currency.
Quantity theory	Inflation rate equals the growth rate of money supply.
Rational expectations	Expectations formed by intelligent agents on the basis of all available information, including information about the structure of the economy and current and prospective policies. Forecast error is random with zero mean. New classicals use rational expectations to criticize the idea of adaptive expectation which is based on simple extrapolation of past values.
Real appreciation	A decrease in the real exchange rate, which decrease the quantity of domestic goods that can be purchased with a given quantity of foreign goods. Real appreciation adversely affects exports by raising their relative price to foreigners.
Real balance	Amount of money held by the public divided by the price level.
Real business cycle theory	A version of the new classical theory which states that business cycles are caused by productivity. shocks and inter-temporal labour-leisure substitution by workers.
Real exchange rate	The amount of domestic goods that can be purchased with one unit of foreign good. A reduction stands for real appreciation of the domestic currency.
Real GDP, GNP	The value of national income measured in terms of prices of some fixed base period.
Real interest rate	Nominal interest rate minus the rate of inflation.
Real wage	Remuneration of labour measured in terms of goods, nominal wage divided by the price level.
Recession	A period of falling output and employment.
Ricardian equivalence proposition	For a rational consumer whose consumption is based on lifetime income, taxation and government debt are equivalent because debt is deferred taxation. With government spending unchanged, cut in taxation will leave current consumption unchanged.
Saving	Current disposable income minus consumption spending.
Saving rate	The fraction of income that is saved.

Seignorage	Government revenue raised through money creation. Same as inflation tax.
Stabilization policy	Government policy aimed at reducing fluctuations in output and employment.
Stagflation	A situation of falling output and rising prices.
Steady state	A situation in which output per worker, capital per worker and consumption per worker are constant.
Sterilization	A foreign exchange transaction followed by an offsetting open market operation that leaves the monetary base unchanged.
Sticky prices	See price stickiness.
Stock variable	A variable that can be expressed as a quantity at a specified point in time. Examples: wealth, money supply.
Structural deficit	See cyclically adjusted deficit.
Structural unemployment	Chronic unemployment caused by mismatch between the skill and other characteristics of the existing workforce and the needs of employers.
Supply side economics	A school of economic thought that emphasizes the importance of incentives to work and to invest for economic growth. It strongly advocates reduction in government intervention in the economy.
Tobin's q	The ratio of the market value of capital to its replacement cost. Also called q-ratio.
Total factor productivity (TFP)	The overall efficiency with which an economy uses inputs to generate output.
Trade balance	The excess of the value of exports over imports. Also called net exports.
Transfer payments	Payments made by the government to individuals that are not in exchange for current economic activity. Examples: unemployment benefit, pensions.
Transitory income	Income that is earned in only the current period and not expected to continue into the future. Opposite of permanent income.
Unemployment	The number of people who are willing to work, searching for work but are unable to find work.
Unemployment rate	The fraction of labour force that is unemployed.
User cost of capital	The sum of the real interest rate and the depreciation rate. Also called the rental cost of capital.
Value added	The value of output of a firm minus the value of intermediate inputs purchased.
Velocity of circulation	The number of times the money stock turns over in any period. Nominal GDP divided by the money stock.
Wage rigidity	The failure of wages to adjust to make demand and supply equal in the labour market. Another name for wage stickiness.
Wealth	Assets minus liabilities of an economic agent. Also called net worth.

References

Abel, A.S. and B.S. Bernanke: *Macroeconomics*, fourth edition, Pearson Education, Delhi, 2005.

Athey, M. and Reeser W.: 'Asymmetric Information, Industrial Policy and Corporate Investment in India', *Oxford Bulletin of Economics and Statistics*, Vol. 62, 2000.

Balakrishnan, P., K. Surekha, and B. Vani : 'The Determinants of Inflation in India', *Journal of Quantitative Economics* Vol. 10, 1994.

Basu, K. (ed.): *India's Emerging Economy*, Oxford University Press, New Delhi, 2004.

Dornbusch, R., S. Fischer, and R. Startz: *Macroeconomics*, eighth edition, Tata McGraw-Hill, New Delhi 2002.

Froyen, R.T.: *Macroeconomics: Theories and Policies*, sixth edition, Prentice Hall, 1996.

Goldar, B. 'Econometrics of Indian Industry', in K.L. Krishna (ed.): *Econometric Applications in India*, Oxford University Press, 1997.

Jha, R. (ed.): *Indian Economic Reforms*, Palgrave Macmillan, New York, 2003.

Joshi, V. and I.M.D. Little: *India's Economic Reforms* 1991–2001, Oxford University Press, New Delhi, 1996.

Kohli, R.: *Liberalizing Capital Inflows*, Oxford University Press, New Delhi, 2005.

Krishna, K.L. (ed.): *Econometric Applications in India*, Oxford University Press, New Delhi, 1997.

Parikh, K. (ed.): India Development Reports 1997–2000, Oxford University Press, New Delhi, 2000.

Parikh, K. and R. Radhakrishna (eds): India Development Report 2002, Oxford University Press, New Delhi.

—— (eds): India Development Report 2004–05, Oxford University Press, New Delhi.

Mankiw, G.N.: *Macroeconomics*, fifth edition, Worth Publishers, 2004.

Minhas, B.S. (ed.): *National Income Accounts and Data Systems*, Oxford University Press, New Delhi, 2002.

Mishkin, F.: *The Economics of Money, Banking and Financial Markets*, fifth edition, Addison-Wesley, 1997.

Rao, Manohar: 'Monetary Economics: An Econometric Investigation', in K.L. Krishna (ed.), *Econometric Applications in India*, Oxford University Press; New Delhi, 1997.

Rangarajan, C.: *Perspectives on Indian Economy*, UBS, New Delhi, 2000.

Reddy, Y.V.: 'Managing Public Debt and Promoting Debt Markets in India', *RBI Bulletin*, 2000.

Reddy, Y.V. *Monetary and Financial Sector Reform in India*, UBS, New Delhi, 2000.

Sen, K. and R. Vaidya: *The Process of Financial Liberalization in India*, Oxford University Press, New Delhi, 1997.

Sikdar, S.: *Contemporary Issues in Globalisation An Introduction to Theory and Policy in India*, Oxford University Press, New Delhi, 2004.

Statistical Outline of India: Tata Services Limited (based on *Economic Surveys*), GOI, 2002–3.

Index